THE HISTORY OF
THE ENGLISH NOVEL

THE HISTORY OF
THE ENGLISH NOVEL

By Ernest A. Baker, D. Lit., M.A.

THE HISTORY
OF THE
ENGLISH NOVEL

By Ernest A. Baker, D. Lit., M.A.

Volume IV

Intellectual Realism: from
Richardson to Sterne

New York

BARNES & NOBLE, INC.

First published 1936
Reprinted 1966 by special arrangement with
H. F. & G. WITHERBY, LTD.
326 High Holborn, London, W. C. 1

Printed in the United States of America

27410

PREFACE

THE present volume deals with the most decisive period in the history of the English novel, that of Richardson, Fielding, Smollett, and Sterne. So their names stand in the order of time, but not in that of relative importance. For the cardinal achievement of the period was the establishment of what I have called at a venture, intellectual realism, which is synonymous with the novels of Fielding. What intellectual realism is I have endeavoured to make clear in the following pages. It is the method that has prevailed in English fiction down to to-day, or at any rate yesterday.

This is not the moment to look too far ahead and anticipate a sequel which I may read differently when I reach it by the highroad. But a book which came into my hands since the contents of this volume were nearly all written prompts some remarks that must stand that risk. The book in question is *Messages (première série)*, by Ramon de Fernandez (1926), in which one chapter in especial, "Le Message de Meredith," seems to me to have a peculiar bearing on Fielding, who is not even mentioned.

French criticism, with its firm grasp of the philosophical issues underlying the history of literature in its relations to human history and the history of ideas, is paying an intelligent attention to the work of Meredith which contrasts curiously with the misappreciation and disparagement of him by our own younger critics. This by M. Ramon de Fernandez, though quite brief, seems to me the most penetrating study of our greatest modern novelist that I have yet come across. It follows one on "L'Art de Conrad," still shorter, but equally penetrating. Thus the two English novelists who are responsible—if we omit James as an American and Mr D. H. Lawrence as not yet assessable —for the most profound changes in the technique of fiction are suggestively bracketed together.

5

M. Fernandez' main contention is that Meredith invented— or at least used for the first time *avec profondeur*—a new method of psychological investigation and of literary expression, the method of dramatic analysis, reconciling two tendencies which romanticism had opposed to each other.

Grâce à la parfaite harmonie qui règne chez Meredith entre l'intuition et l'analyse, entre l'intuition qui voit l'individu sentir et agir, et l'analyse qui explique et définit ses sentiments et ses actions, les personnages de ses romans mènent une double vie, une vie réelle et une vie possible, celle-ci étant suggérée par le jugement qui accompagne l'expression de celle-là. . . . Ils nous révèlent inconsciemment ce qu'ils pourraient ou devraient être sous l'influence d'une autre discipline intellectuelle et morale, sans jamais nous enlever la certitude qu'ils ne peuvent être actuellement autrement qu'ils ne sont. (P. 126.)

Donc, psychologie prospective, mais psychologie normative aussi. Le jugement de fait se double d'un jugement de valeur, explicite ou non, qui suit (au lieu de précéder, comme dans le roman à thèse) l'intuition dramatique d'une personnalité. . . . L'idéal meredithien n'est pas introduit dans la vie comme un corps étranger : il se confondrait avec l'action elle-même si celle-ci devenait absolument transparente à l'intelligence de celui qui agit. (P. 127.)

Meredith, au contraire [de Dostoïevsky], nous convainc bientôt que l'exercice de l'intelligence est indispensable, non seulement pour la pleine compréhension, mais encore pour la parfaite réalisation de la vie, que l'on vit plus intensément et mieux à proportion qu'on est plus lucide. D'autre part il démontre par son œuvre que toute connaissance valable de la vie est le résultat d'une réflexion sur l'homme dans le moment où il agit, où il subit l'épreuve de l'expérience. (P. 218.)

Hence to know the individual we must not merely contemplate him, we must make him live, and to make him live it is necessary to know him, to think him, for thought does not fasten upon life merely to satisfy the refined curiosity of an *élite*, " *elle participe comme agent nécessaire à sa création*." And since thought must make use of the facts of life, and have due regard to their correlations, knowledge of mankind and the dramatic expression of the individual are combined in one same act of creation, at once intuitive and rational. Meredith's aim is to harmonize the act of creation and the act of judgment, and, up to a point, to identify them, without confounding their distinct characteristics.

Now a great deal of this might also be said of Fielding. Had M. Fernandez been as well versed in the earlier history of English fiction as he is in the work of Meredith and Conrad, he would probably acknowledge that the method of Meredith is essentially a further development of Fielding's intellectual realism, and that, accordingly, it was not quite so revolutionary as he has made out. In the passages which I have quoted from *Tom Jones*, the reader will perhaps recognize a less advanced but radically similar technique at work. True, Fielding's characters are not so conscious of themselves as Meredith's ; they are not self-analysts, nor possessed by that apprehension of an ideal self and an ideal life which is so peculiarly Meredithian. It is the author who judges them at the moment of action, inviting us to concur with his judgment. Meredith, writing his novels when the Darwinian revelations of man's history were suggesting far-reaching views of man's progress, embodied an evolutionary philosophy of his own in the human drama set forth in his novels. It was essentially a practical philosophy, envisaging an attainable goal for human effort, in the perfecting and complete affirmation of man's true self. His philosophy was an advance upon Fielding's, and his technique adapted itself thereto.

But Fielding had already shown how to combine the act of creation and the act of judgment ; he too had practised a method of dramatic analysis. His interpretation, his running commentary, is given simultaneously, with and in the drama, as will clearly appear in the passages quoted later, where the sequence of motives and actions is analysed and evaluated on the instant of occurrence. Fielding moreover continually, by precept and by the eloquent results of the dramas of life enacted in his novels, inculcated and illustrated a doctrine like Meredith's—the imperative need for intelligence, both for the full comprehension of life and for its perfect realization.

In the chapters on Richardson, I have pointed out the influence of that novelist also upon Meredith. The latter seems to combine the intuitive method of Richardson with the interpretative and critical method of the intellectual realist. M. Fernandez does not mention Richardson ; but the Meredithian procedure, which is based on a sense of the *unité vivante* of the individual, whose character and actions are seized by a dramatic intuition, is, up to a point, identical with Richardson's. Meredith goes on to apply the reflective intelligence, thus achieving that creative technique which is at once intuitive and rational. M. Fernandez' study seems to confirm my own views on the profound and continuous effect of Fielding's work upon the course of English fiction since his day, and also on the fact of a return, late in the nineteenth century, especially by Meredith, to what was profound and valuable in the method of Richardson.

My thanks are due again to Dr F. S. Boas for his kindness in reading the proof-sheets.

E. A. B.

Christmas, 1929

CONTENTS

FROM RICHARDSON
TO STERNE

CHAPTER I

RICHARDSON'S *PAMELA*

In the history of English fiction there is no clean break, no *The quiet* definite ending and new beginning, between the age of romance *transition* and the age of realism ; the transition was gradual and almost *from* *romance* imperceptible.   It was different in France, where the change *to novel* from romance to novel was brought about to the accompaniment of protest, ridicule, and revolt.   There yawns a gulf fully as wide between *Aretina* and *Tom Jones* as between the *Grand Cyrus* and *Manon Lescaut*.   But English writers made the transit quietly and almost without perceiving it, the French with their usual revolutionary trumpeting.   Thus it is wise to keep the eye firmly fixed on English writers in studying the course of English fiction, and not miss the track by sweeping too wide an horizon.   The effects of international influence are easily exaggerated.   French works were read in this country, were even translated into English, that escaped the attention of those who might have learned from them a good deal which had to be learned by experiment.   This is what happened to the anti-romances, the best of which were read with profit later on by Fielding and his followers, but not until the objects of the satire had been long defunct.   In France, the sardonic version of life presented by Furetière and Scarron as an antidote to the absurdities of the high romantic school had been a chief agency in the rise of a new school who endeavoured to see and show things as they are. After the romancers had idealized and the anti-romancers had depreciated human nature, it was the turn of a sober, intelligent, and inquiring age to undertake an unbiased if sympathetic appraisal.   Sorel, Furetière, and Scarron, accordingly, were succeeded by Marivaux and Prévost.   But *Zelinda*, *Incognita*, and the *Adventures of Covent Garden*, if they showed which way the wind was blowing, did not put an end to outworn modes or initiate a new way of writing. On the contrary, the job of extinguishing the last embers of romanticism and heroic extravagance had to be done a long while later by Fielding, Carey, and Mrs Lennox, when other circumstances had prepared the way for the realistic novel of manners.[1]

A series of gradual changes   Thus the English novel came into being through a series of slow and gradual changes, in response to changes of interest and taste. Those changes can be traced even more clearly in the work of the students of charactery and the periodical essayists.[2] It is impossible to put a finger on the point where the romance ceases to be romance, or to lay one's hand on a book and say, this is a novel, the first English example of its kind. In applying the term even to *Robinson Crusoe* or *Moll Flanders*, qualifications are necessary ; it has to be admitted that neither corresponds exactly to what we now mean by a novel. Mrs Behn seized upon the name for stories animated with the high-flown romanticism of heroic drama, though she justified the term to some extent by her reductions of scale, by the playwright's concentration of interest, and an effort to attain actuality both in externals and in the mental anatomy of her characters. Mrs Manley, Mrs Haywood, and the other women who gained a precarious livelihood by writing fiction with but the vaguest understanding of what they were at, dealt with themes less and less pretentious as they gained experience, came lower and lower in the social scale in their choice of characters, made gallant if clumsy attempts to depict the world they lived in, and even succeeded in some measure in telling a story through the experiences and emotions of the principal actor. Subjective fiction—that is to say, the modern novel—was well in sight. Indeed, we can describe their books only as bad novels ; whatever the depreciatory adjective, they were at any rate novels of a sort.

The demand for novels ;   And for these products of a nascent industry there was a growing body of consumers. Novels were becoming the regular light goods in the literary mart. Those that hit the public taste

[1] Fielding's *Tom Thumb the Great* (1730) and *Covent Garden Tragedy* (1731), and Carey's *Chrononhotonthologos* (1734), were aimed at bombast and affectation on the stage. *The Female Quixote* (1750) of Mrs Lennox satirized the foolish readers of romances that had no relation to life.

[2] See Volume II., chapter xiv.

sold in repeated editions, fresh supplies were eagerly awaited. *reading*
Talent could obtain a living, genius might win immortal fame *more*
by entering the new profession and turning the craft into an *popular*
art. At the beginning of the eighteenth century the theatre was *than*
the most lucrative avenue for literary enterprise ; long before the *play-going*
end it was the successful novelist who reaped the larger gains.
This was owing in part to the badness of most contemporary
plays, but still more to the great multiplication of readers, which
also had something to do with the continuous decline of the
drama. There were far more readers than in any previous age,
and the majority belonged to classes that had hitherto been left
in the wilderness. The middle classes were better off, better
educated, more leisured. They now formed the bulk of those
who read for enjoyment. Reading was so much more popular
than theatre-going that many preferred to read even plays. It
was of course on the familiar pattern of the printed play that
Bunyan and Defoe had set out their dialogue in dramatic fashion.
Richardson, who has several allusions to the private reading of
plays, kept up the practice, so arranging many of the dialogues
quoted by his correspondents, and prefacing *Clarissa* and *Sir
Charles Grandison* with lists of the dramatis personæ.

The inextinguishable desire of mankind to see itself in some *Decline of*
sort of glass had been satisfied till now by the theatre. But art *drama*
provides many kinds of mirrors, and for a generation growing in
self-consciousness there was an evident superiority in the fuller
and more heart-searching portrayal of life possible in the novel
than in the concentration and hurry of an evening's play. The
theatre made futile attempts to adapt itself to the times. Audiences
had lost interest in the machine-made comedies, empty farces,
and ranting melodrama of playwrights who copied set patterns
instead of looking for subjects in the world around them. " In
banishing humour from the stage," as Fielding said, " which was
tantamount to banishing human nature, the dramatist made the
stage as dull as the drawing-room." A few writers whose attention
was not fixed on the box-office made serious attempts to bring
the theatre once more into touch with life. Steele in *The Conscious
Lovers* (1722), Gay with *The Beggar's Opera* (1728), Lillo with
his tearful ballad-melodrama of the City apprentice, *George*

Barnwell (1731), and with *The Fatal Curiosity* (1737), and Fielding, in a rapid succession of pieces in which he staged the scandals and grievances of the day, sometimes under the respectable cloak of an adaptation from Molière, sometimes in a fashion far more direct, and caricatured the sham heroics and sentimentality of this effete drama : all these tried hard, in divers ways, to supply what was soon to be supplied better and more abundantly by the novel of manners. Fielding's efforts were checked, before he had time to put forth his full powers in the drama, by the Licensing Act of 1737. This was undesignedly a blow for the novel ; but even without it, such was the appeal of the printed page, the theatre would probably not have put down its upstart rival.

How Richardson and Fielding "slipped" into novel-writing   But, though readers were now familiarized with novels as a means of amusement always ready to hand, the two writers who were to lift fiction to a higher level and find it a place side by side with poetry and the drama were not simply successors who deliberately adopted an existing form and developed and improved it. Fielding and Richardson, in fact, became novelists in as unexpected and accidental a fashion as any writers in history. Richardson was a flourishing printer with a facile pen who, like others before him, discovered that story-telling was the aptest method of teaching morals and decorum. Fielding was a playwright and theatrical manager out of work, who turned to the law for his living and to writing fiction as an outlet for the humour and satire and social criticism which the closing of his theatre had repressed. If Richardson had not been commissioned to write a manual of practical advice for the conduct of life, and had not been prompted by the recollection of a suggestive incident to tell a story instead of merely stringing together maxims and anecdotes, he would never have written *Pamela* or *Clarissa* or *Sir Charles Grandison*. If *Pamela* had never been written or Fielding had been kept fully employed in providing his Little Theatre with plays, perhaps there would have been no *Joseph Andrews*, to be followed by *Tom Jones* and *Amelia* when he found where his genius lay.

Like Defoe before him and George Eliot later, Samuel Richardson (1689-1761) commenced novelist in late middle age.

There exist documents enough on his life to furnish material for *Samuel* a voluminous and most uneventful memoir. The paucity of *Richard-* incident renders Scott's brief sketch an adequate account of the *son's life* main facts, which have been faithfully repeated by every later *and character* biographer.[1] He was born somewhere in Derbyshire,[2] the son of a joiner, and his serious and thoughtful disposition would have bespoken him for the Church, had his parents been able to give him a suitable education. In default of this, Samuel, after but a moderate schooling, was apprenticed to the printing trade, worked diligently for an exacting master, and reaped his reward by marrying his master's daughter and succeeding to the business. He was never afraid of drudgery, and by dint of honesty and hard work his became one of the most prosperous concerns in the City ; he was elected Master of the Stationers' Company, and was employed to print the Journals of the House of Commons. He had a country house—at Hammersmith and later at Parson's Green—as well as a dwelling on his commodious business premises in Salisbury Court. He was married twice, the second time to the daughter of a bookseller in Bath, and had twelve children, of whom only four daughters outlived infancy and childhood. Though energetic, he lived a sedentary life, and had poor health in his latter years. His holiday at Tunbridge Wells in 1748—at the time when *Clarissa* was coming out in instalments —is famous through Loggan's sketch of the crowd of notable people, including Richardson, who were then at the spa, and through Thackeray's account of the incident, under a different date, in *The Virginians*. By this time Richardson was himself a personage. Everybody of taste and feeling had read *Pamela*, everybody was at that very moment trembling with apprehension for the fate of Clarissa. In the years of his literary success, he was the centre of an admiring circle of intellectual friends, mostly women, and the conversations and the letters they exchanged, which have been for the most part preserved and a large propor- tion of them printed, are as voluminous as those in his novels.

With Richardson, said his friend and confidant Aaron Hill, " verbosity became a virtue." It was the secret of his method,

---

[1] *Lives of Eminent Novelists and Dramatists* (1825).
[2] On the Richardson family see *Notes and Queries*, 1922-1923.

The fineness of his sensibility

of his untiring expatiation on the little things of life, which, he considered, are none of them unimportant and sum up to an aggregate in which the smallest counts. Every act, every feeling, every gesture should be deliberately scrutinized, if man, and especially woman, is to lead an upright, dignified, and happy existence. Richardson established the novel of sensibility. Feelings of the utmost refinement and perceptivity must be cultivated by those who aim at a worthy life. His criterion of character was intensity and quality of feeling. His heroines—we can hardly speak of his heroes [1]—seem to do little but study and register their emotions to the minutest beat : his vicious characters are persons whose feelings have been blunted or allowed to degenerate into passion, that lamentable infirmity. Fine feelings are the indispensable basis of fine manners, and with Richardson manners and morals were all but synonymous. [2] Through this intensive study of sensibility he was actually to create or prepare the way for something greater than the novel of sensibility. In an age when the individual was regarded by philosophers and statesmen merely as one of the many units comprised in the body politic, his particular value depending upon his place in the social scheme, the lot assigned him by Providence, Richardson had glimpses of a loftier ideal of personality ; and with that ideal before him he conceived actions and situations in which individuals were shown asserting their private, intrinsic worth, in opposition to tyranny, disaster, obloquy. He gave our literature the first example of that novel of personality, that history of the struggle for self-realization, which was to wait a century, for the recognition of a more enlightened scale of values, before other novelists could take it up and develop it. But of this, which was the real greatness of his achievement, Richardson was unaware, or aware very obscurely ; nor did his contemporaries see what he was doing. To them and to himself he was simply the novelist of

---

[1] Austin Dobson speaks of "the pleasant gibe that Sir Charles Grandison is one of the author's chief feminine characters" (*Richardson*, English Men of Letters, 1902).

[2] As Grandmamma Shirley expresses it, in Richardson's third novel, "My dear loves" [to the younger ladies], "let a good man, let life, let manners be the principal motive of your choice—in goodness will you have every sanction, and your fathers, mothers, relations, friends, every joy" (*Works*, xii., pp. 200-201).

sensibility, and it was the value and interest of human feeling, as exhibited in his three novels, that riveted attention. No one observed that this was necessarily bound up with a new sense of the value and inexhaustible interest of the individual man or woman.

Absorption in the tiniest details of behaviour and deportment *His interest in behaviour* seems to have been congenital in Richardson. From his earliest years he showed a propensity to interest himself in other people's behaviour ; and, not content only to shun the pitfalls himself into which he saw them stumbling, he was generous with his services as a moral expert. They nicknamed him " Serious and Gravity " at school ; and according to his own account, although he did not care for games, he was popular with his schoolfellows for his talent at telling them stories, all of them fitted with a useful lesson. It is strange that there is only one instance recorded of his getting into trouble through his readiness to offer advice to the erring ; this is the well-known incident of the letter written before he was eleven years of age to a widow old enough to be his grandmother, expostulating with her for her uncharitable conduct, and exhorting her in the style of a person of years and experience to amend her ways.

From childhood to old age, Richardson was inordinately given *A confirmed letter-writer* to letter-writing, to what he fondly termed " epistolary correspondence " ; it was an outlet even more congenial than his other recreation, intimate talk, for his constitutional verbosity. Not long after his unfortunate experience with the widow, he was commissioned by various young women, almost exactly as Thomas Hardy confesses to have been employed, to compose or correct or embellish their love-letters. He was always more intimate with women than with men, and it was in such ways as these that he acquired his wide empirical knowledge of the female heart. He also tells how he kept up a long correspondence, during his prentice days in the printing establishment, with a gentleman who was a "master of the epistolary style." Their subjects were various, including things observed in foreign travel ; and, as he hints, this must have been an invaluable part of Richardson's education.

But he was over fifty and had long been in a prosperous way

of business when, as he puts it, he " slipped " into the profession
of novelist. From time to time small literary tasks had been
entrusted to his hands, prefaces and dedications and the like, in
which he had acquitted himself with credit. He was an accomplished indexer—witness the exhaustive analytical index which he
appended to his edition of *The Negotiations of Sir Thomas Roe in
his Embassy to the Ottoman Porte* (1746). The cross-references
afterwards carefully inserted in his long epistolary novels, and
the *Collection of Moral and Instructive Sentiments . . . Digested
under Proper Heads*, which he eventually made from all three,
are further evidences of the methodical and meticulous tendency
Richardson of his mind. In 1739 two of his particular friends, Mr Charles
invited to Rivington and Mr John Osborn, London booksellers, pressed
write a him to turn his peculiar talents to account by putting together
volume of a small volume of *Familiar Letters*, which were to be at once
"Familiar models of this style of writing and illustrations of " how to think
Letters" and act justly and prudently, in the common Concerns of Human
Life." It was in carrying out this delicate task that Richardson
hit upon the germ of *Pamela*. He was writing two or three
letters " to instruct handsome girls, who were obliged to go out
to service, as we phrase it, how to avoid the snares that might be
laid against their virtue," when he recalled a seasonable story
that had come to his ears long ago. In a letter to Aaron Hill,
he replies to the question whether there was any groundwork of
fact for the story of Pamela.[1]

The actual   Richardson says that, some twenty-five years since, a gentleman
germ of whom he intimately knew—perhaps, as Scott suggests, his old-
"Pamela" time correspondent—whilst staying at a country inn, had been
told the story how Mr B., owner of the great house close by,
had married his wife, a lady of great beauty and the finest character. As a young girl, the child of humble parents, who had
brought her up in the best principles of rectitude and piety, she
had been engaged by the squire's mother to attend on her person.
After that lady's death the young squire tried, " by all manner
of temptations, to seduce her. . . . She had recourse to as many
innocent stratagems to escape the snares laid for her virtue ;

---

[1] The passage is quoted by Clara Thomson (pp. 153-155), and Austin
Dobson (pp. 28-30), from Mrs Barbauld's edition of the *Correspondence*, i. 69.

once, however, in despair, having been near drowning. . . . At last, her noble resistance, watchfulness, and excellent qualities, subdued him, and he thought fit to make her his wife." In her new station, " she behaved herself with so much dignity, sweetness, and humility, that she made herself beloved of everybody, and even by his relations, who at first despised her ; and now had the blessings both of rich and poor, and the love of her husband." In short, this was the story of Pamela, which only required filling out with details by Richardson's intense, matter-of-fact imagination, to make the novel which he at once proceeded to write.[1]

The *Familiar Letters* were put aside for the time being ; but Richardson eventually completed them, and the volume was published two months after *Pamela*, with the title, *Letters written To and For Particular Friends, On the most Important Occasions. Directing not only the Requisite Style and Forms to be Observed in Writing Familiar Letters ; But How to Think and Act Justly and Prudently in the common Concerns of Human Life. Containing 173 Letters ; none of which were ever before Published* (1741). It is another of the Puritan conduct-books, combined with practical instructions for all sorts of likely contingencies ; and combines experience of the world, sound sense, and insight into the shortcomings of human ability, with the old prejudices against play-going, musical and other entertainments, extravagant and immodest fashions in dress. There are recommendations of servants, applications for a daughter's hand in marriage, letters from creditors and excuses for non-payment of debts, letters of congratulation and letters of condolence, warnings against the insidious arts of fortune-hunters, directions how to act in business matters, and, characteristically, discreet advice on the momentous issues of courtship and matrimony. Touches of humour are sometimes evident, and there are many glimpses of contemporary life and manners ; promising little stories are begun, and cut short all too soon.[2] Many of the letters do not

The "Familiar Letters"

---

[1] The story of Amanda (*Spectator*, No. 375, 10th May 1712) by Hughes has been suggested as a possible original. But the idea of a woman resisting a man of wealth and station, who at length offers marriage, was not one that required any very daring effort of imagination at that period.

[2] Nicholas Breton's *Packet of Mad Letters* (see Volume II. 152) curiously anticipated Richardson.

fill a page. The book appeared anonymously till after the death of its author, who used to speak of it rather shamefacedly. Apparently it was the " lowness " of the style, adapted for the use of the comparatively unlettered, not of the subjects treated or the maxims recommended, that he felt to be beneath the dignity of the author of *Pamela*, for the book is an inquire-within for people in almost every rank and occupation.

" Pamela: or Virtue Re- warded" —outline of story   Having set out to write a series of letters, Richardson kept to this form in relating his story.   Pamela is indeed " a mighty letter-writer."   " I have got such a knack of writing," she says, " that when I am by myself, I cannot sit without a pen in my hand."   Her first letter is to inform her parents of the death of her good mistress, and has a postcript telling them that her new master had come in unexpectedly and found her writing, had read the letter, and paid her a compliment on her pretty hand. She is all confusion, but thinks no harm.   Her parents, however, write at once to put her on her guard.   The young squire had given her money, which looks as though he had improper designs ; and they conjure her to watch over that jewel, her virtue, the loss of which " no riches, nor favour, nor anything in this life," can make up for.   But it is not till the seventh letter that Pamela begins to show uneasiness at her master's attentions.   He soon declares himself.   When Pamela resists, and he finds that blandish- ments, bribes, threats, and promises are of no avail, he tries to entrap or coerce her.   She is reduced to all sorts of shifts to keep in communication with her parents, on whose knowledge of what is going on she feels that her security depends.

Dramatic function of the letters   It will be noticed that the letters are not only Richardson's chosen method of relating the story, but also a vital factor in it. In all three of his novels the writing and transmission, the copy- ing out and reading out of the correspondence to sympathetic relatives and friends, are an important and often exciting part of the drama.   We are continually told what a source of delight and edification it was to everybody to read their friends' letters. Clarissa and Harriet Byron are as untiring as Pamela with their pens.   Evidently they all regarded verbosity as a virtue.   At length Pamela is reduced to the last straits, and her letters being stopped records what happens in a journal.   It is through this journal coming into her master's hands that he is brought to a sense of his wickedness and of her exceeding worth, and changes his heart. Before that happens, he calls her a slut who minds her pen more than her needle, for he is well aware that Pamela is writing to her parents and that they will be allied against him. But Pamela outwits even the Argus eyes of the villainous Mrs Jewkes, an old bawd whom Mr B. sets over her as jailer when he has transferred her to his other house in Lincolnshire. Mrs Jewkes tells her: "Though you are as innocent as a dove, yet you are as cunning as a serpent."

Richardson is not above using the hackneyed device of two letters put in the wrong envelopes. Pamela receives the one intended for Mrs Jewkes ; and terrified by her master's threats—for he finds out that she has been appealing for help to the parish clergyman and letting him fondle hopes of marrying her—she makes an attempt to escape, and being intercepted tries in a half-hearted way to drown herself. The ugly incidents that ensue show how far Richardson was at fault in reading the character of his own sex. That his Mr B. should try compulsion when he had met with such steady resistance, and remain unmoved by Pamela's transparent goodness, is incredible, as well as inconsistent with the character afterwards attributed to Mr B. But a crisis is not long delayed. Mrs Jewkes gets hold of Pamela's journal, and hands it over to her master. His eyes at last are opened, and he tells Pamela that he will defy the world and the world's censures ; if it be in the power of his whole life, he will make her amends for the hardships she has undergone.

But Pamela has received a private intimation that he may try to impose upon her with a sham ceremony. Hence she replies : "Your poor servant is far unworthy of this great honour ; for what will it be but to create envy to herself, and discredit to you ? Therefore, sir, permit me to return to my poor parents, and that is all I have to ask." At this, Mr B. flies into a passion, and bids her begone. Quite bewildered, Pamela sets out in her master's coach and attended by two of his men. And now she suddenly realizes that to quit her master's house is not the object that her heart of hearts desires. "What could be the matter with me, I wonder ?—I felt something so strange, and my heart was so impish !—I wonder what ailed me ?—But this was so *unexpected !*—I believe that was all !—Yet I am very strange still. Surely, surely, I cannot be like the old murmuring Israelites to long after the onions and garlic of Egypt, when they had suffered there such heavy bondage ? " One of the servants escorting her has been entrusted with a letter, to be handed to her next day when she is nearly home. But Pamela's curiosity and anxiety prevail on him to give her a sight of it beforehand. She writes, for she is still writing, although she expects to bring what she has written in her pocket : "Well, my dear father and mother, I have got the letter, on great promises of secrecy, and making no use of it." So she opens it without breaking the seal, copies out the contents, and returns it to the bearer. Next day it is handed to her at the hour appointed, and she retires as if to read it. Innocent Pamela ! But Richardson thought that even a Sir Charles Grandison would condone eavesdropping and similar tricks, and, instead of protesting, be the first to take advantage of the report of a private conversation by a shorthand-writer posted in a cupboard.[1]

Mr B.'s change of attitude　In the sealed letter, Mr B. makes a clean breast of his feelings. The tables have been turned, and he is now in more danger from her than she from him. He has let her go, but only because he could not trust his own weakness. And now Pamela finds that she can no longer trust hers. She admits to herself that her heart has been long " too partial in his favour " ; " she has made an escape to be more a prisoner." When a further letter arrives, acquainting her that he finds it vain to struggle against his affec-tion, and humbly imploring her to come back, Pamela is torn between triumph and doubt. Can he mean that he will honestly marry her ? For it must be confessed that Mr B. even now has not made her a hard and fast offer. Or is there still the risk of a bogus wedding ? In Pamela's candid self-communings, Richardson shows himself an accurate reader of a doubting and hesitating but hopelessly enamoured heart.

Oh my exulting heart ! How it throbs in my bosom, as if it would reproach me for so lately upbraiding it for giving way to

[1] He expresses himself suitably, however, on Father Marescotti's eaves-dropping during his interview with Clementina (*Works*, xi. 293).

the love of so dear a gentleman ! But take care thou art not too credulous neither, oh fond believer ! Things that we wish, are apt to gain too ready credence with us.[1]

She returns, and finds the love-sick gentleman ill in bed. He, too, is a victim of sensibility. Her failure to respond to the magnanimity of his self-sacrifice, when he owns himself vanquished yet leaves the terms of capitulation still undefined, has wounded him to the soul.

But the game is now in Pamela's hands, so long, that is, as she *Pamela's* does not throw away the advantages which her long resistance *father,* has given her. She has taken a certain risk in coming back, but *Goodman* the odds are in her favour. And it is not long before Mr B. *Andrews* announces that they are to be made man and wife in his private chapel. On the eve of the wedding, some of the squire's more intimate friends are invited to make her acquaintance, when who should arrive but Pamela's father, who is still in fear that she has ceased to be an honest woman. She sends a full account of the incident to her mother.

He put on a clean shirt and neckcloth (which he brought in his pocket) at an alehouse there, and got shaved ; and so, after he had eaten some bread and cheese, and drank a can of ale, he set out for my master's house, with a heavy heart, dreading for me, and in much fear of being brow-beaten. He had, it seems, asked, at the alehouse, what family the 'squire had down here, in hopes to hear something of me : And they said, A housekeeper, two maids, and, at present, two coachmen, two grooms, a footman, and a helper. Was that all ? he said. They told him, there was a young creature there, belike who *was*, or *was to be*, his mistress, or somewhat of that nature ; but had been his wife's waiting-maid. This, he said, grieved his heart, and confirmed his fears.[2]

Goodman Andrews is a sturdy peasant drawn to the life. His apprehensions are gradually removed. He is greeted with compliments on his matchless daughter, and forced reluctantly to sit down with the quality whilst Pamela is sent for. The meeting of father and daughter is a touching scene, in spite of the floods of tears, the restoratives, and the excess of gratitude for everybody's condescension in treating Pamela almost as one

1 *Works*, ed. Leslie Stephen, i. 284.   2 *Ibid.*, i. 331.

of themselves. But her account of the wedding sounds, to the modern reader, almost like a burlesque of this odious servility.

Mr Peters gave me away ; and I said, after Mr Williams [the clergyman with whom Pamela cannot be acquitted of playing fast and loose], as well as I could, as my dear master did with a much better grace, the words of betrothment ; and the ceremony of the ring passing next, I received the dear favour at his worthy hands with a most grateful heart ; and he was pleased to say afterwards in the chariot, that when he had done saying, *With this ring I thee wed*, etc., I made a courtesy, and said, Thank you sir. Maybe I did; for I am sure it was a most grateful part of the service, and my heart was overwhelmed with his goodness, and the tender grace wherewith he performed it.[1]

Richardson's own view of the differences between what are lumped together as misalliances is put unmistakably in the dispute between Mr B. and his sister, Lady Davers, after the marriage.

Said he, Does your pride let you see no difference in the case you put ? None at all, said she. Where can the difference be between a beggar's son married by a lady, or a beggar's daughter made a gentleman's wife ?

Then I'll tell you, replied he ; the difference is, a man ennobles the woman he takes, be she who she will ; and adopts her into his own rank, be it what it will ; but a woman, though ever so nobly born, debases herself by a mean marriage, and descends from her own rank to his she stoops to.[2]

The story continued after the marriage

Pamela's troubles are not entirely over when she is safely married; there is still the implacable Lady Davers to be reckoned with. This truculent person, a sort of Lady Wishfort with the manners of a fishwife and a scolding tongue in place of wit, comes one day when the squire is away to find out from Pamela what is the truth of the rumours that have reached her ears. She is attended by a silly young spark, Lord Jackey, who is quickly put down by Pamela's neat repartees. Lady Davers tries to make Pamela wait upon her at table. The quondam servant-maid is a match for the witless lordling, but she quails before the woman of condition.

And indeed I began to be afraid ; for I have but a poor heart, after all. But Mrs Jewkes hearing high words, came in again,

[1] *Works*, i. 394.   [2] *Ibid.*, ii. 66.

with the second course, and said, Pray your ladyship, don't so discompose yourself. I am afraid this day's business will make matters wider than ever between your good ladyship and your brother : For my master doats upon madam.

Woman, said she, do thou be silent ! Sure, I that was born in this house, may have some privilege in it, without being talked to by the saucy servants in it !

I beg pardon, madam, replied Mrs Jewkes ; and, turning to me, said, Madam, my master will take it very ill if you make him wait for you thus. So I rose to go out ; but my lady said, If it was only for *that* reason, she shan't go.—And went to the door and shut it, and said to Mrs Jewkes, Woman, don't come again till I call you ; and coming to me, took my hand, and said, Find your legs, miss, if you please. I stood up, and she tapped my cheek ! Oh ! says she, that scarlet glow shows what a rancorous little heart thou hast, if thou durst show it ! But come this way ; and so led me to her chair ; Stand there, said she, and answer me a few questions while I dine, and I'll dismiss thee, till I call thy impudent master to account ; and then I'll have you face to face, and all this mystery of iniquity shall be unravelled ; for between you, I will come to the bottom of it.

When she had sat down, I moved to the window on the other side of the parlour, looking into the private garden ; and her woman said, Mrs Pamela, don't make my lady angry. Stand by her ladyship, as she bids you. Said I, Pray, good now, let it suffice *you* to attend your ladyship's commands, and don't lay *yours* upon *me*.—Your pardon, sweet Mrs Pamela, said she. Times are much altered with you, I'll assure you ! Said I, Her ladyship has a very good plea to be free in the house that she was *born* in ; but you may as well confine your freedoms to the house in which you had your *breeding*. Why, how now, Mrs Pamela, said she ; since you provoke me to it, I'll tell you a piece of my mind. Hush, hush, *good woman*, said I, alluding to my lady's language to Mrs Jewkes, my lady wants not your assistance ;—Besides, I can't scold !

The woman was ready to flutter with vexation ; and Lord Jackey laughed as if he would burst his sides : G—d d—n me, Beck, said he, you'd better let her alone to my lady here ; for she'll be too many for twenty such as you and I !—And then he laughed again, and repeated, I *can't scold*, quoth-a ! but, by gad, miss, you can speak d—d spiteful words, I can tell you that ! Poor Beck, poor Beck !—'Fore gad, she's quite dumbfoundered ! [1]

[1] *Works*, ii. 28-30.

The whole scene is vivacious comedy ; but it is tiresome to read the recapitulation when Pamela reports to her husband, who would have taken summary vengeance, but is persuaded by the sagacious Pamela to make terms with his irate sister. The instrument that subdues this fierce lady is Pamela's journal: as in Richardson's succeeding novels, nothing can withstand virtue combined with epistolary genius.

Pamela's character   It is easy to criticize Pamela as a woman. She is obviously an epitome of the excellences dearest to the Puritan mind. She stands there to enforce a lesson, not, unfortunately, the beauty of goodness, but what through Richardson's matter-of-factness looks too much like the policy of being honest. She has her vanities and weaknesses, however, which save her from being too offensive a paragon: in truth, she is often a minx, who certainly does not fascinate the reader of a different epoch as she did the friends of Mr B. and lovers of sensibility in 1740. But it can be said with more appropriateness of Pamela than the poet Young said of the more ambitious but less successful figure of Lovelace : " 'Tis the likeness and not the morality of a character we care about."[1] Her self-portrait betrays an infinity of those tiny, almost imperceptible touches of nature, the quirks of temperament, the feminine foibles, that Richardson had been quietly observing all his life, which slip unconsciously from her pen when the didactic purpose has for the moment been forgotten. Pamela was the first creation of that kind in our literature, and, however much we may criticize and even dislike her, there is no challenging her perfect lifelikeness. She is painted on full-size canvas, not a feature slurred, not an eyelash omitted, with the solidity of an old master. The Fleet Street printer was himself Pamela, heart and soul, as he wrote her letters and plotted how to outwit her unscrupulous admirer.[2]

Other Characters   The young woman's parents and fellow-servants, though minor figures, are drawn with a firmness and sureness that belie Richardson's disclaimers of any intimate acquaintance with

---

[1] *Correspondence*, ed. Barbauld, ii. 4.

[2] Though he got the germ of her story from hearsay, the character of Pamela was his own making. He had very little actual acquaintance, he said, with young women of that class, and had to rely here on his own imagination. (See a remarkable letter to Thomas Edwards, 1752, cited by Mr Paul de Castro in his edition of *Joseph Andrews*, p. 12.)

people of that class.   He is not so unerring when he deals
with the gentlefolk.   Mr B. the would-be seducer and Mr B.
the married lover are two different persons, and the difference
is not accounted for by his alleged reformation.   Lady Davers
derives from post-Restoration comedy rather than from personal
experience.   In bringing such characters as Mrs Jewkes on the *Mrs*
scene, Richardson resorts to the old English lampooning device *Jewkes a*
of making the exterior proclaim the internal ugliness—English *character*
in the preference of depicting to describing, though it has been *verging on*
used with most point and venom by Scots.   The portrait of *caricature*
Mrs Jewkes is in a style that Smollett was soon to make a
favourite and Sterne used with a finer skill :

> Now I will give you a picture of this wretch : She is a broad,
> squat, pursy, fat thing, quite ugly, if anything human can be so
> called ; about forty years old.   She has a huge hand, and an arm
> as thick as my waist, I believe.   Her nose is fat and crooked, and
> her brows grow down over her eyes ; a dead spiteful, grey,
> goggling eye, to be sure she has.   And her face is flat and broad ;
> and as to colour, looks like as if it had been pickled a month in
> saltpetre : I daresay she drinks :—She has a hoarse, man-like
> voice, and is as thick as she is long ; and yet looks so deadly
> strong, that I am afraid she would dash me at her foot in an
> instant, if I was to vex her.—So that with a heart more ugly
> than her face, she frightens me sadly ; and I am undone to be
> sure, if God does not protect me ; for she is very, very wicked
> —indeed she is.[1]

Even Lady Davers is outraged by her brother's patronage of
the hideous Mrs Jewkes ; and, when at last she resolves to make
the best of a bad job and accept Pamela as a sister, she blames
her for suffering the repulsive creature about her, after what has
passed.[2]   Readers will side with Lady Davers rather than with
Richardson, for letting his heroine be so poor-spirited as to make
friends with this ignoble tool of her perfidious master.

Such was the novel that appeared with the title, *Pamela : or
Virtue Rewarded.   In a Series of Familiar Letters from a beautiful Young Damsel, to her Parents.   Now first published in order*

---

[1] *Works*, i. 121.   *Cp.* the alleged parson engaged by Sir Hargrave Pollexfen
to marry him to Miss Byron, in *Sir Charles Grandison* (*Works*, ix. 185).
[2] *Ibid.*, ii. 200.

*to cultivate the Principles of Virtue and Religion in the Minds of
the Youth of both Sexes. A Narrative which has its Foundation
in Truth and Nature ; and at the same time that it agreeably
entertains, by a Variety of* curious *and* affecting *Incidents, is
entirely divested of all those Images, which, in too many Pieces
calculated for Amusement only, tend to* inflame *the Minds they
should* instruct (1740). Marivaux had published his *Vie de
Marianne* a decade ago (1731-1741) ; an English translation
was now coming out in instalments (1736-1742), and was as
yet incomplete.[1] Had Richardson read it ? The resemblances
are evident and striking. In both novels, a heroine in humble
circumstances is pursued with the attentions of her social
superiors, and rewarded for her virtuous resistance by a prosperous marriage. In both, the intimacy and the minute detail
of the reflective and emotional passages are remarkable and
unprecedented. Marivaux makes his heroine recount her experiences years later to a confidential friend. Richardson adopts
the analogous device of autobiographical letters. These are the
main resemblances. Against the view that they tend to support
must be set Richardson's express statement that the tale was
based on fact, his ignorance of French, the absence of any
evidence that he had read even the incomplete translation, and,
lastly, certain very profound differences in his attitude and in
the character he gives his heroine. Marianne, it is true, finds
herself in poor circumstances and at the mercy of a designing
world. But she is no simple peasant. She convinces herself
from the outset that she was the child of persons of quality ;
and, whether or no that can be proved, she has a very lively
sense of her own worth, and is determined not to let her beauty
go to the first bidder. She is, indeed, a very subtle creature,

*Question
of
Richard-
son's
obligations
to
Marivaux*

---

[1] There were three parts available in English before the date of *Pamela*,
and of course Marivaux may have had some influence on the later *Clarissa*.
But it is much likelier the resemblances merely show that both Marivaux and
Richardson were strongly affected by the domestic tragedies and sentimental
comedies which were in vogue. There were three English translations of
Marianne published when Richardson was writing *Clarissa* (see " Translations of the Vie de Marianne," by Helen Sard Hughes (*Mod. Phil.*, xiv. 1917-
1918, pp. 491-512). No stress should be laid on the reference to Marivaux in
the preface to volume iv. of *Clarissa* (1748), which has been shown to be by
Warburton, not by the author of the book (see " Richardson, Warburton and
French Fiction," by R. S. Crane, *Mod. Lang. Rev.*, xvii., 1922, pp. 17-23).

with that keen intuition which makes up in a Frenchwoman
for mature experience of life. Pamela, on the other hand, is
essentially simple. Though she is in love with her master, and
manages in the end to conquer him by remaining unconquerable,
she is not a coquette. She is not innocent, but learns through
her parents' admonitions and her own experience to be very
wideawake. But from first to last, in spite of the pleasure she
takes in the compliments paid her, and in spite of her delight in
reckoning up her articles of apparel and her hopes of making
a fine figure with her singing and dancing, she remains the
little peasant girl, the little prude, with the well-brought-up
country girl's strict regard for what is befitting in every station.
Both Marivaux and Richardson are minute in their analysis
of every sensation ; both Marianne and Pamela continually stop
to make reflections on the situation which, put together, would
fill out a small volume of maxims. But, on the whole, one is
inclined to believe that there was neither imitation nor rivalry
but merely a coincidence of theme and of reflective treatment
due to the same social feelings and interests that were astir in
both countries. If Richardson came under French influence at
all, it is to be looked for rather in *Clarissa* and *Sir Charles
Grandison*, with their affinity to the sentimental romances of
the Scudéry type.[1] If Marivaux influenced any English writer
considerably, it was Sterne rather than Richardson, the sentimentalist rather than the moralist.

Pamela was exactly the sort of book that Richardson's grave *Pamela in*
and tender-hearted contemporaries were waiting for. Everybody *high life*
read it, without distinction of class, everybody in polite society
was prepared to talk about it. Pope said it would " do more
good than many volumes of sermons." It was recommended
from the pulpit. In less than six months it had gone into a
fourth edition. Before a year was out a fraudulent sequel was
published, entitled *Pamela's Conduct in High Life* (1741). A
few objected, including the venerable Dr Isaac Watts, to the

[1] French critics are inclined to take Richardson's obligations to Marivaux
as proved (*e.g.* G. Larroumet's *Marivaux, sa vie et ses œuvres*, 310-318). Clara
L. Thomson (*Samuel Richardson*, 147-153) sums up in the opposite sense, and
Austin Dobson (*Richardson*, 48-50) agrees with her, laying stress on the
chronological difficulties.

questionable moral inculcated by Pamela's discreet and well-remunerated behaviour, and a slashing parody, *An Apology for the Life of Mrs Shamela Andrews*, appeared, probably from the pen of Fielding, which will be examined when that writer's more famous *Joseph Andrews* comes up for discussion. The result of the sham continuation was that Richardson decided to carry on the story himself, and accordingly he published two further volumes giving the history of her married life. Mrs B. and Lady Davers are the principal correspondents in these supplementary letters, in which Richardson showed that he was gaining skill in the exchange of dialogue and the hitting off of small social foibles. But, in the absence of any central interest, he had to spin out a book by going over the old ground again, making Mr B. relapse into his previous courses and once more reform, and amplifying all this with lectures on the minor problems of life and Pamela's reflections on reading Locke's treatise *On Education*. It is a dull book. Warburton thought that Richardson would have done better to have given Pamela's comments on high life from the point of view of simple nature. But Richardson was neither a Montesquieu nor a Goldsmith, and in any case the advice was received after the book had been written.

CHAPTER II

CLARISSA

WHEN Richardson actually commenced *Clarissa* is unknown, but *"Clarissa"* he had made some progress with it by 1745, at which date Aaron Hill mentions " the charming Miss Harlowe." [1] Hill, in fact, had been invited to criticize the new work, and not merely took it upon himself to propose an abridgment, but even sketched out a plan and suggested alternative titles for such a compressed version. [2] Richardson, very wisely, refused to alter his method or reduce his scale. Whether the new novel was to any extent the outcome of his having realized, after the remonstrances received from various quarters, that the doctrine to which he had given his blessing in *Pamela* was not a very lofty or inspiring one, is not a question to be answered too positively. Richardson never admitted the justice of any such criticism. But, at all events, *Clarissa* propounds a very different and far more elevated ideal ; there is no crass materialism in the motives commended here. It is indeed curious that Richardson's second and third novels seem each to correct the ethical attitude of the one next before. The morality of Pamela is far from disinterested, nor does it go without reward. Clarissa looks for heavenly compensation alone. And perhaps her creator and a few of his readers more than half discerned that she exemplified a different order of poetic justice, and that her true reward was her spiritual triumph. [3] No deeper contrast could be imagined than that between the morals to be deduced from these two books. Lastly,

[1] Thomson, 41.   [2] *Ibid.*, 42-43.
[3] Richardson's (and Clarissa's) view was that she would receive her due reward hereafter : see the long postscript to the novel in which he discusses ancient and modern theories of poetic justice, and points out that every one of the worthy or unworthy participants in Lovelace's villainy receives his or her deserts (*Cp.* also p. 75, later). Richardson could not shake off his materialist preconceptions even in questions of high spiritual finance : there must be something to pay.

the character of Sir Charles Grandison was evolved as a reply to the objection that he had made the wicked Lovelace too attractive. Richardson announced that he wished to present " the example of a man acting uniformly well through a variety of trying scenes, because all his actions are regulated by one steady principle. A man of religion and virtue ; of liveliness and spirit ; accomplished and agreeable ; happy in himself, and a blessing to others." [1]

Richard-son's account of his method   *Clarissa* appeared (1747-1748) first in seven volumes, and then in an edition of eight, with " Letters and passages restored from the original manuscript " (1749-1751).[2] It is the longest of Richardson's works, numbering considerably more than five hundred letters, and aggregates, on a rough estimate, about a million words. The four chief correspondents, as is intimated in the preface, are " two young ladies of virtue and honour, bearing an inviolable friendship for each other, and writing not merely for amusement, but upon the most *interesting* subjects ; in which every private family, more or less, may find itself concerned " ; and " two gentlemen of free lives, one of them glorying in his talents for stratagem and invention, and communicating to the other, in confidence, all the secret purposes of an intriguing head and resolute heart." The preface also emphasizes the moral purpose of the book, declaring that " the principal of these two young ladies is proposed as an exemplar to her sex," and sets forth the theory of epistolary fiction. " All the letters are written while the hearts of the writers must be supposed to be wholly engaged in their subjects (the events at the time dubious) : so that they abound not only with critical situations, but with what may be called *instantaneous* descriptions and reflections (proper to be brought home to the breast of the youthful reader) ; as also with affecting conversations ; many of them written in the dialogue or dramatic way." " Much more lively and affecting," he goes on, quoting from one of his own characters, " must be the style of those who write in the height of a *present* distress ; the mind tortured by the pangs of uncertainty (the events then hidden in the womb of fate) ; *than* the dry, narrative, unanimated style of a person relating difficulties and dangers surmounted, can

[1] Preface (*Works*, ix. 10).   [2] Dobson, 82-83.

be ; the relater perfectly at ease : and if himself unmoved by his own story, not likely greatly to affect the reader." [1]

Richardson had happened, more by luck than by calculation, on a method rich in artistic possibilities, and one vastly superior to the haphazard and groping methods of his rivals in fiction. *Advantages of the epistolary method* The actors in his tragic play write out their own parts ; they reveal their emotions, fears, desires, suspense, whilst in the thick of the action. Each incident is set down before the next has given it a new significance, before the issue can be foreseen. It is a method radically superior to the most effective then in vogue, autobiography ; which is historical and retrospective, recording only what is past and finished, and which, moreover, is confined to a single point of view. When several correspondents are made to collaborate, the advantages of different points of view are secured without forgoing the authority of the *ipse dixit*. Each presents his or her own aspect of the case, his or her own attitudes and motives ; all contribute to the fullness and solidarity of the whole. Richardson, with his matter-of-fact imagination, intent upon points of behaviour and shades of feeling, has a certain analogy with Defoe, to whom he was, as it were, the feminine counterpart. The one produced a close likeness of the world as we see it by the steady accumulation of hard, tangible facts ; the other, preoccupied with the inner world of feeling and motive, was as thorough and exhaustive in the registration of mental facts. But there was a vast difference between Defoe, the busy man of the world, and Richardson, shut up in his printer's office. Defoe, when he started work as a novelist, had an almost inexhaustible fund of material to hand, collected from many-sided experiences, keen observation, much reading ; and he was continually adding to his capital. Thus he had plenty of stuff for his imagination to work upon. Richardson, on the contrary, was badly off in this respect ; he had little direct knowledge of the social circles in which his scenes are laid, and had to make up for his ignorance by enormous overdrafts on the imagination. And so, being short of bricks and also of straw, he built up a curiously artificial world, now very like and now remarkably unlike the real one. The device of a voluminous correspondence

[1] Preface to *Clarissa* (*Works*, iv. 12).

was the best a man so handicapped could have chosen, but the results of the handicap were always evident. Let us watch his method at work.

Summary of the story The Harlowes, in Richardson's new novel, are of like social standing to the B. family in *Pamela*, they belong to the upper grades of the middle class which he depicted, more or less correctly, in all his three novels. Clarissa is the beautiful, cultivated, high-spirited younger daughter of a wealthy gentleman, who is hard and avaricious, and nurses ambitions of raising his family to the rank of the nobility. Just before the novel opens, her elder sister Arabella had had attentions paid her by a Mr Robert Lovelace, who, however, after proposing in such a manner as could hardly lead to an acceptance there and then, had taken her coy negative as final, and speedily transferred his addresses to Clarissa. This conduct had been violently resented by Arabella and her brother James, who had forced a duel on Lovelace and come off wounded. The first letter is from Clarissa's bosom-friend, Miss Howe, asking for full particulars of the affair, which Clarissa in several letters proceeds to give. Before long, the reader is in clear possession of the facts. Lovelace, a young man of fortune, with a terrible reputation for profligacy, was recommended by his uncle to pay court to the beautiful and accomplished younger daughter of Mr Harlowe, who had just inherited the fortune of her grandfather and was in every way a great catch. Through his uncle's blundering, he addressed himself to the wrong sister ; but, quickly finding his mistake, he got out of it with a finesse that was one of the talents on which he most prided himself, and transferred his suit to the person originally intended.

Arabella is mortified by his treatment and bitterly jealous of her sister. Her brother James, a hectoring young man, whose one object in the world is to aggrandize the Harlowes and so himself, the prospective head of the family, joins her in moving heaven and earth in opposition to Lovelace's proposals. Clarissa is as yet indifferent to Lovelace, and biased unfavourably by his notorious character. But resistance only excites that person's pertinacity, and he induces her on various pretexts to keep in communication with him. The animosity and greed of her brother and sister force her into a more risky situation. James

Harlowe wants her to marry a Mr Solmes, whose estate lies contiguous to that which he will inherit, and might be exchanged for the one he owns in Scotland and so enable him to round off the property. The whole family unite to push Clarissa into the arms of the insufferable Mr Solmes. She is in despair. Her only help and adviser is Lovelace, who is determined to take every advantage of the situation. That unscrupulous plotter has sworn vengeance on the purse-proud Harlowes, and is now forming the resolve to humble their arrogance, not merely by carrying off the lady, but by the worse indignity of making her his without marriage, even though he should marry her afterwards. He writes to his comrade Belford : " My REVENGE and my LOVE are uppermost by turns. If the latter succeed not, the gratifying of the former will be my only consolation : and by all that's good, they shall feel it ; although for it I become an exile from my native country for ever." [1]

With a forced marriage to Mr Solmes staring her in the face *Clarissa's* Clarissa is at her wits' end. Even the discreet Miss Howe *dilemma* counsels flight, and offers to accompany her. Lovelace begs her to accept the protection of his aunts. For a while she assents. Then her heart misgives her, and she writes to revoke her half-promise. That crafty schemer well perceives that such a decision is imminent, and carefully refrains from taking the letter announcing it from the loose bricks in the wall used as their post-box. She can give him her message only by word of mouth, and she unbolts the garden door to speak to him. Lovelace has one of the servants in his pay ; and when, after listening to his urgent appeals, she turns to re-enter, this man raises an alarm, and she believes that the whole house has discovered her absence. Insane with terror, she suffers herself to be led, half-running, half-fainting, to where Lovelace has his chariot stationed, with two armed servants of his own and two of his kinsman, Lord M.'s, on horseback.

Thus Clarissa is tricked into flight, without the safeguard of her friend Anna Howe's presence. And now that she is in his power, Clarissa finds the conduct and demeanour of her lover change. Miss Howe advises her to marry Lovelace, and Clarissa

[1] Letter 35 (*Works*, iv. 221).

still thinks she has it in her power to accept or refuse him. But there is something in his expression that puzzles and alarms her.

> I watch every turn of his countenance : and I think I see very deep lines in it. He looks with more meaning, I verily think, than he used to look ; yet not more serious ; not less gay—I don't know how he looks—but with more confidence a great deal than formerly ; and yet he never wanted that.[1]

Though she lost her presence of mind at a critical moment, Clarissa is not wanting in penetration. But his complete lack of scruple, the falsehoods that he entwines with his seemingly candid admission of venial offences, his delight in villainy for its own sake, are beyond her comprehension. She cannot believe that a man " so young could be so wicked as he had been reported to be." Yet she is aware that he sets no value on his reputation, and is at the head of a set of libertine friends who will stick at nothing. What may she not apprehend from such a man, in such a position ! "Would to heaven—but what avail wishes now ?—To whom can I fly, if I would fly from him ? " [2]

Lovelace's strategy   Lovelace meanwhile is waiting upon opportunity. He thinks that her resistance is breaking down, that she is beginning to be in love with him. He contrives opportunity by a deep-laid train of stratagems, with the aid of his four faithful Mohocks and a set of abandoned women who are entirely his tools. He makes a show of pressing her to marry him. He is an adept at tendering an offer that courts a refusal. Having taken lodgings for her under the pretence that she is his wife, he pretends to urge her to make the deception unnecessary.

> Since you dislike what I have said, let me implore you, dearest Madam, to give the only proper sanction to it, by naming an early day. Would to heaven that were to be to-morrow ! For God's sake, let it be to-morrow ! But, if not [was it his business, my dear, before I spoke (yet he seemed to be afraid of me) to say, *if not* ?], let me beseech you, Madam, if my behaviour shall not be to your dislike, that you will not to-morrow, at breakfast-time, discredit what I have told them. . . . What could I say ? What could I do ?—I verily think, that had he urged me again, in a

[1] *Works*, v. 167.   [2] *Ibid.*, v. 241.

proper manner, I should have consented (little satisfied as I am with him) to give him a meeting to-morrow morning at a more solemn place than in the parlour below.[1]

He returns to the question over and over again, but always in the same guarded way.

Would to heaven, my dearest life, added he, that, without complimenting *any*body, to-morrow might be the happiest day of my life !—What say you, my angel ? with a trembling impatience, that *seemed* not affected.—What say you for *to-morrow* ?

It was likely, my dear, I could say much to it, or name another day, had I been disposed to the latter, with such a *hinted delay from him.*

I was silent.

Next day, Madam, if not to-morrow ?

Had he given me *time* to answer, it could not have been in the affirmative, you must think—but, *in the same breath*, he went on —Or the *day after that* ?—and taking both my hands in his, he stared me into a half-confusion. Would you have had patience with him, my dear ?

No, no, said I, as calmly as possible, you cannot think that I should imagine there can be reason for such a hurry. It will be most agreeable, to be sure, for my Lord to be present.

I am all obedience and resignation, returned the wretch, with a self-pluming air, as if he had acquiesced to a proposal *made by me*, and had complimented me with a great piece of *self-denial*.

Is it not plain, my dear, that he designs to vex and tease me ? Proud, yet mean and foolish man, if so !—But you say all punctilio is at an end with me. Why, why will he take pains to make a heart wrap itself up in reserve, that wishes only, and that for his sake as well as my own, to observe due decorum ?[2]

But form and decorum are by now the least things at stake, *Clarissa* as she speedily finds. Lovelace is only throwing dust in her eyes *at bay* when he harps on an early day, talks at large about marriage settlements, and wonders when it will be convenient for his noble relatives to attend the ceremony. The longer her durance continues, the more hopelessly is Clarissa at his mercy. She is even in love with him a little. Bewildered and annoyed by his tergiversation, she yet confesses to Anna that he has made an

[1] *Works*, v. 418-419.   [2] *Ibid.*, vi. 52.

impression on her heart, which becomes plain to her when he suddenly falls ill.

'Tis true I have owned more than once, that I could have liked Mr Lovelace above all men. I remember the debates you and I used to have on this subject, when I was your happy guest. You used to say, and once you wrote, that men of his cast are the men that our sex do not *naturally* dislike : while I held that such were not (however *that* might be) the men we *ought* to like. . . . If love, as it is called, is allowed to be an excuse for our most unreasonable follies, and to lay level all the fences that a careful education has surrounded us by, what is meant by the doctrine of subduing our passions ?—But, oh, my dearest friend, am I not guilty of a punishable fault, were I to love this man of errors ? And has not my own heart deceived me, when I thought I did not ? And what must be that love, that has not some degree of purity for its object ? [1]

Lovelace, for his part, is violently in love with her ; but nothing can divert him from his resolve. " Hard-heartedness as it is called," he writes in one of four letters given only in part, " is an essential of the libertine's character. Familiarized to the distresses he occasions, he is seldom betrayed by tenderness into a complaisant weakness unworthy of himself." About the marriage settlements he continues :

I am in earnest as to the terms. If I marry her (and I have no doubt that I shall, after my pride, my ambition, my revenge, if thou wilt, is gratified), I will do her noble justice. But by my soul, Belford, her haughtiness shall be brought down to own both love and obligation to me. . . . At the very altar, our hands joined, I will engage to make this proud beauty leave the parson and me, and all my friends who should be present, though twenty in number, to look like fools upon one another, while she took wing and flew out of the church door, or window (if that were open, and the door shut) ; and this only by a single word.[2]

She shall be his, though his damnation were to be the purchase.

Improbabilities of the story It may be asked, it has often been asked, why did not Clarissa throw herself on the compassion of some stranger, or appeal for redress to a magistrate. " Justice Fielding," Scott remarked,

[1] *Works*, vi. 207-208. [2] *Ibid.*, vi. 56.

"would have afforded her his most effectual protection."[1]
Would the Harlowes have allowed even an erring daughter to
disappear in such suspicious circumstances without raising a
hue and cry ? Would Belford, whose pity and admiration revolt
against his chief's brutality, when it is too late, have remained
subservient so long ? His remonstrances before the fatal deed
are futile. The exigencies of Richardson's underlying purpose
required that Clarissa should suffer, and he put a severe strain
on probability to attain his end. Even in Georgian London, in
the lawless days of the Mohocks, it is incredible that a lady
of wealth and fashion should be maltreated and held a close
prisoner with impunity, or that a conspiracy in which so many
were implicated should not leak out.[2] The case of Pamela, only
a poor maidservant, and the abduction of Harriet Byron, in
Richardson's third novel, which was an affair of promptitude
and surprise and after all failed of success, are not quite fair
comparisons.[3] As in some other tragic histories, what may be
described as certain external improbabilities must be overlooked,
for the sake of the truth and greatness of the inner drama.
Richardson's method makes this more difficult, since we are
shown the letters passing on both sides, and keep asking ourselves why Clarissa, with her keen insight, fails to see through
her lover's specious strategy and does not detect his wiles in
time. But to insist on these evident weaknesses would be almost the same as ranging ourselves on the side of Richardson's
contemporaries, who entreated him to spare Clarissa and let her

escape the pursuer's toils. The mental story has a coherence, and the impending tragedy has an inevitableness, beyond these questions of the adequacy or inadequacy of the machinery. The shortcomings of Richardson's practical experience of the world must be forgiven, when we centre attention on the lofty figure conjured up by the poetic vision of the middle-aged printer.

The catas- Clarissa does make bootless efforts to escape. After a ruffianly
trophe and attempt to surprise her, she actually gets away, but has nowhere
Clarissa's better to go than to Hampstead, whither Lovelace traces her, and
moral by the persuasions of two courtesans, dressed up to impersonate
victory his kinswomen Lady Betty Lawrance and Miss Montague, decoys her back to the house in London kept by the abominable Mrs Sinclair. There by the aid of drugs he reaps his sorry triumph. He tries to brazen it out, when Belford reproaches him for the monstrous wrong he has committed. "When all's done, Miss Clarissa Harlowe has but run the fate of a thousand others of her sex—only that they did not set such a romantic value upon what they call their honour ; that's all." If she hates him, she will forgive, and it shall then be the study of his whole life to make her happy. But the lady's piteous and incurable anguish wakens even his remorse.

Cæsar never knew what it was to be *hipped*, I will call it, till he came to be what Pompey was ; that is to say, till he arrived at the height of his ambition : nor did thy Lovelace know what it was to be gloomy, till he had completed his wishes upon the most charming creature in the world.

But, if remorseful, he is still unrepentant.

And yet why say I *completed* ? when the *will*, the *consent*, is wanting—and I have still views before me of obtaining that ? [1]

Holding to her noble ideals of womanhood, with the inflexible resolution of the Harlowes, Clarissa refuses to accept a vile seducer as a husband. She tries again to escape, and confronts Lovelace and the women who are set to guard her. He describes the scene to Belford. They hear her coming downstairs, and know that she cannot get out, " the street door . . . doubly secured, and every shutter to the windows round the house

[1] *Works*, vii. 56.

fastened, that no noise or screaming could be heard " ; and then she enters,

confiding in her own innocence ; and with a majesty in her person and manner, that is *natural* to her ; but which then shone out in all its glory !—Every tongue silent, every eye awed, every heart quaking, mine, in a particular manner sunk, throbless, and twice below its usual region, to once at my throat :—a shameful recreant !—She silent too, looking round her, first on me ; then on the mother, as no longer fearing her ; then on Sally, Polly, and the culprit Dorcas !—such the glorious power of innocence exerted at that awful moment !

She would have spoken, but could not, looking down my guilt into confusion. A mouse might have been heard passing over the floor : her own light feet and rustling silks could not have prevented it ; for she seemed to tread air, and to be all soul. She passed backwards and forwards, now towards me, now towards the door several times, before speech could get the better of indignation ; and at last, after twice or thrice hemming to recover her articulate voice — Oh, thou contemptible and abandoned Lovelace, thinkest thou that I see not through this poor villainous plot of thine, and of these thy wicked accomplices ?

Thou, woman (looking at the mother), once my terror ! always my dislike ! but now my detestation ! shouldst once more (for thine perhaps was the preparation) have provided for me intoxicating potions, to rob me of my senses—And then, thus, wretch (turning to me), mightest thou more securely have depended upon such a low contrivance as this!

And ye, vile women, who perhaps have been the ruin, body and soul, of hundreds of innocents (you show me *how*, in full assembly), know that I am *not* married—ruined as I am, by your help, I bless God, I am not married to this miscreant—and I have friends that will demand my honour at your hands !—and to whose authority I will apply ; for none has this man over me. Look to it, then, what further insults you offer me, or incite him to offer me. I am a person, though thus vilely betrayed, of rank and fortune. I never will be his ; and to your utter ruin, will find friends to pursue you : and now I have this full proof of your detestable wickedness, and have heard your base incitements, will have no mercy upon you ! [1]

Lovelace continues : " They could not laugh at the poor figure I made. — Lord ! how every devil, conscience shaken,

[1] *Works,* vii. 157-158.

trembled !" Even the wretched women who had abetted him, half-believing the pretence that she was his wife, are struck with pity. Never, they told him afterwards, had they beheld such a scene. "Then, taking one of the lights, she turned from us ; and away she went, unmolested.—Not a soul was *able* to molest her." [1]

Importance of the letters relating Clarissa's inflexible repudiation of Lovelace

It takes more than two hundred letters and many hundreds of pages to relate what follows this climax, for, although the dramatic scenes are played out and the one event of consequence that remains is the death of Clarissa, this, in a profound sense, is the most important part of the book. Still an outcast from her family, but entreated by her loyal friends to accept the reparation offered by Lovelace, Clarissa remains firm ; her heart is broken, and she prepares by meditation and by affectionate messages to all who love her for entry upon that state of existence where alone justice is apportioned. Her trust in the eternal goodness never falters. As the end draws near, she has no desire to see even her dearest friends. " God will have no rivals in the hearts of those he sanctifies." She appoints the repentant Belford her executor, with orders to collect and arrange her correspondence. She directs that her coffin shall be made and placed in her room. "Who, that makes a will, should be afraid of a coffin ? " She says to the women at her lodgings who are shocked to see it carried up : " I love to do everything for myself that I can do. I ever did. . . . Minutenesses may be observed, where greater articles are not neglected for them. I might have had this to order, perhaps, when less fit to order it, I have no mother, no sister, no Mrs Norton, no Miss Howe, near me. . . . I shall not die the sooner for such a preparation."

Richardson dwells on these pathetic details, not merely because the age of sentiment relished them, but because it was in the last phase of her tragedy that the whole significance lay. It is not Clarissa's resistance to Lovelace that constitutes her greatness, but the magnanimity and dignity of a character that rises superior to earthly dishonour. Her purity of soul remains untarnished by another's outrage. So intensely living was the creation which Richardson's genius had brought into the world,

[1] *Works*, vii. 162.

that while her fate was trembling in the balance thousands waited in awe-struck suspense to know the issue of her trials. She became, as she was meant to be, an example to all mankind. And in this wonderful being evolved by the moral Richardson, who in so much of his writing appears a pedantic, small-minded person,[1] art, as it were through an unconscious instrument, triumphed over reality at all points.

When she is dead, Mrs Howe, who had put a stop to the correspondence with her daughter when she thought Clarissa compromised by Lovelace's treatment, realizes that " never did there live a lady more deserving of general admiration and lamentation than Miss Clarissa Harlowe ; and never was there a stronger friendship dissolved by death than between her young lady and her." But Richardson, by a clever stroke, makes the reformed rake Belford the mouthpiece of his own sentiments and of the proper application of her story. He writes to Lovelace : " I never knew what a virtuous, a holy friendship, as I may call mine to her, was before. But to be so new to it, and to be obliged to forgo it so soon, what an affliction! " And, when she is gone, he gives his friend the whole history of her last days, pointing out the final lesson of what has taken place : to crush that hellish delusion " that a reformed rake makes the best husband." *The retribution dealt out to the evil-doers*

How, indeed, can it be, if this point be duly weighed, that a man who thinks alike of all the sex, and knows it to be in the power of a wife to do him the greatest dishonour man can receive, and doubts not her will to do it, if opportunity offer, and importunity be not wanting : that such a one, from principle, should be a good husband to any woman ? And indeed little do innocents think, what a total revolution of manners, what a change of fixed habits, nay, what a conquest of a bad nature, and what a portion of divine GRACE, is required, to make a man a good husband, a worthy father, and true friend, from principle ; especially when it is considered that it is not in a man's power to reform when he

---

[1] Coleridge said : "I confess that it has cost, and still costs, my philosophy some exertion not to be vexed that I must admire, aye, greatly admire, Richardson. His mind is so very vile a mind, so oozy, so hypocritical, praise-mad, canting, envious, concupiscent! . . . Richardson felt truly the defect of Fielding, or what was not his excellence, and made that his *defect* —a trick of uncharitableness often played, though not exclusively, by contemporaries " (*Anima Poetæ*, 166-167).

will. This (to say nothing of my own experience), thou, Lovelace, hast found in the progress of thy attempts upon the divine Miss Harlowe. For whose remorses could be deeper, or more frequent, yet more transient than thine ? [1]

By another irony, Clarissa's family, who had stood aloof during her distress, write repentant and regretful letters when it is too late for any earthly reconciliation, and are left with their share in her undoing to embitter the remainder of their lives. To the one kinsman whose loyalty was never impugned, her cousin and guardian Colonel Morden, who had unfortunately been away during the critical months, Clarissa had left a letter in condemnation of duelling, fearing he would undertake to avenge her. But Lovelace, a branded wanderer like Cain, gives him an opportunity to meet him. A duel is fought, and Lovelace falls mortally wounded, his last words being : " Let this expiate ! "

" Un-flinching realism" *of certain* *scenes* *depicted* Retribution falls likewise on other of the foremost actors.[2] Belton, one of the gang of roisterers who had aided and applauded Lovelace, dies in terrible convulsions, sure that he is going straight to eternal torment. Still more gruesome is the death-scene of Mrs Sinclair, keeper of the bagnio where Clarissa had endured such atrocities. Going to bed drunk, she had fallen and injured her leg ; the limb had gangrened, and in agonies of fear she had sent for Belford, who knew all about her part in the Harlowe affair. Belford describes, with a realism that would have done credit to a Zola, the inmates of the house of ill-fame in their morning deshabille :

. . . just up, risen perhaps from their customers in the forehouse, and their nocturnal orgies, with faces, three or four of them, that had run, the paint lying in streaky seams not half blowzed off, discovering coarse wrinkled skins ; the hair of some of them of divers colours, obliged to the black-lead comb where black was affected ; the artificial jet, however, yielding apace to the natural brindle ; that of others plastered with oil and powder ; the oil predominating ; but every one's hanging about her ears and neck in broken curls, or ragged ends ; and each at my entrance taken with one motion, stroking their matted locks with both hands under their coifs, mobs, or pinners, every one of which was

---

[1] *Works*, viii. 351.
[2] See Postscript (*Works*, viii. 531-532).

awry. They were all slip-shoes ; stockingless some ; only under-petticoated all ; their gowns, made to cover straddling hoops, hanging trollopy, and tangling about their heels ; but hastily wrapt round them, as soon as I came upstairs. And half of them (bunpadded, shoulder-bent, pallid-lipt, limber-jointed wretches) appearing from a blooming nineteen or twenty perhaps over-night, haggard well-worn strumpets of thirty-eight or forty.[1]

The pen of the moralist exposing the ugliness of unrighteous-ness is very evident. But what is to be said of the realism ? We may be sure that Richardson himself had never been inside the doors of such an establishment ; he was no modern investigator of the seamy side, content with nothing less than direct personal observation. He learned his facts from sources open to any interested inquirer. It is, in short, but another example of his ordinary method. As in the portrayal of Lovelace or Clarissa—as in depicting so many scenes of life with which he could have no intimate acquaintance—Richardson's " strong matter-of-fact imagination," and, no doubt, what he had learned from his friends, produced, to quote Hazlitt again, " an artificial reality, which is nowhere else to be met with." [2]

The authors of *Mr Badman* and of *Nana*, could they have combined forces, might have equalled the scene to which this is the introduction. Belford is ushered into the bedroom of the dying prostitute, whose writhing " quaggy carcase " is described in the colours of repulsion. The hideous half-dressed crew huddle round the bed of their mistress, who yells curses at them for leaving her to the mercies of two ignorant surgeons, talking the jargon of their trade and caring for nothing but their fees. (Both here and in the Belton scene Richardson has a spiteful dig at the medical fraternity.) The nauseating sights and smells and noises are described with overpowering vividness ; but it is the dying anguish of the worn-out sinner that is the chief subject of the piece. Neither in *Moll Flanders* nor in *Roxana* had Defoe attempted anything of quite this kind :

[1] *Works*, viii. 342.
[2] Richardson's footnote on the passage cited is characteristic: " Whoever has seen Dean Swift's lady's dressing-room, will think this description of Mr Belford's not only more *natural*, but more *decent painting*, as well as better justified by the *design*, and by the *use* that may be made of it " (*loc. cit.*)

As soon as she saw me, her naturally big voice, more hoarsened by her ravings, broke upon me : O Mr Belford ! O sir ! see what I am come to !—See what I am brought to !—To have such a cursed crew about me, and not one of them to take care of me ! . . . Cursed, cursed be every careless devil !—May this or worse be their fate, every one of them ! And then she cursed and swore most vehemently, and the more, as two or three of them were excusing themselves on the score of their being at that time as unable to help themselves as she. As soon as she had cleared the passage of her throat by the oaths and curses which her wild impatience made her utter, she began in a more hollow and whining strain to bemoan herself. And here, said she—Heaven grant me patience (clenching and unclenching her hands) am I to die thus miserably !—of a broken leg in my old age !—snatched away by means of my own intemperance !— Self-done !—Self-undone !—No time for my affairs ! No time to repent !—And in a few hours (Oh !—Oh !—with another long-howling O—h !—U—gh—O ! a kind of screaming key terminating it) who knows, who can tell *where* I shall be ?— Oh, that indeed I never, never had had a being !

Belford, confounded and helpless, advises her to get into a better frame of mind. Then she remembers her injury to Miss Harlowe, and curses the man who had led her into this, the most crying of all her sins. Belford begs her again to compose herself, then at least she would die with more ease.

But the word die put her into a violent raving, and thus she broke in upon me. Die, did you say, sir ?—Die !—I will not, I cannot die !—I know not how to die !—Die, sir !—And must I then die ?—Leave this world ?—I cannot bear it—And who brought you hither, sir ?—(her eyes striking fire at me) Who brought you hither to tell me I must die, sir ?—I cannot, I will not leave this world. Let others die, who wish for another ! who expect a better !—I have had my plagues in this ; but would compound for all future hopes, so as I may be nothing after this !

And then she howled and bellowed by turns. By my faith, Lovelace, I trembled in every joint ; and looking upon her who spoke thus, and roared thus, and upon the company round me, I more than once thought myself to be in one of the infernal mansions.[1]

[1] *Works*, viii. 344-345.

Thirty-two characters are enumerated in the list of the *The figure* principal persons at the beginning of the novel ; of these half *of Clarissa* at least are drawn with great care and fullness, all are clearly individualized, two are among the most memorable creations in literature. In *Pamela*, Richardson had managed to endue a sturdy, commonplace figure with life, in a manner hitherto un-exampled in English fiction. But as an artistic creation Pamela was marred by Richardson's crude didacticism. In *Clarissa* a fine idea took hold of him and carried him beyond the orbit of his pedagogic vision: the idea of the natural purity and excellence of a woman's heart, and her power to suffer shames untold with-out surrendering her personal dignity ; and so he conjured up a mind and soul that could not be stuffed into the pigeon-holes of any prudential scheme of morality, but had to run its course to the death. Clarissa is exquisite and true. She is one of the noblest creations in literature, and perhaps the most complete. Her charm, her pride, her modesty are salient qualities. But Richardson, the head of his salon of intellectual women, the friend of Miss Mulso—the superfine Mrs Chapone to be—of the Fielding sisters, Mrs Delany, Miss Carter, and the rest, was bent upon showing that she had a mind,[1] that she was not merely one of those creatures, all heart and emotion, for whom Meredith would have prayed : " More brain, O Lord, more brain ! " Her discussions with Miss Howe, or the conversations in which she holds the redoubtable Lovelace at bay and confutes his sophistries, would take too much space to quote. But there is room for a few of her aphorisms.

How neatly she exposes the foolishness of the mean man, in her judgment of Mr Solmes :

When the difference between the obtaining of a fame for generosity, and incurring the censure of being a miser, will not, prudently managed, cost fifty pounds a year.[2]

The world, as I have often thought, ill-natured as it is said to be, is generally more just in characters (speaking by what it *feels*) than is usually apprehended ; and those who complain most of

[1] Sir Charles Grandison was afterwards to assure Harriet Byron that he had never left *mind* out of his notions of love (*Works*, x. 223).
[2] *Works*, iv. 111.

its censoriousness, perhaps should look *inwardly* for the occasion oftener than they do.[1]

There never was a rogue who had not a salvo to himself for being so.—What a praise to honesty, that every man pretends to it, even at the instant that he knows he is pursuing the methods that will perhaps prove him a knave to the whole world, as well as to his own conscience ![2]

I fancy, my dear, however, that there would hardly be a guilty person in the world, were each suspected or accused person to tell his or her own story, and be allowed any degree of credit.[3]

Loving sensibility, she knows it can only be enjoyed at a price. She writes to Anna Howe of her sister Arabella's bullying, and her involuntary reminder of happier days when the family peace was undisturbed :

I met only with insult for this—Bella has not a feeling heart. The highest joy in this life she is not capable of : but then she saves herself many griefs, by her impenetrableness—yet, for ten times the pain that such a sensibility is attended with, would I not part with the pleasure it brings with it.[4]

The figure of Lovelace The character of Lovelace is more difficult to assess, and strangely diverse have been the sentences passed upon him by distinguished critics. The contradiction is not surprising, since Richardson had to fashion, out of his inner consciousness as usual, a being that would fulfil contradictory requirements. Lovelace had to be fascinating and not without some sterling merits, else he could never have interested Clarissa : he had to be vile, else he would never have betrayed so worshipful a creature.[5] He had to be veritably in love, yet be capable of the most un-adulterated baseness towards the object of his affection. The result is a conglomeration of virtues and vices, human and inhuman attributes, such as neither Richardson nor anybody else ever saw in real life ; a being compounded of ingredients that were never intended to mix, made up, as it were, on a prescription for a therapeutic purpose. To say that " Lovelace is a lady's

---

[1] *Works,* iv. 111.
[2] *Ibid.,* 220.
[3] *Ibid.,* 234.
[4] *Ibid.,* 275.
[5] This " regality " fascinated Hazlitt, who very injudiciously characterizes Grandison as a poltroon and a blockhead (" Why the Heroes of Romances are Insipid," *Sketches and Essays,* 183-184). Into such absurdities is even a critic led by the *ignis fatuus* of antithesis.

villain, as Grandison is a lady's hero," is merely to observe that he is drawn by Richardson, who in his attempts to draw men always seems an outsider. He simply did not know that sex. He is interested, fascinated, puzzled by the task : one can see him painfully doing his best, modifying the character as the tale goes on, yet never succeeding in making it quite natural ; whereas his women come to life as if he were painting from flesh and blood.

To look for the original of a Lovelace seems, on the face of it, absurd. If Richardson had ever met anyone like him he would never have seen through his external pretences. For, again, he was of the wrong sex. Richardson had once had some business transactions with the brilliant reprobate, Philip, Duke of Wharton, who has been put forward as a possible model for Lovelace. But there is no evidence that Richardson and his aristocratic client ever came into personal contact.[1] A more reasonable idea is that Lovelace was suggested by the " gay Lothario " in Rowe's *Fair Penitent*.[2] But why particularize ? Lovelace belongs to a numerous and well-known lineage. He is of the same seed as the superfine, conquering rakes of post-Restoration drama, of the patrician seducers in Mrs Behn's and Mrs Hayward and Manley's novels, of the Villiers, Rochesters, and Ethereges of real life. He is the apotheosis, if the word can be so twisted, of a Gramont libertine.

Lovelace is no mere sensual egotist, but an incarnation of the spirit of mischief and the love of intrigue for its own sake, with a ruthlessness which spares nothing that stands in its way. He asks Jack Belford :

How will the good folks account for it, that Satan has such faithful instruments, and that the bond of wickedness is a stronger

---

[1] The suggestion is discussed by Miss Thomson (pp. 14-16, 199) and Austin Dobson (pp. 12-13). The question of Mr B. is also involved. Richardson told Hill : " I am a good deal warped by the character of a gentleman I had in my eye, when I drew both him and Mr B. in *Pamela*. The best of him for the latter ; the worst of him for Lovelace, made still worse by mingling the worst of two other characters, that were as well known to me, of that gentleman's acquaintance. And this made me say in my last, that I aimed at an uncommon, altho' I supposed, a not quite unnatural character " (Letter to Aaron Hill, 26th June 1747, *ibid.*, 88-89).

[2] The resemblances are shown in detail by H. G. Ward. See "Richardson's Character of Lovelace" (*Mod. Lang. Rev.*, vii., 1912, pp. 494-498). Richardson's quotations from Rowe and references to Lothario confirm the supposition.

bond than the ties of virtue ? as if it were the nature of the human mind to be villainous ? . . . . Cannot our fraternity in a hundred instances give proof of the like predominance of vice over virtue ? And that we have risked more to serve and promote the interests of the former, than ever a good man did to serve a good man or a good cause.[1]

To the service he has deliberately chosen, he dedicates his fault-less courtesy, keen intelligence and unfailing wit, a social address there is no withstanding, presence of mind and resourcefulness, indomitable courage, and a generosity that acknowledges great-ness in others. But he remains a manufactured article rather than a creation of imaginative art. Lovelace has often been pronounced an impossible character, and condemned by Aris-totelian canons. It is argued that we can imagine such a monster as Caliban, but not such a man as Lovelace.[2] This argument misses the point, or, rather, inverts it. Such characters as Lovelace and Sir Charles Grandison are examples of the possible but highly improbable, whilst Caliban is probable but impossible. But neither the improbable nor the impossible has any place in fiction that purports to be realistic. Lovelace is one of the greater improbabilities in the novel *Clarissa*, which contains a good many things that might possibly have happened in real life, but are far too abnormal for fiction. Little more can be said in defence than Scott has said : " Some exaggeration must be allowed to the author of a romance ; and considering the part which Love-lace had to perform, it was necessary that his character should be highly coloured." [3] And this leaves us with the same criticism in another form, that Richardson undertook a representation of real life but imported into it elements allowable only in romance.

Other   The Harlowe family are admirably true and lifelike. The *characters* stern, tyrannical father would be incredible in any other period of English social history, but was then not very extraordinary. Such a father, such a household ! The crushed and broken-spirited mother ; the son, conceited, grasping, and obstinate ; the sister, envious and spiteful ; the servants, some sympathetic,

[1] *Works*, vii. 108.
[2] Twining's edition of Aristotle's *Poetics* (see Dobson, 91).
[3] *Lives of the Novelists*, 401.

one a traitor, all obsequious : these form a domestic background to the heroine's sufferings incomparably richer in life and variety than any novelist before Richardson and Fielding had attempted. The vivacious, clear-sighted, loyal, but impish Miss Howe provides, not only a humorous commentary, but also throughout something of that sane and critical poise which is a function of the chorus in Greek drama. For, although it is not at all likely that Richardson had calculated these effects, and he confessed himself " a very irregular writer," who " can form no plan, nor write after what I have preconceived," he identified himself with his characters, and absorbed himself in the drama that was going forward, with such an intensity that he was dead to everything, including the moral theorem to be demonstrated, except his engrossing vision of life. His characters moved in his mind, as it were of their own volition, into the situations that gave the fullest scope and precision to the clash of personality. And the result was the balance and shapeliness that are the signs of great art.

In the prefaces to his books, and in the very titles, however, he *The* deprecated any such attitude. He regarded himself, not as an *didactic* artist or entertainer, but as a responsible teacher. In offering *purpose in* *"Clarissa"* this to the public, he wrote : " Considerate readers will not enter upon the perusal of the piece before them as if it were designed only to divert and amuse. It will probably be thought tedious to all such as dip into it, expecting a light novel, or transitory romance ; and look upon the story in it (interesting as that is generally allowed to be) as its sole end, rather than as a vehicle to the instruction." [1] He entitled it, *Clarissa ; or the History of a young Lady, comprehending the most important concerns of private life, and particularly showing the distresses that may attend the misconduct both of parents and children in relation to marriage,* clearly advertising the practical object. There is no question that he regarded his books primarily as edifying treatises on conduct, more serious than those of a previous age because more concerned with religion. He returned to the point in the preface to *Sir Charles Grandison,* where again he explains his object in writing the history of Clarissa, " a truly Christian heroine . . .

[1] Preface to *Clarissa* (*Works,* iv, 12-13).

whose letters, it is hoped, afford many useful lessons to the gay part of mankind, against that misuse of wit and youth, of rank and fortune, and of every outward accomplishment, which turns them into a curse to the miserable possessor, as well as to all around him." And he gives the same caution with regard to this, the third novel, that it " is not published ultimately, nor even principally, any more than the other two, for the sake of entertainment only. A much nobler end is in view." [1] There was actually a supplement to *Clarissa* in which the moral and religious end monopolized attention. This was a small volume with the title *Meditations collected from the Sacred Books ; and adapted to the different Stages of a deep Distress ; gloriously surmounted by Patience, Piety and Resignation. Being those mentioned in the History of Clarissa as drawn up for her own Use* (1750). It contains thirty-six of the meditations which the heroine transcribed into her note-book during her last days on earth ; four of them are given in the novel.

Richardson's artistic sense versus his didacticism   But it was Richardson's sense of dramatic propriety,[2] not his moral convictions, that determined the shape of *Clarissa*, and made him turn a deaf ear to all entreaties that he should respite the heroine and contrive a happy ending to her story. The most grotesque of these appeals for his forbearance was from Colley Cibber's friend, the effusive Lætitia Pilkington, who wrote, after describing Cibber's violent outbreak when he heard of the proposed martyrdom of the heroine, " Spare her virgin purity, dear Sir, spare it ! Consider, if this wounds both Mr Cibber and me (who neither of us set up for immaculate chastity), what must it do with those who possess that inestimable treasure ? " More interesting is the fact that a similar appeal came from Fielding, who had praised the early volumes of *Clarissa* in *The Jacobite's Journal.* His brother novelist Scott held no such heterodox opinion.

---

[1] *Works*, x. 10.
[2] He speaks of *Clarissa* as a " Dramatic Narrative " in the interesting Postscript (*Works*, viii. 525).
[3] *Correspondence*, 130-131.

CHAPTER III

SIR CHARLES GRANDISON

THERE can be little doubt that the appearance of Fielding's *Tom Jones* (1749) had something to do with the inception of Richardson's third novel, *The History of Sir Charles Grandison* "*Sir in a Series of Letters published from the Originals* (1753-1754). *Charles* Richardson, however, intimates in the preface that he had all *Grandison*" along planned a sort of trilogy, of which this was to be the final portion. He also speaks of the insistence of his friends that " he should produce into public view the character and actions of a man of *true honour.*"[1] His friend Lady Bradshaigh had hoped that he would provide a masculine counterpart to the saintly Clarissa, enforcing the request with animadversions on the popularity of *Tom Jones* and its pernicious moral influence. As already noted, the fascinations of Lovelace seemed to call for some creation that would serve with susceptible young readers as an antidote. Fielding's claims to have written a book recommending " Goodness and Innocence, to convince men that their true interest directs them to a pursuit of Virtue," and to have furnished in this work " a stronger Picture of a truly benevolent Mind than is to be found in any other," must have been deeply irritating to one who professed disgust at the freedom and levity with which licentious scenes were treated in this great comic survey of every phase of English life. Still more annoying to Richardson's thin-skinned self-esteem were the acclamations that greeted *Tom Jones* : his supremacy was challenged by a rival who had wounded him beyond forgiveness by his ridicule of *Pamela*, in *Joseph Andrews*, and also, he was convinced, in the scurrilous *Shamela*. The author of *Clarissa* regarded himself, not erroneously, as the recognized champion of those who took life as a solemn and serious affair and were outraged when

[1] *Works*, ix. 9-10.

problems of conduct became the subject of raillery. Once more war was declared between the forces of Puritanism and respectability and the free-lances of wit, and art, and intellect ; once more was the strife renewed between the modern spirit, the spirit of freedom and humour, and the old standing army of intolerance and restraint.

Sir Charles Grandison, a novel in seven volumes,[1] almost as long as *Clarissa*, and by no means so absorbing as a story, is not for the present age ; but it did not fail of success in its own day : Richardson's defensive blow was a shrewd one. His genius was more sure of itself than ever. General admiration had given him the utmost self-confidence, and had contributed to the development of his peculiar art, if it had not strengthened his original powers of insight and imaginative creation. In this last novel his technique is at its best ; if the story lacks the sustained interest of *Clarissa*, it is full of lively episodes and moving situations. Although there is no single figure so inimitably true and living as Pamela or so impressive as Clarissa, there is a larger multitude than in either of the previous books of distinct characters well representative of the genteel world of that day. Nearly fifty names are included in the list of principal persons, and are grouped under the three heads of men, women, and Italians. Of chiefest importance are three : the heroine who eventually carries off the hero, a faultless and colourless young lady, whose interest for the reader is almost entirely comprised in her being, so to speak, the extremely sensitive optical instrument through which we study the perfections of the hero ; Sir Charles Grandison himself, who is also contemplated, through other correspondents, from every possible viewpoint ; and the pathetic Clementina, who loves and loses Sir Charles, or rather, sacrifices her affections to the higher claims of religion.

Outline of the story Our first introduction is to Miss Harriet Byron, who for formality's sake may be described as the heroine. A young lady of moderate fortune, she has just come to London, and without delay finds herself surrounded by candidates for her hand. The persons and comparative merits of her adorers are discussed with Richardson's accustomed minuteness, in letters and conversations

---

[1] A six-volume edition simultaneously.

between a large number of friends. But a mere summary of the plot will be enough at this stage. Two suitors stand out as specially interesting : Mr Greville, who nearly dies, and in the end actually goes mad, for the lady he fails to win ; and the handsome and self-conceited roué, Sir Hargrave Pollexfen, Baronet, who tries high-handed measures when fair courtship proves unavailing. Decisively refused by Miss Byron, he carries her off after a ball, but is accidentally intercepted by Sir Charles Grandison, an incident that brings on the scene, with suitable éclat, this central figure. Miss Byron inevitably falls in love with the knight-errant who has done her so signal a service. He becomes the idol of her circle ; he has long been that of all who know him. Her devotion is soon no secret to any-one about her : she confides her sentiments to her dear friend Miss Selby ; they are communicated to or easily detected by everybody at Selby House, and are soon the theme of general discussion and benevolent sympathy.

At a much later date, Sir Charles Grandison divulges the fact that he too was conscious of her regard and fain to return it. But, alas, he was fettered by other ties. One day, he has a quiet talk with Harriet, and relates his history. He had but recently come back to England after spending some years in Italy, in the course of which he had chanced to render the most valuable of services to a scion of a very noble Italian family living at Bologna. They had entertained their son's preserver, whose graces of mind and person won him the usual homage, and unfortunately made a fatal impression on the heart of their daughter, Clementina della Porretta. On his departure, this young lady had fallen into such a state of melancholia that the family had been obliged to send for him to return, and, though he was a foreigner and a heretic, were prepared to accept him as a son-in-law if he would agree to become a Roman Catholic and settle in Italy. Sir Charles could not submit to these condi-tions, and the proposals fell through. But now it appeared that Clementina had had a relapse, and he was invited to return to Italy and discuss new terms for an alliance, as the lady's reason and perhaps her life were at stake. Sir Charles felt himself bound in honour to submit to their wishes, although his own feelings towards Clementina were those of generous compassion rather than anything warmer.

Suspense during the conferences with Clementina's family   The baronet sets out for Bologna, leaving not only Harriet, but also his ward Emily Jervois and another Italian lady who had followed him to England, weeping at the imminent downfall of all their hopes. For months, Harriet, with a large body of well-wishers, remains in poignant suspense. Her tender heart has been wrung with pity for the other helpless victim of her lover's attractions ; she is above petty jealousy, yet she cannot but hope against hope that her rival may somehow find happiness without annihilating hers. The time drags wearily on. At intervals there is news from Bologna, where Sir Charles is engaged in solemn conference with all the assembled members of the Porretta family, the parents, the brothers, the bishop, the general, and the rest of them, and reports every stage with exhaustive minuteness to his revered friend Dr Bartlett. Everything is pointing to a successful end of the negotiations, and Harriet is in acute distress. But, when all difficulties have been removed, Clementina herself realizes that a union is impossible with one of an opposite creed whose soul she fears is marked for perdition. Sir Charles loyally entreats her not to persist in this resolve ; but she declares that it is her intention to take the veil, and begs him to marry one of his own countrywomen.

The sequel may be guessed, but it takes nearly two volumes to relate it. Once free, Sir Charles offers himself to Miss Byron, and the rest of the story consists of an account of the engagement, the congratulations of Harriet's friends, the wedding, and the happiness of the united pair, with such episodes as an outbreak on the part of Greville, who wants to fight Sir Charles, but is neatly disarmed, the death of Sir Hargrave Pollexfen, who leaves most of his property to Sir Charles and Lady Grandison, and Clementina's flight to England, whither she is pursued by her parents, who persuade her at last to look favourably on the suit of the Count of Belvedere, the lover whom Grandison had eclipsed.

Richardson was pestered with requests to carry on the story still further ; but he pointed out that as the events already narrated had reached the present year of grace, this was out of the question.[1] In a concluding note, he dealt with some objections to the character of Sir Charles Grandison. His hero's willingness to compromise with the Porretta family on the score of religion was declared by some to be " a blot in the character." Others objected that he was too faultless, and went beyond nature. Others, again, not without justice, complained that it was all very well for a hero of Grandison's prowess to condemn duelling and refuse to fight, but the average man who neither wanted nor was able to defend himself against a skilled adversary would gain nothing but humiliation if he imitated him. To all these strictures Richardson patiently replied, and in a footnote cited the Articles of War, in which duelling is strictly prohibited in the army, a fact which he recommended to the attention of all military men.

Richardson concluded with a paragraph from Tillotson rebutting the view that it is a mistake to portray a pattern of " so great perfection, as is above our reach to attain. . . . No man can write after too perfect and good a copy ; and though he can never reach the perfection of it, yet he is like to learn more than by one less perfect. He that aims at the heavens, which yet he is sure to come short of, is like to shoot higher than he that aims at a mark within his reach." [2] In a didactic work, the attempt to delineate such a pattern is certainly justifiable. But, though Richardson admittedly set his didactic purpose first, he could not have denied that he aimed at something further, and at something which from the point of view of literary criticism was infinitely more important, even if he could not allow its superior claims. The figure of Sir Charles Grandison has to be appraised on its artistic merits. On that side, the character has not met with unanimous approval. There are some who would dismiss him as a colossal prig ; to some he is the " faultless monster that the world ne'er saw." But the gibe is hasty and uncritical, and Grandison is by no means the improbable kind of creation that Lovelace was. Sir Charles, though so far above the ordinary run of mankind, is no abstraction that omits to be alive. In a comparison with Fielding's Squire Allworthy, the

The perfect gentleman —Sir Charles Grandison

[1] Grandison leaves Bologna for Vienna at the time of the Chevalier's undertaking—*i.e.* in 1745 (*Works*, x. 231-232).

[2] *Works*, xiii. 474.

fairest that could be demanded, the advantage in lifelikeness is not altogether with the realist as opposed to the confessed idealist. As we read his letters, his conversations, his friends' accounts of his kindly ways, a genial as well as an excellent man grows distinct before us, and, what is still more to the purpose, a very capable, clear-headed, and clear-sighted man. The method of self-portrayal, however, in conjunction with Richardson's didactic purpose, rendered it almost impossible to avoid giving him the figure of a prig. To do justice to his conception of faultlessness, Richardson would have had to change his method completely. Grandison's misfortune was to have to collaborate with a host of worshippers in objectifying his author's idea of masculine perfection.

Grandi-son's self-conscious-ness due to the Richard-sonian method

Self-consciousness, nowadays, is not accounted a virtue, still less an ingratiating trait, though, on abstract grounds, it would be admitted that self-scrutiny is a duty. It is held to be the infallible sign of priggishness. Richardson himself could hardly be absolved of that mean and factitious self-righteousness which differentiates the prig ; and it is hastily assumed that if he tried to portray a good man the portrait must inevitably betray the priggishness of the author. But a pygmy may draw a giant, the timid man can imagine bravery, the weak of will, strength and resolution. Richardson knew how to rise above his personal limitations and delineate goodness unalloyed with his own infirmities. But he attempted too much. He painted too incredible a galaxy of faultless ladies and gentlemen not to shatter any impression we might have had that we were seeing with our own eyes in a world similar to the world we know. Almost everybody is so inhumanly virtuous, so incapable of doing or even thinking anything wrong ! An odd reprobate thrown in as makeweight does not bring the balance anywhere near probability. We have nothing personal against Harriet Byron, or against any of these admirable people : better if we had ; they would not only be more interesting, but it would correct absurdities, make the atmosphere less oppressive. Could Richardson have brought off one Grandison successfully, a crowd of them would still have been a gross offence against verisimilitude.

Sir Charles, to expose him still more to the imputation of priggishness, has, so to speak, a double dose of self-consciousness. There is that with which he must be endued as one of Richardson's chief correspondents, one of the most active collaborators in writing the novel. For this, having accepted the convention that a novel may consist of letters exchanged between the characters, we make due allowance. But Richardson in this case undertook the superhuman task of making his hero openly demonstrate how the good life is to be lived. And, however edifying it may be to watch a person trying to put the loftiest principles into action, trying also to help his fellow-creatures by precept as well as example, the spectacle of a man studying the beauties of his own mind and calling attention to his admirable behaviour cannot help being ludicrous. Granted the worthy baronet's self-consciousness does not run to conceit, that it is consistent with genuine modesty. But a cultivated modesty repels when natural diffidence would be enchanting. Thus, when Sir Charles describes to Miss Byron how he had long taken the approval of Dr Bartlett as the touchstone of his conduct, whilst the reader can but applaud, he cannot help some slight feeling of discomfort.

I found the following questions often occur to me, and to be of the highest service in the conduct of my life—" What account shall I give of this to Dr Bartlett ? "—" How, were I to give way to temptation, shall I report it to Dr Bartlett ? "—Or, " Shall I be a hypocrite, and only inform him of the best, and meanly conceal from him the worst ? "

Thus, madam, was Dr Bartlett in the place of a second conscience to me : and many a good thing did I do, many a bad one did I avoid, for having set up such a monitor over my conduct. And it was the more necessary that I should, as I am naturally passionate, proud, ambitious ; and as I had the honour of being early distinguished (pardon, madam, the seeming vanity) by a sex of which no man was ever a greater admirer ; and possibly the *more* distinguished, as, for my safety's sake, I was as studious to decline intimacy with the gay ones of it, however dignified by rank or celebrated for beauty, as most young men are to cultivate their favour.[1]

[1] *Works*, x. 221-222. As the Marchese della Porretta whispers to Father Marescotti, there is " too great solemnity in all this ! "

This is preaching, and would be cited by depreciation as an instance of the hero's priggishness. But preaching was a part of the character, as it was of Bunyan's good men, and, to take a modern example, of George Eliot's Dinah Morris. They, too, would no doubt seem priggish had they depicted themselves in the same deliberate way as Sir Charles was compelled to do by his author's scheme. Clearly, it is Richardson's method that is at fault, not the character portrayed. Nevertheless, it must be said that Sir Charles Grandison would have been all the more likeable and lifelike had the shocks and vicissitudes of circumstance, less coolness of disposition, and some powerful temptation to err, tried the mettle of his rectitude as Pamela's and Clarissa's was tried. Richardson does not put him to any severe test. He might with advantage have been a little less reticent about the affair with the siren Olivia. It seems doubtful whether Sir Charles was by nature as vulnerable as other men are.

Richard-son's advance in technique   Richardson's mature technical dexterity could be illustrated by innumerable passages in this last novel. His narrative skill and command of fluent dialogue are well-nigh perfect. He still shows faults of taste, and was censured by Lady Mary Wortley Montagu for presuming to depict high life without being conversant with its manners and usages.[1] But this is a trifling defect compared with the inherent vivacity of the social scenes and of the interplay of character. Sir Hargrave Pollexfen's proposal to Miss Byron may have given hints for the more celebrated declaration of Mr Collins, in *Pride and Prejudice*.

You *cannot*, madam, *encourage my addresses*? And express yourself so seriously? Good heaven! (He stood silent a minute or two, looking upon me, and upon himself, as if he had said, foolish girl! knows she whom she refuses?) I have been assured, madam (recovering a little from his surprise), that your affections are not engaged. But surely it must be a mistake : some happy man——

Is it, interrupted I, a necessary consequence, that the woman who cannot receive the addresses of Sir Hargrave Pollexfen, must be engaged?

Why, madam—as to that—I know not what to say—but a

[1] Mrs Andrew Lang took the trouble to note instances of his mistakes in "Morals and Manners in Richardson" (*National Review*, November 1897).

man of my fortune, and, I hope, not *absolutely* disagreeable either in person or temper ; of *some* rank in life—He paused ; then resuming—What, madam, if you are as much in earnest as you seem, can be your objection ? Be so good as to name it, that I may know whether I cannot be so happy as to get over it.[1]

Puzzled, but still incredulous, Sir Hargrave soon returns to the charge.

Your objections ? I insist upon knowing your objections. My *person*, madam—Forgive me, I am not used to boast—My *person*, madam——
    Pray, Sir Hargrave.
    —Is not contemptible. My *fortune*——
    God bless you, sir, with your fortune.
    —Is not inconsiderable. My *morals*——
    Pray, Sir Hargrave ! Why this enumeration to me ?
    —Are as unexceptionable as those of most young men of fashion in the present age.
    (I am sorry if this be true, thought I to myself.)
    You have reason, I hope, sir, to be glad of that.
    My *descent*——
    Is honourable, sir, no doubt.
    My *temper* is not bad. I am thought to be a man of vivacity, and of cheerfulness.—I have *courage*, madam—And this should have been seen, had I found reason to dread a competitor in your favour.
    I thought you were enumerating your *good* qualities, Sir Hargrave.
    Courage, madam, magnanimity in a man, madam——
    Are great qualities, sir : courage in a right cause, I mean. Magnanimity, you know, sir, is greatness of mind.
    And so it is, I hope——
    And I, Sir Hargrave, hope you have great reason to be satisfied with *your*-self : but it would be very grievous to me, if I had not the liberty so to act, so to govern myself, in essential points, as should leave me as well satisfied with *my*-self.[2]

Grandison's tactful handling of Lady Beauchamp in her difference with her spouse on the thorny question of the amount of generosity to be extended to the latter's son, towards whom she entertained more than a stepmother's spite, is a good example

[1] *Works*, ix. 97-98.   [2] *Works*, ix. 134-135.

of his social address.[1] Briefer and more amusing in its rapid
character-drawing is the interview with the bullying Irishmen
who want to sponge upon him in the name of the disreputable
Mrs Jervois, mother of the baronet's ward. One of the rascals
claims to be the lady's husband, and the three propose to make
a concerted appeal for an increase of her regular allowance. Sir
Charles dexterously divides the enemy's forces by refusing to see
them together.

They gave themselves airs of importance and familiarity ; and
the major motioned, as if he would have taken my hand.

I encouraged not the motion. Will you, gentlemen, walk this
way ?

I led the way to my study. The woman arose, and would have
come with them.

If you please to stay where you are, madam, I will attend you
presently.

They entered, and, as if they would have me think them con-
noisseurs, began to admire the globes, the orrery, the pictures
and busts.

I took off that sort of attention—Pray, gentlemen, what are
your commands with me ?

I am called Major O'Hara, sir : I am the husband of the lady
in the next room, as she told you.

And what, pray, sir, have I to do either with you or your
marriage ? I pay that lady, as the widow of Mr Jervois, 200*l.* a
year : I am not obliged to pay her more than one. She has no
demands upon me ; much less has her husband.

The men had so much the air of bullies, and the woman is so
very wicked, that my departed friend, and the name by which she
so lately called the poor Emily, were in my head, and I had too
little command of my temper.

Look ye, Sir Charles Grandison, I would have you to know——

And he put his left hand upon his sword-handle, pressing it
down, which tilted up the point with an air extremely insolent.

What am I to understand by that motion, sir ?

Nothing at all, Sir Charles. D—n me, if I mean anything by it.

You are called *major*, you say, sir—do you bear the king's
commission, sir ?

I *have* borne it, sir, if I do not now.

That, and the house you are in, give you a title to civility. But,

[1] *Works*, x. 413-429.

sir, I cannot allow that your marriage with the lady in the next room gives you pretence to business with me. If you have, on any other account, pray let me know what it is?

The man seemed at a loss what to say; but not from bashfulness. He looked about him, as if for his woman; set his teeth; bit his lip, and took snuff, with an air so like defiance, that, for fear I should not be able to forbear taking notice of it, I turned to the other: Pray, Captain Salmonet, said I, what are *your* commands with me?

He spoke in broken English; and said, he had the honour to be Major O'Hara's brother: he had married the major's sister.

And why, sir, might you not have favoured me with the company of all your relations?—Have you any business with me, sir, on your own account?

I come, I come, said he, to see my brother righted, sir——

Who has wronged him?—Take care, gentlemen, how—But Mr O'Hara, what are your pretensions?

Why look ye, Sir Charles Grandison—(throwing open his coat, and sticking one hand in his side, the other thrown out with a flourish)—Look ye, sir, repeated he——

I found my choler rising. I was afraid of myself.

When I treat *you* familiarly, sir, then treat *me* so; till when, please to withdraw.

I rang: Frederick came in.

Show these gentlemen into the little parlour. You will excuse me, sirs; I attend the lady.

They muttered, and gave themselves brisk and angry airs; nodding their heads at each other; but followed the servant into the parlour.[1]

The lady is treated with more gentleness but not less firmness. When the two bravos are invited to escort her away, they draw their swords, which gives Sir Charles an opportunity of exhibiting his famous feat of disarming an opponent whilst refusing to fight a duel.

I drew, put by Salmonet's sword, closed with him, disarmed him, and, by the same effort, laid him on the floor.

O'Hara, skipping about as if he watched for an opportunity to make a push with safety to himself, lost his sword by the usual trick whereby a man, anything skilled in his weapons, knows how, sometimes, to disarm a *less* skilful adversary.[2]

[1] *Works*, x. 155-157.   [2] *Ibid.*, 159.

Sir Charles is that charming combination, a humane man and a man of courage. On an earlier occasion, when he declined to accept Sir Hargrave Pollexfen's challenge, and was explaining his attitude to duelling, he gave a pithy account of how he once treated a swashbuckler who dealt him a box on the ear to provoke him to draw.

Mr Merceda. And *did* you draw, sir ?
Mr Bagenhall. To be sure, you *then* drew ?
Mr Jordan. Pray, Sir Charles, let us know. You could not then *help* drawing ? This was a provocation that would justify a saint.
Sir Charles. He had forgot, in that passionate moment, that *he* was a gentleman. I did not remember that *I* was one. But I had no occasion to draw.
Sir Hargrave. What a plague—You did not cane him ?
Sir Ch. He got well, after a fortnight's lying by.
Sir Har. Damnation !
Sir Ch. I put him into possession of the lodgings I had taken for myself, and into proper and safe hands. He was indeed unable, for a day or two, to direct for himself. I sent for his friends. His servants did me justice as to the provocation.[1]

It is pleasant to think of Richardson, who probably never saw a nose bleed in anger in his life, enjoying himself in recording these muscular deeds. But the sedentary man is often the best chronicler of scenes of action. Richardson had not failed in this particular in his previous novels, and among other brisk pieces of narrative it is hard to resist the temptation to quote the spirited account of Harriet Byron's abduction by Sir Hargrave Pollexfen. The reader is more excited by these episodes than by the too-languid dramatic interest of Grandison's matrimonial dilemma or Harriet Byron's suspense.

The comic element in Richardson's fiction

Humour, also, is not lacking, though it is predominantly a malign humour. There is comedy in the passages just quoted ; but it is a one-sided comedy, tinged with contempt. Richardson's exemplars of all the virtues are above the laughter as they are above the criticism of their fellow-mortals. The inferior wretches are let off lightly by the condescending good nature of a being

---

[1] *Works*, ix. 310-311.

superior to all human weaknesses. In *Pamela*, Lady Davers ; in *Clarissa*, Miss Howe ; in the present novel, Charlotte Grandison, are allotted the express duty of furnishing comic relief. There is a family likeness between them : Lady Davers is a vulgar harridan ; Anna Howe, the only sufferable person among them, treats her unfortunate Mr Hickman too overbearingly, and is inclined to show off her superiority to all the world. Charlotte is another Miss Howe, but not equal to her original. She, too, condescends to marry one of the inferior sex, the adoring, submissive Lord G., who exasperates her with his dog-like patience and devotion. Richardson himself points out the likeness between the two couples ; he makes Harriet Byron say :

Lord G. appeared to advantage, as Sir Charles managed it, under the awful eye of Miss Grandison. Upon my word, Lucy, she makes very free with him. I whispered her that she did. A very Miss Howe, said I.

To a very Mr Hickman, rewhispered she.—But here's the difference : I am not determined to have Lord G. Miss Howe yielded to her mother's recommendation, and intended to marry Mr Hickman, even when she used him worst. One time or other (archly continued she the whisper, holding up her spread hand, and with a countenance of admiration) my Lord G. is to show us his collection of butterflies, and other gaudy insects : will you make one ?—

Of the gaudy insects ? whispered I.—

Fie, Harriet !—One of the party, you know, I must mean. Let me tell you, I never saw a collection of these various insects, that I did not the more admire the Maker of them, and of all us insects, whatever I thought of the collectors of the minute ones.[1]

"Miss Grandison has a way of saying ill-natured things in such a good-natured manner that one cannot forbear smiling, though one should not altogether approve of them." So thinks Harriet Byron ; and there is not much more to be said for her, either as a comic character or as a plausible portrait.

"The bright Clarissa," exclaims Hazlitt, "the divine Clementina ! "[2] What is to be said of Harriet Byron's rival for the hand of Sir Charles Grandison ? At all events, she out-rivals the

---

[1] *Works*, ix. 275-276.
[2] "On Reading Old Books" (*The Plain Speaker*).

*The
tragic
figure of
Clemen-
tina*

English young lady in the interest that reaches the heart. She
has the deeper nature that seems to be marked down for tragedy,
and her fate is almost as pathetic as Clarissa's. Rent between a
love that seizes her like fatality and the tenets of an exclusive
creed, she loses her reason, and recovers only to immolate her
earthly happiness to her belief in a life hereafter. Richardson
must be allowed the credit of a poetic conception, though not the
credit of realizing it to the full. Most of the Italian chapters are
as tedious as the minutes of interminable committee meetings.
They are a good example of his skill in unthreading a thick
entanglement of motives. But few readers persevere to the
end, and most are wearied by the monotonous reappearances of
the tortured heroine. Richardson never understood how griev-
ously pathos becomes diluted by being long drawn out. Yet it
is in the history of Clementina, though he weakens the effect by
her dutiful submissiveness in giving ear at last to the Count of
Belvedere, that Richardson affords his one glimpse of passion
in the poetic sense, not the disreputable aberration which he
condemns so puritanically in the Lady Olivia.[1]

*Moral
reflections
in the
three
novels*

Richardson took the trouble to draw up and publish *A Collection
of the Moral and Instructive Sentiments, Maxims, Cautions, and
Reflections, contained in the Histories of Pamela, Clarissa, and
Sir Charles Grandison. Digested under proper Heads, with
References to the Volume, and Page, both in the Octavo and
Twelves, in the respective Histories* (1755). This was not a
difficult task, but it was ill-advised of him to perform it. All
three novels abound in quotable sayings, but they lose more than
half their force when removed from their context. " Bad habits
are of the Jerusalem-artichoke kind : once planted, there is no
getting them out of the ground," is pithy, but its point lies in
its being a comment on the supposed reformation of Sir Hargrave
Pollexfen. And Sir Charles Grandison's reflection after catching
Father Marescotti in the act of eavesdropping hardly bears de-
taching from its place : " I have more than once, Dr Bartlett,
experienced the irreconcilable enmity of a man whom I have
forgiven for a meanness, and who was less able to forgive me
my forgiveness than I was him his fault. But Father Marescotti

---

[1] Who tries to stab Sir Charles Grandison (see *Works*, xi. 59).

cannot be such a man. He is capable of generous shame : he could hardly hold up his head all the time I stayed."

H. D. Traill pointed out that " The sufferings of Clarissa are those of an imprisoned princess in a fairy-tale : the cruelty and power of Lovelace is that of the giant ogre of the same order of fable." [1] To put it another way, *Clarissa*, and for that matter, *Pamela*, are modernized variations on the favourite themes of the popular old romances. If we follow up this indication, we cannot help seeing that Richardson's novels perpetuate a good deal that was most characteristic of the later and more sophisticated romances. The labyrinthine plots, on which innumerable episodes are threaded ; the multitude of characters, each furnished with portrait and history ; the indefatigable analysing of sentiment and balancing of motive ; the close identification of manners and morals, the apotheosis of courtliness, grace, dignity ; and the love-suits, rivalries, intrigues, duels, abductions, rescues : all are relics of the long-winded histories that were in their heyday a generation or two before. Richardson had not discarded the romantic apparatus, in spite of his professed realism, which, after all, was a kind of realism towards which the later sentimental romances were themselves tending. The link between him and them was not Marivaux, who was a contemporary rather than a predecessor, but Madame de la Fayette, author of *La Princesse de Clèves* (1678), which Harriet Byron's grandmother, Mrs Shirley, read when she was young, and felt relief when someone pointed out that the whole sequence of the heroine's woes was based on an idle supposition. This is at once a novel, almost of a modern type, and a survival of heroic romance. The complexity is simplified, the artificiality and the vapid sentimentalism are purged away by the intensity of real emotion. It may have been inspired by the writer's feelings towards La Rochefoucauld, who is even said to have had a hand in the book. At any rate, here is a deeply moving situation, between real, live people, who still, however, have those attributes of high rank, prowess, and ultra-refined feelings which were conventional to Scudéry romance ; and it is dramatized with a new sincerity that

The romantic element in Richardson's stories

---

[1] "Samuel Richardson," by H. D. Traill (*Contemporary Review*, October 1883).

strikes direct to our human sympathies.[1] Sentimental romance is giving birth to the novel of sensibility, and that to the novel of personality.

Richard-   Richardson's romantic prepossessions did not blend well with
son's   the prudential code of ethics pertaining to his age and class ;
romanti-   hence, partly, the questionable views of life and morality that
cism shown   provoked Fielding's satire. They interfered less with his por-
in his   trayal of spheres of society that his predecessors had thought
class   beneath their dignity. Drama had recently been seeking its
prejudices subjects lower in the social scale. Richardson's first novel, in particular, followed the lead. His plain country girl is drawn to the life ; his mistake was to make her a romantic heroine. The unreality of a high-pitched romanticism, again, is over the showy figure of Lovelace. It is not literally untrue to speak of Richardson as a novelist of the middle classes, but the phrase requires careful qualification. It is misleading to go on and talk about " the fundamentally democratic character of his novels," [2] on the strength of the lady's-maid heroine in the first, the exposure of aristocratic vices in the second, and the purely human virtues of Grandison in the third, which are supposed to be independent of rank and wealth. Richardson did not give us the life of a London apprentice or make a hero of a master-printer ; he did not depict the manners of City tradesmen and their families, though he belonged to them. He was far too romantic and too conservative in his reverence for caste. Nearly all his characters belong to the middle classes, but to the upper grades. Pamela comes from the lower orders ; but the point of her story is that as the reward of distinguished virtue she is graciously admitted to the ranks of the upper ten thousand. Richardson stresses the

---

[1] The plot of *La Princesse de Clèves* is as follows. Mlle de Chartres is united in a *mariage de convenance* to the Prince de Clèves, who loves her devotedly. She has the misfortune to be attracted by the Duc de Nemours, a courtly Don Juan, who conceives a sincere passion for her. She avoids his attentions, and feeling her own weakness resolves to reveal her danger to her husband and beg him to take her into the country, where she will be out of reach of temptation. The Prince is deeply distressed, yet believes in her perfect innocence. But when he learns that the Duc de Nemours has been seen prowling round her château at night, he becomes convinced that she has given way. He dies broken-hearted, not, however, before she has cleared herself of the suspicion of guilt. Now that the lovers are free, the Princess declines to marry the man who has been the cause of her husband's death.

[2] W. H. Hudson, *A Quiet Corner in a Library*, 235-236.

view that only a woman can be thus elevated, ability to raise her being one of the prerogatives of a well-born husband. The Harlowes belong to the wealthy higher strata of the middle class that are about to merge in the aristocracy ; the Grandisons and their intimates have merged already. The romantic printer had his full share of what is now termed class-consciousness, due in his case to a romantic admiration for his superiors in the social hierarchy. The kind of social structure he would approve, if he had been asked for his considered opinion, would be one based on liberality, respect, and mutual loyalty ; but not on too much liberty, and assuredly not on equality. Lady G. puts his reflections on the subject sententiously when she says of her brother :

He . . . is most likely to resemble him, who has an unbounded charity and universal benevolence to men of all professions, and who, imitating the Divinity, regards the heart rather than the head, and much more than either rank or fortune, though it were princely, and yet is not a leveller, but thinks that rank or degree entitles a man who is not utterly unworthy of both, to respect.[1]

Richardson was the grandsire of all the ladies who write romantic novels about people of title.

But Richardson is not a novelist of society, as Fielding was. His depth is the converse of Fielding's width of survey. He is the novelist of personality. To show personality asserting and fulfilling itself was, whether he saw it clearly or not, the prime object of all his three novels ; this was the real achievement of *Pamela*, and *Clarissa*, and *Sir Charles Grandison*. To regard him as merely an analyst of the emotions would be as inadequate as to think of him as a sentimentalist, like Sterne. The study of feeling leads directly to the study of motive ; the whole system of volitions and actions is opened up. Personality in action becomes the central theme. Richardson's main instrument was the imagination, rather than, as in Fielding's case, the intelligence working upon the accumulated material of experience. By a profound intuition he put himself at the centre. He identified himself with the characters whom he had conceived and launched into the world of being, lived in them, thought and felt in unison

The Richardsonian method of dealing with character

---

[1] *Works*, xii. 203.

with their whole psychic activity.   Even his by-characters are
vivified by this same act of self-identification.   Even such a
one as Lovelace, who lay outside his natural province, and was
compounded of qualities abstracted intellectually rather than of
the vital elements furnished by a genuine intuition, has a certain factitious life due to his being thus animated from within.
Richardson had got inside the automaton.   It is relevant here to
insist again on the feminine traits in both Lovelace and Grandison.

*The
artificial
reality
that he
created*

Hence the risk of classing Richardson with the general body of
realists.   Are there not two very different sorts of realism ?   There
is that which produces as close a likeness as may be of the life
we see around us, and there is the realism which gives the sem-
blance of reality to an imagined version of life.   Other novelists
observe the world ; novelists of the Richardson class observe themselves.   Borrowing the terminology of the modern psychologist,
we might classify novelists, and other creative artists also, into
two broad divisions, the introverts and the extraverts—those
whose minds for the most part are directed inwards, and those
who look abroad and give an account of what they see, simplified,
ordered, rationalized, more or less, so as to express their personal
comprehension of the world, but interpretative rather than
creative.   Richardson would then, if ever any man, be pre-
eminently the introvert.   Hazlitt, in the subtlest criticism of
Richardson yet written, described him as one " who seemed to
spin his materials entirely out of his own brain, as if there
had been nothing existing in the world beyond the little room in
which he sat writing."   Hence an " artificial reality about his
works " ; " they have the romantic air of a pure fiction, with
the literal minuteness of a common diary." [1]

*Dr
Johnson
on
Richard-
son*

Dr Johnson, also, made various pregnant remarks on Richardson, among them the pompous dictum that " He taught the
passions to move at the command of virtue."   He drew a broad
distinction between what he called " characters of nature and

---

[1] " On the English Novelists " (*Lectures on the English Comic Writers*, 1819).
Hazlitt goes on : " He does not appear to have taken advantage of any thing
in actual nature, from one end of his works to the other ; and yet, throughout
all his works, voluminous as they are—and this, to be sure, is one reason why
they are so—he sets about describing every object and transaction, as if the
whole had been given in on evidence by an eye-witness."

characters of manners," meaning, apparently, the very important one between character and characters, between human nature in its essence and generality, and characters in their singularity and diversity, as mankind were surveyed by Fielding. Comparing his two contemporaries, he went on : " There was as great a difference between them as between a man who knew how a watch was made and a man who could tell the hour by looking at the dial-plate." Boswell did not agree with the preference thus assigned to Richardson. " I cannot help being of opinion," said he, " that the neatest watches of Fielding are as well constructed as the large clocks of Richardson, and that the dial-plates are brighter." [1] Richardson vivisected with a microscope, with infinite labour and patience ; Fielding poured out the abundance of what he knew from a long and catholic acquaintance with the world. They stand at the head of two schools of novelists, and the distinction roughly defined by Johnson holds good throughout.

And now such inquiries as the aforementioned, whether the Duke of Wharton, or anyone else in real life or in fiction, was the original of Lovelace, can be easily disposed of. Such questions arise from a misunderstanding of Richardson's art. He needed no pattern beyond the traditional idea of an aristocratic profligate of superlative brilliance. It might be said, indeed, that Lovelace was his model for Sir Charles Grandison. He had evolved a perfect villain : he would now evolve a perfect man of honour. The consummate scoundrel merely had to be inverted, and his vices turned into their opposites. As he knew more about the well-behaved than he knew about rakes he found the task easier and more congenial, and was tempted to overdo it, more even than he had done, in his inbred tendency to excess, in the evolution of Lovelace. [2] *His characters evolved from his inner consciousness*

Both alike bear the seal of their origin ; they have about them a certain air of unreality, as Hazlitt noted, and they are infected by Richardson's ineradicable self-consciousness. The creatures of his imagination are as self-conscious as he ; how could they be otherwise, when they were members of himself, collaborators *Hence their air of unreality and their self-consciousness*

---

[1] *Life of Johnson*, under date 1768.

[2] It has already been noted that Richardson himself stated that he imagined the character of Pamela (p. 28 n.). He may have received the suggestion from the story he had heard, but the character was his own work.

with him in the task of presenting his image of life ? Each is a lesser novelist, engaged on his or her share of the complicated job. Pamela writes out her own part and makes her contribution to the complete story. The others in that first novel, in which the co-operative method was not yet perfected, have but subordinate functions. But in the next, Clarissa, Lovelace, Belford, and Anna Howe are almost novelists in their own right, each contributing a personal narrative to the joint history. Miss Byron, in the last novel, is of no significance as a person, but she is of cardinal importance as Richardson's most active partner in the writing business. Grandison performs the double duty of playing up to the character of hero and doing his turn at the ledger ; the other collaborators in the symposium, Lucy Selby, Pollexfen, Mr Reeves, Lady G., punctually discharge their allotted tasks. And their self-consciousness is as extreme as their verbosity : with the work they have to do, this latter is more than a virtue, it is an essential qualification.

The superiority of Clementina to the others in " Grandison " It is because she stands aloof from Richardson's team of writers, and has an existence of her own apart from her function as a critical element in the assaying of Sir Charles Grandison, that the Countess Clementina is so much more impressive than the generality of his characters. Pamela and Clarissa escape some of the consequences of persistent self-analysis because in both cases there is an absorbing story to unfold, there is something at stake, something more urgent than the problem of giving the reader an exhaustive view of their characters. But in *Grandison* nothing much is in jeopardy beyond the trifling matter of Miss Byron's happiness, about which we can bear to be rather indifferent. All that the vast story is told for is to display a group of persons emulating each other's virtues for the admiration and admonishment of an imperfect world. Clementina, however, not being one of the author's secretaries and not having to wear the livery of self-consciousness, comes to life through inadvertence, and arrests our interest and our ardent sympathy, as it were by accident. She is one of Richardson's tragic characters, and the novel of personality cannot attain its full scope except in tragedy.

Tragedy the test of In fiction having this theme, the testing as well as the development of character forms the necessary groundwork of each story.

Like Meredith later, who was equally his disciple and Fielding's, *the novel of* and the first to combine the Richardsonian method of portraying *personality* the mind and soul from within with the intellectual survey of a critic of life standing aloof, Richardson constructed his stories in the shape of an ordeal, a process of discipline and trial, from which the self emerges victorious or defeated. Through the accidents of his age and his mental prepossessions he narrowed the issues in his first two novels to the single question of sexual honour; In *Pamela* and *Clarissa* this is the ground of a death-struggle. Chastity is envisaged as woman's chief treasure, her very life. Losing it, she is ruined. Even the humble Pamela contemplates suicide when her virtue is in danger. Clarissa, being a thorough-bred and highly strung, cannot survive the loss of her honour, and succumbs, willingly and not merely resignedly, to her broken heart. In *Sir Charles Grandison*, only happiness and a befitting marriage are at stake ; but these are the goal and guerdon of an exacting course of moral education, the cultivation of character. In previous fiction, character is indeed a factor in the trials of life, but not the counter that is fatally hazarded. It is the security and prosperity of Moll Flanders and Roxana, not their moral being, that is wagered. In these and Defoe's other stories the moral aspects are not overlooked ; they are continually brought forward for inspection and comment ; but they are not the main interest of the story, that which holds us in sympathy, fear, and suspense.

Clarissa might have been even a finer example of tragic art had Richardson not insisted so much on the religious consolations that uphold his heroine in the last trial of her steadfastness. The more sublime tragedy is that which ignores all visions of a compensating justice, and shows the soul victorious over the worst that fate can do, facing even extinction with serenity, in the assurance that it has saved its own integrity. Lear and Cordelia attain a grandeur of spirit that puts them above all the evil in the world. The outcome in failure or success is nothing ; it is the ripeness of personality that is the enduring achievement :

" Nothing is here for tears."

The glory of tragedy is that it represents the triumph of spirit over matter, of the human being over circumstance. It is the greatest thing in art, because it sets forth the final and greatest test and the victory of man.

Richard-son's influence

Richardson's influence on his English successors will be recorded in later chapters. To it was due the long currency of the novel of sensibility. The epistolary form was employed afterwards repeatedly, but those who made a notable success of it adopted the form for totally different purposes, Smollett, Fanny Burney, and Galt, for instance, using it to bring out the comic opposition of different points of view and incompatible ways of meeting the same experiences. Richardson's influence abroad was even more remarkable than in his own country. *Robinson Crusoe* is the only earlier English work of fiction the influence of which on European literature was in any way commensurate with that of *Clarissa*, The author of *Manon Lescaut* translated Richardson ; Diderot paid him the tribute of an extravagant panegyric, and was under his spell in writing *La Religieuse* ; Rousseau was so earnest a disciple in *La Nouvelle Héloïse* that Richardson was annoyed to find that the gospel of sensibility could bear such evil fruit. The German translator of *Pamela* and *Sir Charles Grandison* was Gellert, who tried to copy his master in an unwieldy romance, *Das Leben der Schwedischen Gräfin von G.* Hermes imitated *Pamela* and *Clarissa* in his *Geschichte der Miss Fanny Wilkes*, which he pretended to have translated from the English. Lessing's homage was the prose tragedy, *Miss Sara Sampson*, which has a similar plot to that of *Clarissa*. Musäus satirized the Richardson vogue in *Grandison der Zweite*. Wieland had once extolled, but afterwards decried, the author, whose acquaintance he first made through a French version of *Pamela*. Goethe read and appreciated Richardson sanely; the influence that is apparent in the youthful *Werther* reached him indirectly through Rousseau.

CHAPTER IV

FIELDING: EARLY LIFE, AND *JOSEPH ANDREWS*

THE man who counts more votes than Richardson for the title *Fielding:* of father of the English novel was a son of the upper classes, *contrast in* and in almost every lineament of person and fortune the very *personality with* opposite of his rival. Fielding's was an open, full-blooded, hearty *Richardson* nature, that disposed him to warm sympathy with all classes of Englishmen and a thoughtful delight in every idiosyncrasy and vagary of the human mind. He was the outdoor man, roaming the woods and hills and farming the broad fields of life, whilst Richardson applied intensive cultivation to his human garden and hothouse. The pair were to stand in opposition during their lifetime and after, and to typify two contrasted modes of prose fiction.

His father, Edmund Fielding, an officer who served under *Parentage* Marlborough, was descended from a younger son of the first Earl *and childhood* of Denbigh, thus belonging to a family that claimed to be derived from the Counts of Hapsburg, a circumstance which was to give point to Gibbon's bold prediction, that Fielding's " romance of *Tom Jones*, that exquisite picture of human manners, will outlive the palace of the Escurial and the imperial eagle of the House of Austria " [1]—a prophecy which, so far as regards the latter item of the comparison, has already been fulfilled. Edmund Fielding married Sarah Gould, daughter of a judge, and there is some suspicion that it was a runaway match. At any rate, there was no love lost between Sir Henry Gould and his son-in-law, and he left the small fortune that he bequeathed to his daughter in trust for her sole use or for the upbringing of her children in case she died. Henry was born probably in 1707, at Sharpham Park, Sir Henry's

---

[1] Gibbon's *Memoirs*, ed. G. B. Hill (1900), p. 5.

seat near Glastonbury,[1] where he spent the first two or three years of his life, before his grandfather settled the small family in a house at East Stour, in Dorset. The house and estate were to have been placed in trust for Mrs Fielding and her children ; but the old man died too soon, with the result that there were repeated disputes about the property and the maintenance of the children, between Edmund Fielding, improvident and a gambler, and his wife's relatives. The differences came to a head later in Chancery proceedings (1721-1722). Henry lost his mother when he was eleven years old, and his father quickly married again, the second wife being rumoured to be a woman of doubtful antecedents and an Italian and papist. Henry was sent to Eton ; his four sisters were sent to a boarding-school at Salisbury. Here Lady Gould established herself to look after them, and here Henry Fielding felt he had a second home of a more friendly kind than that of his father and stepmother at East Stour. It was to his grandmother at Salisbury that he made his way when on one occasion he ran away from school.

Education: This was but a passing escapade. He remained at Eton till he *scholarship* was eighteen or nineteen, and became a proficient Latin scholar, though he did not advance very far in Greek. But, not only did his familiarity with and enjoyment of the chief Latin authors accompany him through life, he afterwards found time to read several of the Greeks. He was always ready with a quotation from Cicero, and more even than his elder, Swift, was he indebted to Lucian for the grace and the felicitous irony of his style. He was well read also in English literature, and fairly so in French. He had devoured the old romantic chap-books as a boy and knew the English Bible and the ordinary books of devotion, the time-honoured histories and other household works, to an extent that can be gauged by the frequency and aptness of his allusions thereto.

Soon after leaving Eton, Fielding was at Lyme Regis, paying attentions to a certain Miss Andrew, an heiress whom he made an unsuccessful attempt to carry off. Little is known of his doings

1 According to another theory he was born in Ireland, probably at Dublin, when Major Fielding was over there. No entry of his birth has yet been found. Miss Godden is convinced that he first saw the light in the Harlequin Chamber at Sharpham Park (Godden, *Henry Fielding*, 1-2).

from this event (1725) till he is found in London (1728), in no very flourishing circumstances, one of a great crowd of adventurers in that literary Bohemia, bringing out his first play, *Love in Several Masques*, at Drury Lane. He was not yet twenty-one, and boasted that "none ever appeared so early on the stage." The Fieldings, never well off, had recently lost money through a levanting broker,[1] and Henry was faced by the alternatives of being a hackney writer or a hackney coachman. His people wanted him to enter the law, nor was Fielding averse. Apparently it was not, however, to study law that he now enrolled himself as a student in the University of Leyden, but in order to continue his literary studies : it was the faculty of letters that he entered, not of law. *At the University of Leyden*

Before two years were up lack of funds compelled Fielding to quit Leyden and plunge again into the crowd of competing play-wrights in London, with a bunch of comedies that procured him at first only a rebuff. The first, *Don Quixote in England*, he afterwards recast, at a time when an election was afoot, introducing scenes caricaturing the wholesale bribery common at such events (1734). The topical hits gained it great applause ; but its only interest now is that, in one of the by-characters, Squire Badger, Fielding struck out the first rude sketch of one of his most memorable creations, Squire Western. *The Temple Beau* was a piece in the Congreve style. As Drury Lane would not have it Fielding tried Odell's new theatre at Goodman's Fields, where it started him on a career that was to keep him active and prosperous for a number of years. But this playhouse was soon closed for a time by royal order, and Fielding's next effort, *The Author's Farce, and the Pleasures of the Town*, a skit in the *Rehearsal* manner, with a burlesque play within the play, was given at the Little Theatre in the Haymarket. It was followed by a shot at more high-flying game, the inimitable *Tragedy of Tragedies, or the Life and Death of Tom Thumb the Great* (1730). *Fielding's first plays*

Tom Thumb, which in the printed version Fielding provided with a serio-comic preface, dealing ironically with the beauties of heroic drama, the majesty of the sentiments, the sesquipedalian diction, and the moral greatness, is a burlesque of Otway, Nat *"Tom Thumb the Great"*

---

[1] His cousin, Lady Mary Wortley Montagu, gives the evidence (see Digeon, 18, n.).

Lee, James Thomson, with his *New Sophonisba*, and other
followers of Dryden and Banks, whose bombastic nonsense still
held the stage. The diminutive hero with the mighty soul loves
Huncamunca, daughter of King Arthur, who slights his consort,
Dollallolla, through his passion for Glumdalca, Queen of the
Giants. The pen which was presently to evoke mock-heroics out
of Newgate, in *Jonathan Wild the Great*, is already evident in the
Billingsgate eloquence of Huncamunca and Glumdalca, parodying
Dryden's *All for Love*, and in such a bit of fustian and delectable
bathos as this snatch of dialogue. The king is welcoming the
captive Glumdalca, secretly in love with Tom Thumb :

> *King.* Think, mighty princess, think this court your own,
> Nor think the landlord me, this house my inn ;
> Call for whate'er you will, you'll nothing pay.
> I feel a sudden pain within my breast,
> Nor know I whether this arise from love
> Or only the wind-cholick. Time must shew.
> Oh Thumb ! what do we to thy valour owe ?
> Ask some reward, great as we can bestow.
>   *Thumb.* I ask not kingdoms, I can conquer those.
> I ask not money, money I've enough ;
> For what I've done, and what I mean to do,
> For giants slain, and giants yet unborn,
> Which I will slay—if this be call'd a debt,
> Take my receipt in full—I ask but this,
> To sun myself in Huncamunca's eyes.
>   *King.* Prodigious bold request.⎱   *[Aside.*
>   *Queen.*—Be still my soul. ⎰
>   *Thumb.* My heart is at the threshold of your mouth,
> And waits its answer there.—Oh ! do not frown ;
> I've tried, to reason's tune, to tune my soul,
> But love did overwind and crack the string.
> Tho' Jove in thunder had cry'd out, YOU SHAN'T,
> I shou'd have lov'd her still—for oh strange fate,
> Then when I lov'd her least I lov'd her most !
>   *King.* It is resolv'd—the princess is your own.
>   *Thumb.* Oh ! happy, happy, happy, happy Thumb ! [1]

This incisive parody, lightened by the incidental fooleries of
the two courtiers, Noodle and Doodle, had a long run ; the first

[1] Act i., scene 3.

version, in which the ghost of Thumb is killed by Lord Grizzle—
the absurdity that made Swift laugh the second time in his life
—still being called for when a new version was acting at another
theatre, the pygmy hero in this latter being swallowed by a cow
and done with. It ought to have been the grace-stroke to bombastic drama; but Carey was still to deal the hydra another blow
in *Chrononhotonthologos*, just as Mrs Lennox was to slay the ghost
of sentimental heroics in *The Female Quixote*.

Gay's *Beggar's Opera* had been spiced with sarcasms at the
rapacity of Walpole, whose contention with Townshend was
travestied in the quarrel of the two rogues, Peachum and Lockit.
Macheath, too, reflected not obscurely on the detested Prime
Minister. In *The Welsh Opera*, under a specious disguise, but
with a parallelism that could not be missed, Fielding now brought
him and the entire Court, with the rivalries, intrigues, notorious
scandals, and equally noted quarrels, on the stage in a slashing
burlesque. This play narrowly escaped suppression, and, when
Fielding rewrote it, adding scenes in ridicule of the literary
cliques who were attacking him, and renaming it *The Grub-Street
Opera*, the Government managed somehow to keep it off the
boards.[1] The best known of his songs, *The Roast Beef of Old
England*, is in *The Welsh Opera*.

Fielding next turned to serious comedy. In the prologue to
The Modern Husband, he claimed to be the honest servant of

> The stage, which was not for low farce design'd,
> But to divert, instruct, and mend mankind.

*Serious
comedy—
"The
Modern
Husband,"
etc.*

But this realistic comedy offered such a repellent picture of
marital venality that it was hissed at the theatre, and aroused a
virulent campaign against its author in *The Grub-Street Journal*,
a scurrilous though able print that, with *The Daily Gazetteer* and
Old England, at a later date, did much harm to Fielding's
reputation. The two plays that followed at Drury Lane, *The
Old Debauchees* and *The Covent Garden Tragedy*, with its row in a
bawdy house, were no addition to Fielding's laurels. Turning
aside from farce he now skilfully adapted two of Molière's plays
to English manners and the English stage, *Le Médecin malgré lui*

---

[1] Cross, *History of Fielding*, i. 108.

and *L'Avare*, reducing the length, tightening up the plot, and adding topical pungency to the dialogue. *The Mock Doctor, or the Dumb Lady Cur'd*, was admittedly a farce, and gave opportunity for smacks at the medical tribe, the aversion of eighteenth-century novelists. Leander pleads that he has not mastered the professional jargon :

If I did but know a few physical hard words——
Gregory. A few physical hard words ! Why, in a few physical hard words consists the science. Would you know as much as the whole faculty in an instant, Sir ?

In *The Miser* Fielding shows a mastery of colloquial dialogue which was to serve him in good stead in his novels. Decoy is persuading Lovegold (Harpagon) to lend five hundred pounds to Frederick (Cléante), all he knows about whom is that he has a very rich father and calls him a covetous old rascal.

Lovegold. Ay, that is the name which these spendthrifts, and the rogues, their servants, give to all honest prudent men who know the world, and the value of their money.
Decoy. This young gentleman is an only son, and is so little afraid of any future competitors, that he offers to be bound, if you insist on it, that his father shall die within these eight months.
Love. Ay, there's something in that ; I believe then I shall let him have the money. Charity, Mr Decoy, charity obliges us to serve our neighbour, I say, when we are no losers by so doing.

Frederick appears. He is as much surprised to find it is his father who has been demanding such extortionate terms for a loan as the latter to find that the would-be borrower is his own son.

Love. How ! rascal, is it you that abandon yourself to these intolerable extravagances ?
Fred. I must even stand buff, and out-face him. (*Aside.*) And is it you, father, that disgrace yourself by these scandalous extortions?
Love. Is it you that would ruin yourself, by taking up money at such interest ?
Fred. Is it you that would enrich yourself by lending at such interest ?
Love. How dare you, after this, appear before my face ?
Fred. How dare you, after this, appear before the face of the world ?

Love. Get out of my sight, villain ; get out of my sight.
Fred. Sir, I go ; but give me leave to say——
Love. I'll not hear a word. I'll prevent your attempting any thing of this nature for the future.—Get out of my sight, villain. —I am not sorry for this accident ; it will make me henceforth keep a strict eye over his actions.[1]

Fielding had brought out no less than sixteen plays, some of them brilliant successes on the stage, though he never pretended that they were literature or anything better than an amusing way of earning his wages, and at the same time exposing the abuses in high places and low that roused his ire. A serious step which he now took enforced a short rest from his theatrical labours. Fielding married. He had long been in love with *Fielding's* Charlotte Cradock, one of two young ladies whom he had cele-*first* brated as the beauties of Salisbury.[2] There are hints that this *marriage* was an elopement, the parties being married in the tiny church of a tiny village nestling in a sequestered combe under Lansdown, near Bath. Charlotte, however, enjoyed her mother's favour, and inherited the widow's small property, which, in fact, came as a windfall to the Fieldings when they were in sore straits. This was the beloved woman whose beauties of mind and person he commemorated imperishably in two characters, Sophia Western and Amelia Booth, if not in a third, Mrs Heartfree, the true-hearted heroine of *Jonathan Wild*. They came to London, where Mrs Fielding was before long to be her husband's chief solace in a season of monetary anxiety and domestic sorrow.[3]

Fielding was now managing partner, with a rather truculent person of American origin, James Ralph, of the Little Theatre in the Haymarket, " then known by the name of Fielding's scandal shop," as Mrs Hayward remarks in *Betsy Thoughtless*. Warfare *Attacks* with the Walpole Government was quickly resumed. His *Pasquin,* *on the* *a dramatic Satire on the Times*, was performed by a troupe of *Walpole* young players from Drury Lane whom Fielding dubbed " The *Govern-* Great Mogul's Company of Comedians." It was almost as *ment*

---

[1] Act ii., scene 2.
[2] There were two Miss Cradocks (Cross, i. 164). Miss Godden refers to the tradition of three beautiful sisters (Godden, 47).
[3] "One from whom I draw all the solid comfort of my Life" (Preface to *Miscellanies*).

popular as *The Beggar's Opera*. *Pasquin* presents the rehearsal
of two plays, " The Election," a comedy, and a tragedy " call'd
The Life and Death of Common-Sense." As might be supposed,
the plays are dull in comparison with the comments of the rival
authors, Trapwit and Fustian, and of the critic, Sneer-Well.
Says Trapwit, explaining " the fable, the design " :

Oh ! you ask who is to be married ! Why, Sir, I have a
marriage ; I hope you think I understand the laws of comedy
better than to write without marrying somebody.
Fust. But is that the main design to which every thing
conduces ?
Trap. Yes, Sir.
Fust. Faith, Sir, I can't for the soul of me see, how what has
hitherto past can conduce at all to that end.
Trap. You can't ; indeed, I believe you can't ; for that is
the whole plot of my play ; and do you think I am like your
shallow writers of comedy, who publish the banns of marriage
between all the couples in their play, in the first act ? No, Sir,
I defy you to guess my couple till the thing is done, slap all
at once ; and that too by an incident arising from the main
business of the play, and to which every thing conduces.

But the scenes of universal bribery, culminating when the
Mayor, having as his wife shows him voted wrong, retrieves
the situation by declaring Lord Place and Colonel Promise, the
defeated candidates, duly elected, are packed with deadly satire.
This did not need to be rubbed in, but the sting rankled all the
more for such a criticism as Trapwit's : " How can a man vote
against his conscience, who has no conscience at all ? " Queen
Ignorance triumphs in the burlesque tragedy, which is a caustic
review of the prevailing taste in plays.[1]

But Walpole at last came to the conclusion that Fielding had
been allowed rope enough. A further satire, *The Historical
Register for the Year 1736*, which was still more outspoken,
decided him to bring in a Bill for putting an end to all offensive
stage plays. It was not the first time that such an Act had been
projected, and he was determined not to court another failure.
A scurrilous farce, *The Golden Rump*, not by Fielding, was pro-

---

[1] *Pasquin* gave Sheridan the suggestion for his admirable political comedy
The Critic (1779).

duced as a specimen of what was to be expected if the nuisance were not stopped; and, in spite of Chesterfield's eloquence in the House of Lords on behalf of a free stage, the Licensing Act *Licensing* was passed (1737). The Little Theatre and two other unlicensed *Act of* houses were closed; the Grand Mogul's Company were thrown *1737* on the streets. Fielding saw his occupation gone. But he wasted no time in repining. He loved the theatre and enjoyed play-writing; yet he had never thought it worth while to put his best into it. He had written more farces than comedies; they are none of them rubbish, but they were all put forth carelessly and at high speed for immediate production on the stage. As he him-self expressed it, he left off writing for the theatre at the moment when he should have begun. He could have been numbered among the dramatists had he gone on. But his was to be the better fortune, to have perfected a sister art, by which the printed book furnishes a stage on which imagination conjures up

> Forms more real than living man,
> Nurslings of immortality !

With characteristic energy and decision, he entered himself forth-with as a student at the Middle Temple, and prepared to earn his bread in a career for which he had always felt he had a real vocation.

Such a step on the part of a man so much before the public did not pass without ridicule. But Fielding applied himself with zeal to his new profession, and was duly called to the Bar (1740), *Fielding* going periodically on the Western Circuit. He took his duties *as lawyer* seriously, especially when later on he was made a magistrate. *and* The library of legal books that he collected was considerable, *journalist* and the annotations in many of the volumes bear witness to the conscientiousness of his legal studies. Yet he did not keep himself long out of the political fray. With the aid of several friends he set up a newspaper, *The Champion*, with Ralph as assistant-editor, and, along with the ordinary periodical writing on subjects at large, he renewed the struggle with the Walpole Government. As Captain Hercules Vinegar, he established another Censorship of Great Britain, with a family of coadjutors like the Bickerstaffs, and made himself the terror of all enemies of virtue, honour, and patriotism.   Incidentally, he also enlarged the circle of his own enemies, and his journalistic activities, and still more the many libels falsely ascribed to his pen, did him no good in his other capacity of lawyer.

Works included in the "Miscellanies"   It is not unlikely that Fielding already had in hand at this period some of the work that afterwards went into his books—into *Jonathan Wild*, for instance, and other parts of the *Miscellanies*, and even into *Joseph Andrews*.   The social criticism that formed much of the contents of *The Champion* foreshadows the riper treatment of men and manners in the novels.   The articles on moral and other topics are forerunners of the prefatory discourses in *Tom Jones*.   There was a fair allowance of narrative pieces, allegories, and the like; the first draft of *A Journey from this World to the Next*, for instance, appeared in *The Champion*.[1] In short, the future novelist was probably learning more from his experience as self-appointed Censor than he had acquired in his feverish dramatic career.   Perhaps to eke out a diminished income, he undertook various other literary jobs.   He translated a life of Charles XII. of Sweden, a task that sharpened his convictions on the true character of what is esteemed greatness.   On that very theme he published a poem, *Of True Greatness*, anticipating in many of its reflections the philosophic irony of *Jonathan Wild*.   Learning as well as wit went to the composition of his *Vernoniad*, a poem celebrating the exploits of Admiral Vernon, which in burlesque of pedantry he pretended to be one of the lost poems of Homer.   In this piece, Mammon is Walpole; elsewhere he is referred to as " a certain great man," " that Enemy which the Devil hath raised up against us," or the Devil himself. The sentiments on rascality masquerading as greatness, and on Sir Robert Walpole as a glaring example of the same, which were to inspire his ironical biography of Wild, were already formed, if that strange masterpiece was not partly the work of these years.[2]

Richardson's *Pamela* appeared in November 1740, and the third edition was followed the next April by a pamphlet of less

[1] Cross, i. 280.
[2] Cross, i. 238, 281 ; Digeon, 38-42.   Digeon thinks *Jonathan Wild* was projected, if not partly written, before *Joseph Andrews* (see p. 57, n., and pp. 145-146).

than sixty pages, bearing the title, *An Apology for the Life of "Shamela" Mrs Shamela Andrews . . . by Mr Conny Keyber.* There is good reason to believe that the writer was Fielding, who was poking fun, not only at Richardson, but also at a favourite butt of his, Colley Cibber, and at Dr Conyers Middleton, whose dedication of his life of Cicero to Lord Hervey, another of Fielding's aversions, is ridiculed in the burlesque dedication.[1] The style looks like Fielding's; Mr B. is already branded as Mr Booby, and Fielding would never have appropriated that masterly thrust without acknowledgment; Mother Andrews babbles the same sort of malapropisms as are to be the hall-mark of Mrs Slipslop; and there are sundry other signs of Fielding, whom Richardson, Horace Walpole, and other contemporaries declared to be the author.[2] There is no need to assume, with Thackeray, that Fielding was instigated by a desire to ridicule the author of *Pamela*, " whom he disliked and utterly scorned and laughed at," either in *Shamela* or in *Joseph Andrews*.[3] He loftily repudiated personalities. It was the book and the spurious morality exemplified in Richardson's worldly-wise vestal that inspired his wrath. Probably, he was as yet unacquainted with the author, of whose coterie of women friends his sister Sarah was afterwards a faithful adherent.[4]

The writer's first drollery is to announce that he will write after the manner of Euclid. A certain Parson Tickletext sends the book to his friend Parson Oliver in the country, with a fulsome recommendation of its edifying virtues outvying the encomiums that had fallen from press and pulpit. Unfortunately, Mr Oliver is acquainted with the egregious heroine, whose real name is Shamela, and who is the offspring of a scamp and an orange-woman at the playhouse. She is a woman with a past. After an intrigue with Parson Williams, a disciple of Whitefield and a rank hypocrite, who preaches the doctrine " Be not righteous over-much," but hold the approved faith—a doctrine that Fielding scorned—the hussy manages to catch Squire Booby,

[1] Cross, i. 306.
[2] *Ibid.*, 307-308 ; Digeon, 63-69 ; see also Miss Thomson's *Richardson*, 38.
[3] *Pamela* had been first issued anonymously and Fielding may have been ignorant of the author's identity ; he may have imputed it to Cibber (see De Castro : Preface to *Joseph Andrews*, 10-11).
[4] Cross, i. 309.

by pretending innocence and artfully playing up to his clownish
advances. She remains on the best of terms with her clerical
paramour, after the foolish young man has made her Mrs Booby.
Even the speeches correspond to those in *Pamela*, but they have
a very different meaning. Her bumpkin of a husband fatuously
proposes to have a book made about their strange courtship, and
is recommended to " a parson (*sic*) *who does that sort of Business
for Folks*, one who can make my Husband, and me, and Parson
Williams, to be all Great People; for he *can make black white*,
it seems." [1] This was nasty for Richardson.

"*Joseph*   Ten months after this vigorous though crude performance,
Andrews" in February 1742, Fielding's first novel, *The History of the
Adventures of Joseph Andrews, And of his Friend, Mr Abraham
Adams*, appeared in two volumes. "Written in Imitation of
The Manner of Cervantes, Author of Don Quixote," said the
title-page, which could not have been said of the ephemeral
pasquinade that had preceded. A longer incubation and a finer
art were required for this more conclusive rejoinder to Richardson's morality-novel, for *Joseph Andrews* is obviously that, if it is
also a great deal more. It is, however, a mistake to suppose that
Fielding began simply with the intention of caricaturing *Pamela*,
but grew so enamoured of the characters that came into his brain
that he went on and wrote a rambling sort of novel. [2] This would
verily have been one of the happiest accidents in the history of
masterpieces. True, the ridicule is there, and first-rate ridicule
it is; but the ridicule is kept in its proper place, entirely subordinate to the main business, the adventures of the two persons
named in the title. The satire of Richardson's model heroine is
carried as far as the occasion demanded, and is all the more telling
for not being pursued too far. Nor, though *Joseph Andrews*
does not portray English life with the completeness of *Tom Jones*,
and has none of the complexities of the greater novel—though
it has on the surface a delusive air of artlessness, like the easy-
going manner of picaresque fiction—is it by any means careless in

---

[1] *Shamela*, 54.

[2] The latest critic to endorse this trite hypothesis is Mr E. M. Forster
(*Aspects of the Novel*, 1927, p. 156). It is so impossible to believe that
Fielding, the rude father of the English novel, could be so clever as to see
his way right from the start! Where would our modern superiority be, if
he were not admittedly rather stupid and a bungler?

design. The plot, a burlesque of romantic plots in general, is present throughout in the background; and, when the moment arrives to bring it forward, the pair of lovers, Joseph and Fanny, are neatly extricated from their painful dilemma, with a final hit at romantic *dénouements* and further merriment at Richardson's expense. Who can forget the classic strawberry-mark on Joseph's breast, or Parson Adams's excited shout, *Hic est quem quæris*; *inventus est!* Fielding had taken adequate time to consider how the specific satire could be compounded with other ingredients to produce this comic delineation of English rural life.

His preface confirms this view. The staple of *Joseph Andrews* is not burlesque but comedy, though he sometimes admits burlesque in the diction, as in the description of battles. Such instances of " a certain drollery in stile " are the Homeric account of Joseph's combat with the pack of hounds let loose on his friend the parson, and, in *Tom Jones*, the similar mock-heroic narrative of Moll Seagrim's doughty deeds in the churchyard. But Fielding deprecates any mixture of the comic and the burlesque; " indeed, no two species of writing can differ more widely " : *[margin: More comedy than burlesque in " Joseph Andrews"]*

For as the latter is ever the exhibition of what is monstrous and unnatural, and where our delight, if we examine it, arises from the surprizing absurdity, as in appropriating the manners of the highest to the lowest, or *e converso* ; so in the former we should ever confine ourselves strictly to nature, from the just imitation of which will flow all the pleasure we can this way convey to a sensible reader.[1]

"What Caricatura is in painting, Burlesque is in writing "; licence and exaggeration are its province. Hogarth has, by the undiscerning, been called a burlesque painter; but there could be no greater mistake about an artist of whose works Fielding admiringly says: " It hath been thought a vast commendation of a painter to say his figures seem to breathe; but surely it is a much greater and nobler applause that they appear to think." Finally, he carefully distinguishes *Joseph Andrews* " from the productions of romance writers on the one hand and burlesque writers on the other "; and protests that he has " no intention to vilify or asperse any one."

[1] Preface.

The first chapter, also, is a prefatory discourse, and so are those of the next two books, like the introductions to the successive books in *Tom Jones*. This discusses the question, " Of writing lives in general, and particularly of Pamela, with a word by the bye of Colley Cibber and others." Richardson's life of Pamela and Cibber's life of himself " represent an admirable pattern of the amiable in either sex," Fielding observes, with suave irony. They are, it is implied, proper objects for ridicule because they are blatant examples of affectation, which is rooted in vanity or hypocrisy. " The former of these " (Cibber's), " which deals in male virtue, was written by the great person himself, who lived the life he hath recorded, and is by many thought to have lived such a life only in order to write it."[1] After this banter, which is not as frivolous as it looks, since it invites the reader to perceive the huge chasm between a character factitiously evolved to illustrate a maxim, sound or delusive, and the real men and women that are about to appear before him, the story begins.

Outline of the story   The first two persons formally introduced are Joseph Andrews and Mr Abraham Adams, the curate. Joseph is footboy at the Boobys', an office to which he has been promoted, on account of his strength and pluck and his good looks, by Lady Booby, the aunt-in-law of Pamela, who is now wedded to Squire Booby, after the events related in Richardson's novel. He has always been supposed to be Pamela's brother, and has read her letters with admiration and the resolve to emulate her chastity. Hence the piquancy of the situation that now ensues. Sir Thomas dies, and Lady Booby takes the household, including the handsome footman, up to London. Parallel to his sister's resistance to the squire, Joseph is depicted indignantly repelling the overtures of his mistress, another wicked person of quality, and a member of the same family. The lady, in a fit of dudgeon, dismisses him, and Joseph sets out on foot for his village in the west, where his fellow-servant and sweetheart, Fanny, has been left behind. He falls among highwaymen, is robbed and beaten, and, being taken half-

[1] Fielding had had several passages of arms with the elder Cibber, and was by many credited with a sarcastic autobiography of the son, Theophilus Cibber: *An Apology for the Life of Mr T . . . C . . ., Comedian. Being a Proper Sequel to the Apology for the Life of Mr Colley Cibber, Comedian* (1740); but there is no proof that he so far forgot his golden rule of eschewing libels.

dead to an inn, kept by the Tow-wouses, would have fared ill but
for the accidental arrival of Parson Adams at the same house.
This is the end of the first book.

In the second, the parson is the more prominent figure. He
was on his way to London to sell nine volumes of his sermons to
a publisher, but, discovering that with his usual absence of mind
he had forgotten to bring the sermons with him, he determines
to go home with Joseph. They are joined unexpectedly by Mrs
Slipslop, Lady Booby's elderly handmaid, who has likewise cast
amorous eyes on Joseph, and has consoled herself by penetrating
her ladyship's secret and threatening to make it public. Fanny,
meanwhile, in fond anxiety on Joseph's account, has set out to
seek tidings of him in London. She falls into the hands of a ruffian
who tries to ravish her, but Parson Adams intervenes in the nick
of time with his stout crabstick. Thus four of the persons chiefly
concerned are now together. But the jealous Slipslop soon takes
flight, when the sight of Joseph's and Fanny's fondness for each
other is more than she can bear. The tale goes swinging on from
one adventure to another, and characters of every complexion
appear at every turn. Fanny, Joseph, and the parson are joined in
the third book by the benevolent Mr Wilson, who tells them the
story of his misguided youth, his downfall, and reformation, and
his retirement to a life according to nature. This edifying history,
like the earlier tale of Leonora, related by a fellow-passenger in
the stage-coach, is one of the features " in imitation of the manner
of *Don Quixote.*" It is not particularly interesting; but the
groans and ejaculations of Parson Adams at the wickedness of
the world are truly comic, and the appearance of Mr Wilson, the
good fairy of the plot, is justified in the end.[1]

In the fourth book all the chief persons are brought together, *The dé-*
as in the last act of a well-knit comedy. Lady Booby, her in- *nouement*
sulted passion for Joseph battling with her resentment, comes
home again, to find Joseph and Fanny preparing for their union,
under the fatherly protection of the parson. Storming and raging,
she forbids Adams to publish the banns, and failing to move him

---

[1] Critics have suggested that Wilson's account of his irregularities, and
especially of his literary struggles, is in part at least autobiographical. As
Parson Adams begat the Vicar of Wakefield, so Wilson begat Mr Burchell.

by arguments or threats, invokes the aid of a rogue lawyer to rid the parish of Fanny and get Joseph committed to gaol. But her schemes are interrupted by a visit from Squire Booby and his wife. This is an opportunity for bringing Pamela into the light of comedy. The parvenue is now as much a stickler for gentility as anyone. It would be a terrible come-down for her brother Joseph, the brother-in-law of Mr Booby, to marry a girl of doubtful origin. But it is suddenly discovered that Fanny is the daughter of the Andrews couple, and therefore Pamela is her sister and Joseph her brother. The disclosure gives scant joy to the impatient lovers. But a further disclosure sets everything right. Mr Wilson reappears. Years ago, as he has already re-counted, he had lost a son. That son is Joseph, who was stolen by gipsies and afterwards exchanged for Fanny, who was sold to Sir Thomas Booby. He is recognized by the famous strawberry-mark on his left breast. He is as good a gentleman as the squire himself. So both Pamela and Fanny have their wishes, and all are genteel together. Even that humblest of men, Parson Adams, comes in for a small fortune, being presented with a living of one hundred and thirty pounds a year—wealth for him beyond the dreams of avarice.

Nature of the plot   It is a thin but sufficient thread of plot on which are strung these consecutive scenes of jovial comedy, but it is a plot of the opposite kind to that of *Tom Jones*. That seems to have the symmetry of a natural growth. It is the collective result of innumerable events which themselves result from the collisions and reactions of a great number of characters in the rough-and-tumble of life; hence it seems as if it has developed from within as a living organism develops. But this of *Joseph Andrews* is merely how Fielding arranges the successive incidents so as to bring them back again to the starting-point in the Pamela affair, without interfering with his freedom to deal as he likes with Parson Adams and the motley population of the road. Plot and the love-affairs of Fanny and Joseph are of secondary importance in comparison with the exploits of their champion, a character of whom it is praise enough that such imitations as Dr Primrose and Uncle Toby are among the immortals of creative literature.

Adams is, in truth, the main hinge of the story, the hinge

between these two sides of it; the allusion to *Don Quixote* in the *The* title signalizes his importance.   And he is given ample room to *character* display his prowess and his blunders, his courage, his childlike *of Parson* innocence, his strength of mind and muscle.   Like the Knight *Adams* of the Rueful Countenance, though with a very different cast of visage, he takes the road, on a steed as eccentric as Rosinante; not in mad quest of adventures, though he meets with adventures without stint.   He is a knight in the finest sense of the word, and he has a mission, not to uphold a defunct ideal, but to teach and in his whole conduct exemplify the standards of a primitive Christianity, unadulterated by the compromises with which the world has tempered its idealism.   His trust in humanity is that of a new-born babe.   No tale of unselfish generosity is extravagant enough to daunt his credulity.   Only the harshest experience can disturb his belief in universal goodness.   And when he is called upon to vindicate the dictates of his simple creed, nothing can withstand the weight of his mighty fist, " rather less than the knuckle of an ox," as ready and alert in the service of the weak and oppressed as was the lance of Don Quixote.   Like that of his prototype, his brain has been crazed with much reading.   Parson Adams lives in a world created by the poets and philosophers of old.   " Knowledge of men," he says, " is only to be learned from books; Plato and Seneca for that! "   When informed that the gentleman of fine promises has only been amusing himself by offering to bestow a living that was never his to dispose of, he can only bless himself and declare he had never read of such a monster.[1]

Fielding's lively interest in the dispute between preachers of *Fielding's* salvation by faith and old-fashioned adherents of the creed that a *attitude to* man should do as he would be done by, must be taken into account *Salvation-* in his portrait of Adams and in numerous passages of the later *ism* novels.   It was the moral side of religion that appealed to him, and he was not one of those who think that religion is not a matter for weekdays.[2]   Fielding would have said that a man is what a man does.   The opposite view is thoroughly demoralizing.   Hence,

[1] Book II., c. 1.
[2] Mrs Adams tells her husband: " It was blasphemy to talk Scripture out of church; that such things were very proper to be heard in the pulpit, but that it was profane to talk them in common discourse " (Book IV., c. 11).

in the wordy discussion with the Rev. Barnabas, Adams calls it roundly, " the detestable doctrine of faith against good works." " Surely," he goes on, " that doctrine was coined in hell; and one would think none but the devil could have the confidence to preach it." Will an all-wise Being damn the good and virtuous for their want of faith, a faith of which they had perhaps never heard? " Can any doctrine have a more pernicious influence on society, than a persuasion that it will be a good plea for the villain at the last day—'Lord, it is true I never obeyed one of Thy commandments, yet punish me not, for I believe them all ' ? " The bookseller to whom Adams offers his sermons, in the sanguine belief that they will bring him in a handsome profit, thanks him and observes: " I am afraid you will find a backwardness in the trade to engage in a book which the clergy would be certain to cry down." Fielding does not hesitate to include Methodists or their most violent opponents among the hypocrites and time-servers who deserve the lash of comedy.

Adams' eccentricities   Parson Adams left his sermons behind when he journeyed to London to sell them. He forgets to pay for his night's lodging. The only thing he does not forget is his lusty appetite. He leaves his horse at the inn and trudges contentedly on foot, till someone else redeems the animal and offers him a mount. Even then the parson does not recognize his property till he is reminded of the affair, and told that they had brought the horse that he left behind. " Bless me ! and so I did ! " is all he remarks. Joseph and Adams agree to ride and walk by turns. Adams strides gaily ahead and soon falls into a contemplation on a passage in Æschylus, which banishes all recollection of his fellow-passenger. At length he comes to a large water filling the road, and tucking up his cassock he wades through, not noticing that he might have taken a footpath on the other side of the hedge and got past dry-shod. Feeling tired and hungry he sits down and pulls out his Æschylus and reads till a country fellow comes by, whom he asks the nearest way to an alehouse. " The fellow, who had just left it, and perceived the house and sign to be within sight, thinking he had jeered him, and being of a morose temper, bade him follow his nose and be d—n'd. Adams told him he was a saucy jackanapes ; upon which the fellow turned about angrily ; but, perceiving

Adams clench his fist, he thought proper to go on without taking any farther notice."

Hypocrites were " a sort of people whom Mr Adams never saw through "; he "never saw farther into people than they desired to let him." Hence it is not till Peter Pounce the usurer, or Lady Booby, with her spiteful attempt to separate Fanny and Joseph, declare themselves in the most unmistakable way that he drops his meek submission. To the furious lady he returns an answer befitting the Christian hero: "Madam, I know not what your ladyship means by the terms master and service. I am in the service of a Master who will never discard me for doing my duty; and if the doctor (for indeed I have never been able to pay for a licence) thinks proper to turn me from my cure, God will provide me, I hope, another. . . . Whilst my conscience is pure, I shall never fear what man can do unto me." In spite of poverty, jeers, and horseplay, Parson Adams never loses his dignity. We love him in spite of his pedantry, his obstinacy, his little vanities. We respect him even when Mrs Tow-wouse has drenched him with hog's blood, and the brutal squire and his myrmidons bait him with the hounds and tumble him into the butt of cold water. The foibles and contradictions are essential to the richness and beauty of such a character.

The pathos and humour of the character of Don Quixote lie *Fielding* in the incongruity between his high-flying idealism and the reality *and Cer-* which he misconceives. That incongruity is made most ludicrous *vantes:* in the contrast between the enthusiastic dreamer and his un- *character-* imaginative squire. There is no Sancho Panza in *Joseph Andrews*; *drawing* but his matter-of-fact stolidity, his sensuality, his greed, his horse-sense, are, as it were, distributed among a vulgar rabble who provide the necessary contrast. Swift said: " I heartily hate and detest that animal called man, although I heartily love John, Peter, Thomas, and so forth." Fielding was no hater of his fellow-men; but, like the generality of novelists, Scott being perhaps one of the rare exceptions, he portrays the majority as a set of nincompoops, knaves, and hypocrites.[1] The characters whom he chooses to paint at full- or half-length are a tiny handful

[1] Meredith reckoned the villains as the larger half of the inhabitants of the globe, see *Evan Harrington*, xlii.

out of the swarm. From the undistinguished mob, Fielding selects a Trulliber, a Peter Pounce, a Beau Didapper, the Towwouses, Mrs Slipslop, and a few others, as specimens worth a little closer attention. One and all, with the exception of Lady Booby—who is there less on her own account than to start the clockwork and send Joseph and the rest on their travels—they belong to the category of low people, even Mrs Slipslop, who has such a strong objection to being classed with Joseph and Fanny.[1] Fielding held that " the highest life is much the dullest, and affords very little humour or entertainment." [2] In portraying their outward features, he confessedly adopts the manner of Hogarth, sailing very near the quicksands of caricature but never going ashore. This is Mrs Tow-wouse :

Her person was short, thin, and crooked. Her forehead projected in the middle, and thence descended in a declivity to the top of her nose, which was sharp and red, and would have hung over her lips, had not nature turned up the end of it. Her lips were two bits of skin, which, whenever she spoke, she drew together in a purse. Her chin was peaked ; and at the upper end of that skin which composed her cheeks, stood two bones, that almost hid a pair of small red eyes. Add to this a voice most wonderfully adapted to the sentiments it was to convey, being both loud and hoarse.[3]

Take for a pendant to this the sketch of Beau Didapper, who foreshadows Smollett's harsh pen :

Mr Didapper, or Beau Didapper, was a young gentleman of about four foot five inches in height. He wore his own hair, though the scarcity of it might have given him sufficient excuse for a periwig. His face was thin and pale ; the shape of his body and legs none of the best, for he had very narrow shoulders and no calf ; and his gait might more properly be called hopping than walking. The qualifications of his mind were well adapted to his person. We shall handle them first negatively. He was not entirely ignorant ; for he could talk a little French and sing two

---

[1] See the dissertation concerning high people and low people (Book II., c. 13). It is noticeable that Fielding calls Lady Booby " the heroine of our tale " (Book I., c. 8). Fanny is, of course, too low to be a " heroine."

[2] *Tom Jones*, (Book XIV., c. 1).

[3] Book I., c. 14.

or three Italian songs ; he had lived too much in the world to be bashful, and too much at court to be proud : he seemed not much inclined to avarice, for he was profuse in his expenses ; nor had he all the features of prodigality, for he never gave a shilling : no hater of women, for he always dangled after them ; yet so little subject to lust, that he had, among those who knew him best, the character of great moderation in his pleasures ; no drinker of wine ; nor so addicted to passion but that a hot word or two from an adversary made him immediately cool.[1]

But it is not by mere description, it is by making his characters *His* speak and act that he puts them before us; and here Fielding *characters* has a knack of making them bare their inmost selves, expose *portray* their essential traits, in the first few syllables uttered. The *them-* *selves:* character-drawing, in short, is in the dialogue itself. Albeit that e.g. dialogue is always shapely literature. Trulliber, for example, *Parson* makes but a brief appearance, and never turns up again ; yet the *Trulliber* man is stamped on the memory, once for all. Adams had gone to this brother parson to borrow fourteen shillings, to enable him to pay the innkeeper's bill, and is taken by that worthy for a customer—for Trulliber farms his glebe and is famous at rearing swine. He hurries his visitor out to see the pigs, for the sty is but two steps from the parlour window. " Do but handle them ! step in, friend ! art welcome to handle them, whether dost buy or no." Parson Adams is down at full length in the filth before he can utter a word. " *Nihil habeo cum porcis* : I am a clergyman, sir, and am not come to buy hogs," he manages to explain; and Trulliber, conceiving no great respect for one of his shabby appearance, takes him into the house, blaming his wife, and adding, " she was a fool, and always committed blunders."

As soon as possible Adams explains the object of his visit. He wants fourteen shillings, " which, peradventure, I shall return to you; but if not, I am convinced you will joyfully embrace such an opportunity of laying up a treasure in a better place than any this world affords." Fielding exhausts his rhetoric in describing the astonishment that seized on Trulliber when Adams had ended this speech.

[1] Book IV., c. 9.

A while he rolled his eyes in silence ; sometimes surveying Adams, then his wife ; then casting them on the ground, then lifting them up to heaven. At last he burst forth in the following accents : " Sir, I believe I know where to lay up my little treasure as well as another. I thank G——, if I am not so warm as some, I am content ; that is a blessing greater than riches ; and he to whom that is given need ask no more. . . . Lay up my treasure ! what matters where a man's treasure is whose heart is in the Scriptures ? there is the treasure of a Christian." At these words the water ran from Adams's eyes ; and, catching Trulliber by the hand in a rapture, " Brother," says he, " heavens bless the accident by which I came to see you ! I would have walked many a mile to have communed with you ; and, believe me, I will shortly pay you a second visit ; but my friends, I fancy, by this time, wonder at my stay ; so let me have the money immediately." Trulliber then put on a stern look, and cried out, " Thou dost not intend to rob me ? " At which the wife, bursting into tears, fell on her knees and roared out, " O dear sir ! for Heaven's sake don't rob my master ; we are but poor people." " Get up, for a fool as thou art, and go about thy business," said Trulliber ; " dost think the man will venture his life ? he is a beggar, and no robber." " Very true, indeed," answered Adams. " I wish, with all my heart, the tithing-man was here," cries Trulliber ; " I would have thee punished as a vagabond for thy impudence. Fourteen shillings indeed ! I won't give thee a farthing. I believe thou art no more a clergyman than the woman there " (pointing to his wife) ; " but if thou art, dost deserve to have thy gown stript over thy shoulders for running about the country in such a manner." [1]

Adams asks him to treat him as a brother Christian, if not as a clergyman, and reminds him of the claims of charity. " I would have thee know, friend," is the reply, " I shall not learn my duty from such as thee. I know what charity is, better than to give it to vagabonds." When Adams invokes his favourite doctrine—" I must tell you, if you trust to your knowledge for your justification, you will find yourself deceived, though you should add faith to it, without good works "— this is the last straw. " Fellow," cries Trulliber, " dost thou speak against faith in my house ? Get out of my doors : I will no longer remain

[1] Book II., c. 14.

under the same roof with a wretch who speaks wantonly of faith and the Scriptures." He clenches his fist, but his wife begs him not to fight, but show himself a true Christian, and take the law of him. "As nothing could provoke Adams to strike but an absolute assault on himself or his friend, he smiled at the angry look and gestures of Trulliber; and, telling him he was sorry to see such men in orders, departed without further ceremony." [1]

The miserly lawyer, Peter Pounce, is drawn with the same *Other* trenchant economy as the clerical miser. And in like manner *figures* we are made acquainted with the innkeeper Tow-wouse and his shrewish wife, with the rakish squire and his pot-companions, who maltreat Adams and Joseph and abduct Fanny, with beggars, postilions, thieves, villagers, and every type of humanity that could be found on the great road to the west.

Next to the parson, Lady Booby's waiting-woman, Mrs Slip-slop, is the most diverting character. She appears again, or some-one very like her, in Sophia's maid, Mrs Honour, in *Tom Jones*. Slipslop is, in fact, the first of a long line, including Sheridan's Mrs Malaprop and the illustrious Mrs Gamp. Her attempts to captivate Joseph with her superannuated charms are infinitely entertaining. Slipslop never forgets that she is of gentle birth, and her alternate fits of cringing and insolence, her contempt for low creatures like Fanny, and her fondness for long words that show her superior breeding, combine to make a low-comedy figure of the finest quality. "O dear madam," she says to Lady Booby, pleading for the coy footman who has disdained both mistress and maid, "is it not a pity such a graceless young man should die a virulent death? I hope the judge will take commensuration on his youth. As for Fanny, I don't think it signifies much what becomes of her; and if poor Joseph hath done anything, I could venture to swear she traduced him to it: few men ever come to a fragrant punishment, but by those nasty creatures, who are a scandal to our sect." [2]

Fielding announced in the preface that he proposed to give the English reader an example of a new kind of writing, differing from serious romance in its fable and action, in that these would

---

[1] Book II., c. 14.
[2] *Cp.* Deloney's malapropisms in *The Gentle Craft* (see Vol. II., p. 175).

be light and ridiculous instead of grave and solemn; in its characters, by introducing persons of inferior rank and therefore of
inferior manners; and lastly, in its sentiments and diction, "by
Comedy preserving the ludicrous instead of the sublime." The result
and its would be a comic romance, which is "a comic epic poem in
source in prose, differing from comedy, as the serious epic from tragedy."
affectation Its province is the ridiculous, and "the only source of the true
Ridiculous (as it appears to me) is affectation. Now affectation,"
he continues, "proceeds from one of these two causes, vanity or
hypocrisy: for as vanity puts us on affecting false characters, in
order to purchase applause; so hypocrisy sets us on an endeavour
to avoid censure, by concealing our vices under an appearance
of their opposite virtues." The discussion is resumed in the
introduction to the third book, where he reiterates his view that
nature will provide the comic writer with all he requires: "life
everywhere furnishes an accurate observer with the ridiculous." [1]
Then he comes to the crucial point: if "everything is copied
from the book of nature, and scarce a character or action produced which I have not taken from my own observation and
experience," is it to be understood that the characters are drawn
directly from actual people? He had already explained that he
had "used the utmost care to obscure the persons by such different
circumstances, degrees, and colours, that it will be impossible
to guess at them with any degree of certainty." He now
declares, "once for all, I describe not men, but manners; not
an individual, but a species."

The lawyer is not only alive, but hath been so these four
thousand years; and I hope G—— will indulge his life as many
yet to come. He hath not indeed confined himself to one profession, one religion, or one country; but when the first mean selfish
creature appeared on the human stage, who made self the centre
of the whole creation, would give himself no pain, incur no danger,
advance no money, to assist or preserve his fellow-creatures;
then was our lawyer born; and, whilst such a person as I have
described exists on earth, so long shall he remain upon it. [2]

Accepting the assurance that he painted from nature, with
the distinction he draws between the satirist and the libeller, we

[1] Preface to *Joseph Andrews*.   [2] Book III., c. 1.

may conclude that, if it were ever possible to unearth Fielding's *How far* originals, we should find that those originals were far from *did* supplying him with the whole physiognomy of the characters *Fielding draw* ultimately bodied forth. Two that seem as if they must surely *from in-* have been drawn from individuals are Peter Pounce and Parson *dividuals?* Trulliber. The former has been identified with a certain Peter Walter, scrivener and usurer, of Stalbridge Park in Dorset, an unneighbourly neighbour of the Fieldings at East Stour. Pope satirized this notorious Shylock, and Hogarth is supposed to have put him into the first plate of *Marriage à la Mode.* He may well have furnished the model for Peter Pounce, who is mentioned again in *Jonathan Wild*.[1] But another sturdy legend, that Trulliber was drawn from Fielding's tutor, Mr Oliver, curate of the adjacent parish of Motcombe, turns out to be unfounded: there is no resemblance.[2]

It is a different question with the finest character of all, Parson *The* Adams. In this case Fielding had an original; the original was *original of* recognized in his own lifetime, in his staunch and estimable *Parson Adams* friend, the Rev. William Young, who was curate at East Stour, and followed Fielding up to London, collaborated with him in a translation of the *Plutus* of Aristophanes, and projected other joint works. About Young there are many anecdotes recording his absence of mind, his learning, and his inability to get on in the world, or understand its ways. Some noticeable traits—such as his powerful but clumsy physique, devotion to Æschylus, and the trick of snapping his fingers—went into the portrait of Adams. But, again, no one would allege that he provided all the features. The wonderfully live yet obviously idealized figure of Parson Adams is the least likely of any creation in the book to be entirely made up from any single one of God's creatures. We might as well search for a complete precedent to Don Quixote himself.

Cervantes was not Fielding's only pattern. There is plenty in *Debts to* *Joseph Andrews* to remind us very distinctly of Le Sage, and *novelists* the author has obviously read the *Roman Comique* and borrowed *other than* from Scarron some hints for his epic of the road. Marivaux also *Cervantes* was well known to Fielding, and both general and particular resemblances have been pointed out between *Joseph Andrews*

[1] Book II., c. 7.   [2] Cross, i. 22-24.

and that author's *Paysan Parvenu*.[1] Fielding was well versed in plays, novels, romances—everything, indeed, that was serviceable to the art he had taken in hand to develop. He followed so far as he chose; but he soon left any beaten track, and took to paths of his own. He discarded both Defoe's method of the conscientious reporter and Richardson's subterfuge of authentic letters. Without making any elaborate pretences, he stationed himself at the point of view of the omniscient spectator, and launched straightway into his prose epic. It was the first time in English fiction that the performers in the story evoked the sense of life by their dramatic self-sufficiency. Even Richardson had wasted our time and his by accumulating superfluous details to assure us that he was retailing fact ; Defoe had been driven into downright fraud. Fielding flung all these tricks aside, and attended to the real business. He tells you he is giving you fiction, and he lets fiction speak for itself. Not the delusive pretence of historical truth but the illusion of art is his object. As Coleridge afterwards put it, he aimed at an imitation, not a copy of reality.

The quality of the realism   The illusion that he achieved was unprecedented in its completeness. It was the first time that anyone had depicted the scene of life with its background and surroundings in perfect verisimilitude. But it is Fielding's reading in the Book of Life, not the Book of Life itself, that we are invited to peruse. He claims the right to explain what may be obscure or open to a wrong interpretation, and of making any comment he thinks fit. He did not let the story, or the characters—even those whom he sympathized with and loved with the greatest tenderness—absorb him and carry him away, as was apt to befall his predecessors. He stood above, like the spirit of Comedy, illuminating all with the flashes of his irony, and at the end, with appropriate gesture, sent the company on their way.

[1] Cross, i. 321-322; Digeon, 72 n.

CHAPTER V

FIELDING'S *MISCELLANIES*

The Joseph Andrews "*Miscellanies*"

FIELDING had apparently, some time before the publication of *The Joseph Andrews*, announced that he was preparing three volumes of *Miscellanies*. For, at the beginning of the June after the February of 1724, when his novel appeared, he issued a circular, the earliest notice now extant, setting forth the contents of the several volumes, and apologizing to his subscribers for the " train of melancholy Accidents " that had hitherto retarded the work. Thus the *Miscellanies*, which appeared at last in April 1743, consist to a large extent of work done at an earlier date, and, further, of some item or items on which he was still engaged in June 1742, and probably later. Pieces that might well have been written in part before *Joseph Andrews* saw the light, but show traces of having been completed after that date, are *A Journey from this World to the Next* and the *Life of Jonathan Wild*, in the second and third volumes respectively. These are, incomparably, the best of the *Miscellanies*. The remainder are odds and ends of verse and prose, a comedy that had failed, *The Wedding Day*, a farce, *Eurydice*, and other trifles. Three essays of considerable length—" On Conversation," " On the Characters of Men," and " Of the Remedy of Affliction for the Loss of Friends "—are of interest for their side-lights on Fielding's mind and heart. By conversation he means good breeding; and he lays down rules by which a well-bred man may, " in his discourse as well as actions, contribute to the happiness and well-being of society." Incidentally, he assigns " those disgracers of the human species," the beau and the fine lady, to the lowest class of either sex. Of the grave and just essay accompanying, the burden is that virtue, like charity, begins at home. Very touching is the third, a meditation on those losses of man's nearest and dearest, of which the writer met with his full share. He applauds the stoical philosophy of Cicero and Seneca, without being able to live up to it.

" A Journey from this World to the Next " *A Journey from this World to the Next* is a Lucianic apologue. Fielding had once projected a translation of Lucian, and declared it was on this author that he formed his style, referring, no doubt, to that of his plays and such a work as *Jonathan Wild*—a style dry, sententious, and nerved with irony, which was gradually transmuted into the limpid, flowing, and not less sprightly style of *Joseph Andrews* and *Tom Jones*. It is the Lucianic attitude that he adopts rather than the theme or shape of any particular work.[1] He tells how he starts one December night, in company with six others, in a stage-coach from Warwick Lane, on the journey to Hades. The drive is recounted with the same sort of humour as enlivens the stage-coach scene in *Joseph Andrews*; but it is difficult to believe that the ampler and richer scene was already penned. Passing through the City of Diseases and visiting the Palace of Death, this a text for sardonic reflections on a vicious social hygiene and that on the holocausts which are the tribute to human greatness, the parties at last arrive at the river Cocytus, and being ferried across finish the journey on foot. They arrive at the gate of Elysium, where a crowd of spirits are waiting for admittance. Each is in turn examined by Judge Minos, and Fielding briefly describes the proceedings.

One very beautiful spirit " began to ogle Minos the moment she saw him. . . . She hoped there was some merit in refusing a great number of lovers, and dying a maid, though she had had the choice of a hundred. Minos told her she had not refused enough yet, and turned her back."

She was succeeded by a spirit who told the judge he believed his works would speak for him. "What works?" answered Minos. "My dramatic works," replied the other, "which have done so much good in recommending virtue and punishing vice." "Very well," said the judge, " if you please to stand by, the first person who passes the gate by your means shall carry you in with him ; but, if you will take my advice, I think, for expedition

---

[1] See Digeon, 119-120, where Rabelais, Scarron, and Le Sage are cited as possible sources for the ideas on the visit to the infernal regions and on reincarnation.

sake, you had better return, and live another life upon earth." The bard grumbled at this, and replied that, besides his poetical works, he had done some other good things ; for that he had once lent the whole profits of a benefit-night to a friend, and by that means had saved him and his family from destruction. Upon this the gate flew open, and Minos desired him to walk in, telling him if he had mentioned this at first, he might have spared the remembrance of his plays.[1]

The playwright is with difficulty restrained from reciting some of his works, to give Minos a fitter idea of their merit. The next candidate is a fine gentleman, of whom Minos says it would be a great pity to rob the world, and therefore desires him to take the other trip. A certain duke, who delivers a long harangue of what he had done in the House, is told that he is " infinitely too great a man for Elysium," and is pushed back with contumely. Then Minos turned to a spirit who, " with fear and trembling, begged he might not go to the bottomless pit."

He said he hoped Minos would consider that, though he had gone astray, he had suffered for it—that it was necessity which drove him to the robbery of eighteenpence, which he had committed, and for which he was hanged—that he had done some good actions in his life—that he had supported an aged parent with his labour—that he had been a very tender husband and a kind father—and that he had ruined himself by being bail for his friend. At which words the gate opened, and Minos bid him enter, giving him a slap on the back as he passed by him.

The judge at last addressed himself to the narrator, " who little expected to pass this fiery trial."

I confessed I had indulged myself very freely with wine and women in my youth, but had never done an injury to any man living, nor avoided an opportunity of doing good ; that I pretended to very little virtue more than general philanthropy and private friendship. I was proceeding, when Minos bid me enter the gate, and not indulge myself with trumpeting forth my virtues.[2]

---

[1] Book I., c. 7.
[2] Of course, it is unfair to identify Fielding with the imaginary narrator, and convict him of youthful dissipations, as it were out of his own mouth. This has been done, however, over and over again. His own loss of a daughter gave poignancy to the incident that follows. But that is a different matter.

In Elysium the first spirit to greet him was the little daughter he had lost several years before, and the interview is related with exquisite tenderness. Leonidas of Sparta, recently gratified by the praises of an English poet; Homer, in close converse with Madame Dacier; Virgil, with Addison under his arm, and other celebrities make their appearance. Addison is convicted of a strange piece of ignorance, but is consoled by Dick Steele, who embraces Addison and tells him he is the greatest man on earth, and that he readily resigns to him all the merit of his own works. " Upon which Addison gave him a gracious smile, and, clapping him on the back with much solemnity, cried out : ' Well said, Dick!'" Next Shakespeare is encountered, to whom Betterton and Booth apply for the right reading of a doubtful line, and he tells them it is so long since he wrote it that he has forgotten his meaning. He further delivers himself of an admirable view of textual criticism : " I marvel nothing so much as that men will gird themselves at discovering obscure beauties in an author. Certes, the greatest and most pregnant beauties are ever the plainest and most evidently striking; and when two meanings of a passage can in the least balance our judgments which to prefer, I hold it matter of unquestionable certainty that neither of them is worth a farthing." All which is good comedy; but two longer and somewhat inconsequent items that are tacked on, an account of the strange transmigrations of Julian the Apostate before he could satisfy Minos, and an autobiography of Anne Boleyn, are laboured, and lacking in humour, though they show with what a critical philosophy Fielding read history. He seems to have wearied of the task and breaks off with ill-disguised abruptness.

Date of composition Some allusions to recent events, and a reference in the introduction to his friend, Parson Adams, indicate that the *Journey* was at least retouched not long before it was published. But, taken as a whole, it is more likely to have been an early work.[1] Together with *Jonathan Wild*, it belongs to a literary species that Fielding never returned to; both seem to pertain to the stage of his mental development preceding the novels, rather than to be

[1] Digeon regards the *Journey* as for the most part a work of Fielding's youth (Digeon, 121). Cross thinks it was begun before *Joseph Andrews* "but mainly written during the weeks immediately succeeding " (Cross, i. 396).

the work of a man who had given the world something so mature
as *Joseph Andrews*. But the question is by no means simple.
There is hardly any light but that guttering candle, internal
evidence, to examine it by; and, unless we take style into consideration as well as matter, we may find references enough in
both works to the period before *Joseph Andrews*, but we can
never be sure that they refer to the time of writing and not to
what had become the past. The references in *Jonathan Wild*
may be left till we have looked at the work as a whole.
Meanwhile, this much can be said on the other point and will be
helpful in weighing such indications as may emerge. The style of
Jonathan Wild is the cool, concise, razor-edged, Lucianic style
that goes so perfectly with satire of the Lucianic stamp. No
finer example of it is to be found in modern literature, not even
in Swift. Fielding's later style is superior, for its own purposes,
but it is superior in respect of those purposes; it is better because
different. It is a reasonable hypothesis that he wrote a large part
of *Jonathan Wild* before he began *Joseph Andrews*, and afterwards made additions, perhaps large additions. But with his
unfailing sense of form he would assuredly cleave to the style
he had first adopted, polishing, no doubt, when he revised and
rewrote, as at the close of his life, in the edition of 1754, he
rewrote and repolished again.[1]

The *History of the Life of the late Mr Jonathan Wild the Great*   "*Jonathan*
(1743) is an ironical biography, like Thackeray's *Barry Lyndon*,   *Wild*"
written in a tone of assumed admiration and applause. The great
criminal is contemplated as the typical great man, with the im-
plication that the great and illustrious are, with rare exceptions,
merely successful criminals. Wild, the infamous organizer of
thieves, the informer with the blood of a hundred betrayed
accomplices on his head, who had been hanged in 1725, and his
deeds celebrated by scores of pens—including that of Defoe—
serves in Fielding's fictitious biography only as a stalking-horse
for satire on the human folly that pays tribute to the kind of
merit implied in the favourite saying, that " nothing succeeds like

---

[1] M. Digeon, in his supplementary volume, *Le Texte des Romans de Fielding*
(1923), shows the textual alterations made by Fielding in the later editions of
his four novels. They form an instructive lesson in prose style, as well as an
illustration of his changes of attitude.

success," and confounds together greatness and goodness, as if Alexander, Charles XII. of Sweden, Louis XIV., and other glorious conquerors were benefactors of mankind. As to the difference between greatness and goodness, Fielding says: "No two things can possibly be more distinct from each other, for greatness consists in bringing all manner of mischief on mankind, and goodness in removing it from them." But, as he ironically maintains, greatness is greatness wherever you find it; and in the career of a ruthless, unblushing, double-dyed scoundrel like Jonathan Wild you have the perfect example, with the perfect climax, the gallows.

For my own part, I confess, I look on this death of hanging to be as proper for a hero as any other; and I solemnly declare that, had Alexander the Great been hanged, it would not in the least have diminished my respect for his memory. Provided a hero in his life doth but execute a sufficient quantity of mischief; provided he be but well and heartily cursed by the widow, the orphan, the poor, and the oppressed (the sole rewards, as many authors have bitterly lamented both in prose and verse, of greatness, *i.e.* priggism), I think it avails little of what nature his death be, whether it be by the axe, the halter, or the sword. Such names will always be sure of living to posterity, and of enjoying that fame which they so gloriously and eagerly coveted.[1]

Not a realistic piece   It would be a waste of time to compare Fielding's version with the actual life of Wild. He read up the subject in old pamphlets and news-sheets, but stuck to fact only when it suited his ulterior purpose, altering whenever he pleased for the sake of philosophic truth. There is hardly any realism in the book.[2] Wild, though he is stated to have had no education to speak of, and who writes a misspelt letter which is a rather feeble specimen of this kind of humour, does not speak the tongue of Newgate, but discourses and reasons in the polished diction that Fielding had adopted for the whole composition. Some of the minor characters, such as Snap the sheriff's officer or the butcher Blueskin—the latter a confederate actually blown upon by the historic Wild—look like

[1] Book IV., c. 12.

[2] Coleridge opined that in putting his scorching wit into the mouth of the hero, Fielding was purposely "unrealizing the story, in order to give a deeper reality to the truths intended" (Blanchard, 322).

sketches from life; but the principals are nicely differentiated types of villainy rather than real persons. They are evolved rather in the manner of Richardson than portrayed in the manner perfected by the author of *Joseph Andrews*. Fielding would indeed like to rewrite the lives of a good many heroes, especially those who missed the final pinnacle of greatness, *videlicet*, the gallows, to complete their characters; their "histories would then have been read with much greater pleasure by the wisest of all ages."

Indeed, we could almost wish that, whenever Fortune seems wantonly to deviate from her purpose, and leaves her work imperfect in this particular, the historian would indulge himself in the licence of poetry and romance, and even do a violence to truth, to oblige his readers with a page which must be the most delightful in all his history, and which could never fail of producing an instructive moral.[1]

Jonathan is represented in a mock genealogical tree as the last *Outline* scion of a very ancient family of light-fingered gentry.[2] He *of the story* learns to thieve almost before he is out of the cradle, and takes the lead among his schoolfellows in their marauding escapades. Having completed his education with a course of reading in picaresque literature, he goes on the grand tour as a convict to the plantations, and returns to make himself, by his superior wits and invincible effrontery, the secret but despotic ruler of a gang of thieves who carry on their operations all over London. Wild himself never takes part in any robbery. He receives the booty, which he disposes of to the owners or other people, giving up only a small fraction of the amount realized to the actual thief. He shows his greatness by the complete ascendancy which he enjoys over his subjects. If any show signs of disaffection, they are handed over without remorse to the authorities and hanged. Blueskin, for instance, tries to keep a watch that he has stolen, instead of surrendering it to his chieftain, and puts himself at the head of a conspiracy of malcontents; whereupon Wild

[1] Book IV., c. 14.
[2] Probably a travesty of Musgrave's in his *History of the Walpole Family* (see Cross, i. 422-423, and Wells, 19).

informs against him. Blueskin is committed to Newgate, and
the profoundest submission is re-established.

All this is pretty much in accord with the history of Wild that
was public property. Fielding amplifies it with episodes of the
rascal's prowess in emptying the pockets of his friends and cheat-
ing them at the gaming-table. Wild exercises his talents even on
the wily Count La Ruse, who bilks him at cards, but is himself
relieved of his gains without being able to convict the friend
that he knows to be the culprit. Wild is not so happy in his
amours. He nurses a passion for Miss Lætitia Snap, daughter
of the keeper of the sponging-house. She repels his attentions
with chaste indignation, but as soon as Wild's back is turned
lets another admirer out of a cupboard. Eventually, however,
he marries this creature, who is probably a character out of a
suppressed comedy of the seamy side.[1] She enslaves, cajoles,
deceives, and in the upshot curses him for leaving her the widow
of a gallows-bird.

Plot interest now comes in with the affair of the Heartfrees.
Heartfree is a London jeweller who has been a schoolfellow of
Wild's, who takes advantage of his complete honesty and the
confidence of old friendship to induce him to entrust a quantity
of valuable jewellery to his accomplice Count La Ruse, who
absconds. Heartfree is robbed even of the sum paid on account,
and finds himself ruined, more than half the jewels being the
property of other tradesmen. He is thrown into Newgate. Wild
has cast lascivious eyes on the poor man's wife, and now entraps
her into fleeing with him to the Continent under the pretence of
saving her husband from bankruptcy. A forcible attempt on the
lady is defeated through the intervention of the captain of the
vessel, and Wild for a punishment is cast adrift in a boat. In
this predicament the intrepid rogue burlesques the part of the
conventional romantic hero. But his finest exploit is to regain
the confidence of his victim Heartfree, now languishing in gaol.
The jeweller, however, rejects his offer of aid; he is too mean-
spirited to attempt an escape at the cost of murdering one or two

---

[1] *E.g.* the dialogue in Book III., c. 8. The sentence, "These words were
spoken with a very great air," was substituted in the 1754 edition for what
was evidently a stage direction, "These words to be spoken," etc. (see
Digeon, *Le Texte des Romans de Fielding*, 25-27).

of the keepers. The great man then determines to have Heartfree put out of the way, and works up a case against him on a false charge of fraudulent bankruptcy. Heartfree is found guilty, and is on his way to the gallows, when Mrs Heartfree reappears. She has recovered most of the stolen property ; and when Firebrand, a member of the gang, splits on his chief the whole plot is exposed, the prisoner is released, and the Heartfrees are restored to affluence.

Wild is at length brought to book. The hero is tried, sentenced to be hanged, and, being foiled in an attempt to cheat the gallows by taking poison, mounts the scaffold in the midst of an execrating crowd, and with admirable firmness swings out of this world. He keeps up his character to the last, picking a bottle-screw out of the pocket of the ordinary who is administering ghostly consolation, and carrying it out of the world in his hand.

Grimmer satire than this cannot be found in English literature. *Satirical* The most corrosive pages in Swift's *Modest Proposal* or the *irony* last book of *Gulliver* are not more deadly. Fielding maintains his calm intellectual attitude right to the end, except for a few unguarded explosions of human feeling in the story of the Heartfrees which scarcely interrupt the sustained irony. It is the sardonic humour of a man who detests heartlessness and hypocrisy, but who never despairs of humanity even in a world that is black with turpitude. And with what incomparable art he keeps control of his weapon, exciting delight and admiration at the perfect ease and grace of the sword-play! How dexterous the wit that could transfix two adversaries with the same flourish, as in the characterization of Blueskin :

This gentleman had two qualities of a great man, viz., undaunted courage, and an absolute contempt of those ridiculous distinctions of *meum* and *tuum* which would cause endless disputes, did not the law happily decide them by converting both into *suum*.

How profound the irony of Wild's famous oration on Honour :

I have heard with infinite pleasure everything which the two gentlemen who spoke last have said in relation to honour, nor can any man possibly entertain a higher and nobler sense of that

word, nor a greater esteem of its inestimable value, than myself.
. . . It is indeed the essential quality of a gentlemen, and which
no man who ever was great in the field, or on the road (as others
express it), can possibly be without. But, alas ! gentlemen, what
pity is it that a word of such sovereign use should have so un-
certain and various an application that scarce two people mean
the same thing by it ! Do not some by honour mean good-nature
and humanity, which weak minds call virtues ? How then ! must
we deny it to the great, the brave, the noble ; to the sackers
of towns, the plunderers of provinces, and the conquerors of
kingdoms ? Were not these men of honour ? and yet they scorned
those pitiful qualities I have mentioned. Again, some few (or I
am mistaken) include the idea of honesty in their honour. And
shall we then say that no man who withholds from another what
law, or justice perhaps, calls his own, or who greatly and boldly
deprives him of such property, is a man of honour ? Heaven forbid I should say so in this, or, indeed, in any other good company !
Is honour truth ? No ; it is not the lie's going from us, but in
its coming to us, our honour is injured. Doth it then consist
in what the vulgar call cardinal virtues ? It would be an affront
to your understandings to suppose it, since we see every day so
many men of honour without any. In what, then, doth the word
' honour ' consist ? Why, in itself alone. A man of honour is he
that is called a man of honour ; and while he is so called, he so
remains, and no longer. Think not anything a man commits can
forfeit his honour. Look abroad into the world : the PRIG, while
he flourishes, is a man of honour ; when in gaol, at the bar, or
the tree, he is so no longer. And why is this distinction ? Not
from his actions, for those are often as well known in his flourishing state as they are afterwards ; but because men (I mean those
of his own party or gang) call him a man of honour in the former,
and cease to call him so in the latter condition.[1]

*What
was
Fielding's
purpose?*
But, comes the question, what impelled Fielding to indite this
long tirade against resplendent villainy? Wild had quitted the
stage of his exploits in 1725, and for his own sake was hardly
worth resuscitating. Was Fielding's object merely to caricature
the still flourishing brand of criminal biography, out of his disgust at a demoralizing form of hero-worship? Or was he bent
on exposing the cynical glorification of rascality that made the
picaresque romances a corrupting influence? If this was his

---

[1] Book I., c. 13.

original aim, he was not the first to treat the theme in some such way. In 1725, just after Wild's execution, a pamphlet life had appeared at Northampton in which the author, without much skill or humour, strikes the ironical attitude, and expatiates on the Machiavellian schemes and the colossal success of Wild's ill-omened genius. The same year an article appeared in *Mist's Weekly Journal* dealing with the career of the grandiose villain in mock-heroic style, and in some degree anticipating the more elaborate irony of Fielding. Could this have been from his pen? He was then a young fellow of eighteen and still at Eton. The suggestion that the book is only an expansion of the article is not very plausible, but it has been broached.[1]

But any of these motives or a combination of them would *"Jonathan* hardly have justified more than a shortish narrative, with some *Wild"; a* disquisition on the lessons to be drawn from such a monstrous *satire on* example; they do not account for the sustained thought which *the Walpole* Fielding put into the book or the murderous energy of the satire. *regime* Some burning question of the day must have roused his deepest feelings and called up all his mental powers. What that question was is clearly revealed in the original edition of *Jonathan Wild* (1743). When his life was drawing to a close, and his enmities had receded into the past, Fielding revised the book very considerably, and cut out or disguised numerous passages hitting unmistakably at the Walpole Government and the wholesale corruption by which that Minister kept in power. Along with the ironical panegyric of Wild and the more discursive satire on false ideals of greatness, on the rapacity and ineptitude of the law, and the state of the prisons, which were cesspools of vice and corruption, there is another object that accounts for all his animus. The Licensing Act of 1737 had deprived the playwright of his living, and of the platform from which he had been railing for years against Walpole's system of jobbers and placemen, and his selfish disregard for the national interests. Dislodged from this post of vantage, he transferred the guerrilla campaign from the theatre to the press. The pages of *The Champion*, especially

---

[1] See the discussion in Cross (i. 408-409) and the article "Fielding's Political Purpose in Jonathan Wild," by J. E. Wells (*Mod. Lang. Assn. of America*, xxviii. 1-55, 1913).

during the period November 1739 to June 1740, are alive with attacks on Walpole, which foreshadow the bitter gibes to be read beneath the surface of *Jonathan Wild*, in the first edition of 1743. Here Walpole and the nefarious hero are continually identified; and, when Wild is not actually a personification of the minister, there are covert strokes at the system of adminis- tration by bribery, and comparisons of a party holding the reins of government and pillaging the country to a gang of footpads. Priggism, the cant word for thieving, is meant to be taken also in another sense; it stands for jobbery, place-hunting, the alleged systematic bribery by means of which Walpole kept his enemies under. References, often in extra-large capitals, to THE GREAT MAN, THE MINISTER, or A PRIME MINISTER—this last a designa- tion first applied to Walpole—to ministerial tools and the like, were afterwards cut out or toned down.[1] These were the regular appellations with which Walpole and his supporters were assailed in the Opposition press.[2] Wild's happy-go-lucky union with the wanton Miss Snap is as palpable a fling at Walpole's loose matri- monial relations as was the affair of Robin and Sweetissa in *The Welsh Opera*, or that of Macheath and his wife and his mistress in *Polly*, a piece that was suppressed for its libellous tendencies.[3]

The ironical version of con- temporary politics   Fielding's personal feeling towards the Minister comes out plainly, among other instances, where he insinuates that one of the strongest bonds of amity between great men, and one of the most reputable at the present time, is that which subsists between the accommodating husband and the gallant—a kind of alliance said to have had the sanction of Walpole's example. His resent- ment at the muzzling of the stage by the Licensing Act is evident in his ironical advice to great men that they should suppress criticism:

Many inconveniences arise to the said great men from these scribblers publishing, without restraint, their hints or alarms to society; and many great and glorious schemes have been thus

---

[1] The toning down is at a minimum in the tirade on "Greatness" (Book II., c. 4).
[2] Walpole was regularly referred to in the Opposition press as "the Great Man" (Wells, 14).
[3] Cross, iii. 408.

frustrated ; wherefore it were to be wished that, in all well-regulated governments, such liberties should be by some wholesome laws restrained ; and all writers inhibited from venting any other instructions to the people than what should be first approved and licensed by the said great men, or their proper instruments or tools ; by which means nothing could ever be published but what made for the advancing of their most noble projects.[1]

But Fielding regarded the whole party machine established by Walpole and run by him and his supporters—most of them bribed by money, place, or title—as an organization not radically dissimilar to Wild's. In the celebrated chapter " Of Hats," differences of political opinion among such a crew are contemptuously dismissed as of no more account than differences in the way they tilted their hat-brims. The satire is more disdainful even than Swift's famous distinctions between the Big-endians and Little-endians or the High-heels and Low-heels.

As these persons wore different *principles*, i.e. *hats*, frequent dissensions grew among them. There were particularly two parties—viz. those who wore hats *fiercely* cocked, and those who preferred the *nab*, or trencher-hat, with the brim flapping over their eyes. The former were called *cavaliers* and *tory rory ranter boys*, etc. ; the latter went by the several names of *wags, round-heads, shakebags, oldnolls*, and several others. Between these continual jars arose, insomuch that they grew in time to think there was something essential in their differences, and that their interests were incompatible with each other, whereas, in truth, the difference lay only in the fashion of their hats.

Wild reminds them that their interests are the interests of the gang.

" To keep up such a ridiculous contention among yourselves, must argue the highest folly and absurdity. When you know you are all prigs, what difference can a broad or a narrow brim create ? Is a prig less a prig in one hat than in another ? If the public should be weak enough to interest themselves in your quarrels, and to prefer one pack to the other, while both are aiming at their

[1] Book III., c. 5.

purses, it is your business to laugh at, not imitate, their folly. What can be more ridiculous than for gentlemen to quarrel about hats, when there is not one among you whose hat is worth a farthing ? . . . Let me hear no more, therefore, of this childish disagreement, but all toss up your hats together with one accord, and consider that hat as the best which will contain the largest booty." [1]

So, when there is sedition in Newgate, and the leader, Roger Johnson, is displaced by Wild, who seizes the spoils of office and dons his predecessor's finery, Fielding points out, in the harangue of the " very grave man," that the exchange of one scamp for another was a matter of indifference. "What a wolf is in a sheepfold, a great man is in society. Now, when one wolf is in possession of a sheepfold, how little would it avail the simple flock to expel him, and place another in his stead? Of the same benefit to us is the overthrowing one *prig* in favour of another. And for what other advantage was your struggle? Did you not all know that Wild and his followers were *prigs*, as well as Johnson and his? What then could the contention be among such, but that which you have now discovered it to have been ? " [2] There is no need here to identify Johnson and Wild with Walpole and Wilmington, or the other way about: the point is that between two covetous gangs, or two political sharpers, there is not a pin to choose: they are all allied to take in the public, and their interests must be identical. It is much the same as Fielding had said before, in *Pasquin* and *The Historical Register*, when he had been silenced by the Government.

A double allegory　*Jonathan Wild*, then, a work in which pure intellect is the creative force rather than the genial and tolerant spirit that gave life and humanity to *Joseph Andrews* and the two later novels, turns out to be a double allegory; the satire has a general and also a particular subject. On examination, the two strands prove to be so closely intertwined that it is difficult to say which is original and which secondary. Perhaps, with the clumsy efforts of previous ironical historians of Wild prompting him to do better, Fielding perceived at once the aptness of his subject both for a caricature of the political situation and for the wider philo-

[1] Book II., c. 6.　　　　　　　　　　　[2] Book IV., c. 3.

sophical satire. The book shows signs of having been amplified from time to time. What may be called the public history of Wild—the doings of the gang and the rivalry for the leadership—does not amalgamate smoothly with the personal history, Wild's conjugal misadventures, and the Heartfree business. It is possible that the whole of this last, necessary as it is to furnish plot interest, or even to convert the story of Wild into a novel at all, was a late insertion.[1]

Fielding probably began *Jonathan Wild* about the end of 1739 *Date of* or the beginning of 1740, when he was in the thick of his war- *"Jonathan* fare in *The Champion* against the Walpole Government. The *Wild"* general and the particular satire expanded together: his outlook was too philosophical ever to keep them separate. The work grew by fits and starts in the intervals of journalistic activity, and was laid aside whilst he was engaged on *Joseph Andrews*. Then, amidst the stress of domestic trials, he took up the unfinished work, and probably recast it. Perhaps it was now that he was struck with the idea of converting it into a sort of novel by interweaving the Heartfree story. It is known that he was writing hard against time, whilst his wife lay dangerously ill, in order to complete the three volumes of the *Miscellanies*; and it could hardly have been such a trifle as the *Journey to the Next World* that kept him from satisfying his subscribers more promptly; this must surely have been the longer and more serious work that fills the last volume. Walpole had resigned in February 1742. The battle was over, and Fielding's combativeness assuaged.[2] Every likelihood points to the conclusion that *Jonathan Wild* belongs in part, especially the satirical part, to the period before the appearance of *Pamela* and Fielding's occupation with *Joseph Andrews*, and in part to the time immediately before the long-delayed issue of the *Miscellanies*. And, since the

[1] Digeon is convinced that it was introduced after Fielding had finished *Joseph Andrews*, seeing in Mrs Heartfree a portrait of the first Mrs Fielding (like Sophia and Amelia) and a parallelism to *Tom Jones* in the general scheme.

[2] Professor Cross supposes the book to have been written in 1742-1743, and curiously suggests that the fall of Walpole was Fielding's occasion for the satire on that minister in *Jonathan Wild*. He seems to think that there is much virtue and consequently a valuable clue in the word "late," in the title *Life of the late Mr Jonathan Wild*. The title may well have been one of the last things composed, and the word "late" would add force to satire penned years earlier (Cross, i. 409-410).

*The
Heartfree
episodes
probably
a last
addition*

Heartfree episodes are a somewhat mechanical affair, apparently written in haste to provide what was lacking to fulfil the conventional requirements of a novel, there is good reason to suppose that these formed the last instalment.   Much of the book was doubtless rewritten; but, if any parts show signs of repolishing, it is certainly not the Heartfree chapters.[1]   The rambling account of Mrs Heartfree's adventures in distant parts of the world, after she got quit of the villain Wild, is a far-fetched excursion from the direct route to the goal Fielding had in view.   One of these chapters, which in the original preface to the *Miscellanies* he said was meant " as a burlesque on the extravagant accounts of travellers," he completely suppressed in the later edition.[2]

*Fielding's
preface to
" David
Simple"*

Fielding wrote an interesting preface for the second edition of that curious example of sentimental romance, *The Adventures of David Simple* (1744), by his sister Sarah, who was three years his junior.   This young lady was one of Richardson's band of female adorers, and after her brother's death, no doubt in acknowledgment of her effusive tributes, received the compliments of the author of *Pamela* upon her knowledge of the human heart. Quoting the remark of " a critical judge of writing," evidently Dr Johnson, Richardson wrote : " Your late brother's knowledge of it was not (fine writer as he was) comparable to yours . . . his was but as the knowledge of the outside of a clockwork machine, while yours was that of all the finer springs and movements of the inside."   Something like it had been said of Richardson's own powers of introspection.   The plan rather than the theme of the book is announced in the sub-title, " Containing an account of his travels through the cities of London and Westminster in the search of a real friend."   But the subject is really—the heart.

[1] Fanny's reflections when Parson Adams rescues her from the ravisher (*Joseph Andrews*, Book II., c. 10)—" She suspected he had used her as some very honest men have used their country ; and had rescued her out of the hands of one rifler in order to rifle her himself "—show that Fielding when he was writing that book had no illusions about the character of the professional politician.   They agree with many of the sallies in *Jonathan Wild*, but throw no light on the question whether these were written earlier or later.   Nor can they be shown to refer specifically to the exit of Townshend or the exit of Walpole and his supersession by Wilmington.

[2] The chapter is reprinted in M. Digeon's study, *Le Texte des Romans de Fielding*, 1923.

The novelist pays tribute to the goddess, " Dear Sensibility,"
and her David at long last finds his ideal in the beautiful and
amiable Camilla.

David Simple falls into two contrasted parts. The earlier *"David*
is critical and satirical, for it is as a censor of society in the *Simple,"*
Addisonian manner that Sarah was at her best ; but the method, *by Sarah*
clumsily enough, is the picaresque. The second, in a series of *Fielding*
fanciful portraits of character, after Richardson, illustrated with
episodes of London life, depicts ideal virtues and the tender and
benevolent sentiments that should be cultivated by all, especially
by those whose talents incline them to triumph in their superiority
to the rest of the world :

"Were all mankind contented to exert their own faculties for
the common good, neither envying those who in any respect have
a superiority over them, nor despising such as they think their
inferiors, real happiness would be attainable, notwithstanding
all that has been said on that subject; and the various humours
and the different understandings with which human nature is
supplied would, instead of discord, produce such a harmony as
would infallibly make the whole species happy."

But to set forth the amiable philosophy that underlies her
criticism of society, the authoress could hardly have chosen a
more unfortunate plan than that of a picaresque story, with its
haphazard episodes and motley succession of characters. Nothing
could be more clumsy than the way she manages her dialogue,
with the names of the speakers formally prefixed as in a play;
nothing more awkward than her stories within the story, and
then again the story told at second or third hand, but still in the
first person, of brothers, lovers, and acquaintances, amid whose
protracted aphorisms we are apt to lose the thread altogether.

But " Sally " was a sensible person and not without wit, as an
extract or two will show :

She spent some time in the deepest melancholy, and felt all the
misery which attends a woman who has many things to wish, but
knows not positively which she wishes most.
If he had but sighed, and been miserable for the loss of her, she
could have married her old man without any great reluctance :
but the thought that he had left her first was insupportable !

Lucretia herself (whose chastity nothing but the fear of losing her reputation could possibly have conquered).

He was not of the opinion, that the more ignorant a man is of any subject, the more necessary it is to talk about it.

And there for some time I will leave him to his own private sufferings—lest it should be thought I am so ignorant of the world, as not to know the proper time of forsaking people.

Sarah's limitations   Miss Fielding never really advanced beyond the Addisonian stage : she was an essayist and commentator rather than a novelist, and could make up an inventory of character with the best, but she did not know how to make her imaginary figures act their parts in a natural way. The following sketch of the censorious critic who introduces David to different phases of London life, good as it is, belongs to an obsolete school :

You are to know, sir, there are a set of men in the world, who pass through life with very good reputations, whose actions are in the general justly to be applauded, and yet upon a closer examination their principles are all bad, and their hearts hardened to all tender sensations. Mr Orgeuil is exactly one of those sort of men ; the greatest sufferings which can happen to his fellow-creatures, have no sort of effect upon him, and yet he very often relieves them ; that is, he goes just as far in serving others as will give him new opportunities of flattering himself ; for his whole soul is filled with pride, he has made a god of himself, and the attributes he thinks necessary to the dignity of such a being, he endeavours to have. He calls all religion superstition, because he will own no other deity ; he thinks even obedience to the Divine Will, would be but a mean motive to his actions ; he must do good, because it is suitable to the dignity of his nature ; and shun evil, because he would not be debased so low as the wretches he every day sees.

Fielding had been credited with the honour of this performance, and his first work in the preface is to disclaim the merit, which he does with graceful modesty and a handsome compliment to his sister's " deep and profound discernment of all the mazes, windings, and labyrinths " which perplex the student of human nature. He then repudiates the charge that he had broken a promise solemnly entered into some years since, never to publish

even a pamphlet without setting his name to it. He complains
that he has been " reputed and reported the author of half the
scurrility, bawdy, treason, and blasphemy, which these last few
years have produced." Hardest and most humiliating of all, he
has had the blame of a wretched lampoon on the Bar, entitled
The Causidicade, laid on his shoulders :

> This accused me not only of being a bad writer, and a bad
> man ; but with downright idiotism, of flying in the face of the
> greatest men of my profession. I take, therefore, this opportunity
> to protest, that I never saw that infamous, paultry libel, till long
> after it had been in print ; nor can any man hold it in greater
> contempt and abhorrence than myself.

Fielding never, apparently, made much of an income at the *Fielding's*
Bar ; doubtless, many looked askance at the dramatist, journalist, *anti-*
and possibly the lurking satirist, who had recently entered upon *Jacobite*
so very different a calling. In spite of his disclaimers, some *journalism*
anonymous pamphlets of this period have been traced to his
authorship. But they were written in a good cause. The army
of the Pretender was on the march from Scotland, and Fielding
in this crisis showed himself a staunch supporter of the Government. Towards the end of 1745 he came forward as editor of
a new journal, *The True Patriot*, in which he kept up a running
fire against the Jacobites and helped to invigorate the spirit of
resistance, which was strangely lacking in earnestness. The
periodical had the usual literary and social features, and Fielding's
humour is evident in the regular section called the " Apocrypha,"
in which he pilloried the baseless reports, the exaggerations, and
the conventional trivialities appearing in the contemporary news-
sheet. When the rebellion was suppressed, this organ was
succeeded by *The Jacobite's Journal* (1747-1748), in which,
under the editorial pseudonym of John Trott-Plaid, Fielding renewed the campaign against all who were still disaffected towards
the Protestant and Hanoverian cause. As he seems to have run
both papers practically single-handed, and to have done some
pamphleteering as well, Fielding, evidently, was not a busy
lawyer. With the close of his anti-Jacobite journalism, however, he found it necessary to cast about for some more regular

employment. He had lost his beloved wife Charlotte in 1744,
and in 1747 he married Mary Daniel, who had been her faithful
maid and nurse. A son was born shortly after. By the interest
of his friend, George, Lord Lyttelton, Fielding was at the end
of 1748 made a Justice of the Peace for Westminster, and shortly
afterwards took over the duties of presiding magistrate at Bow
Street. The emoluments of the office during the tenure of his
predecessors amounted to about a thousand a year. Fielding,
who undertook his new duties with the zeal of a social reformer,
as might be expected from the castigator of venal and incompetent
magistrates and of the evils of defective statutes and a careless
administration of justice, never received a third of that stipend.
He declined to accept some of the perquisites regularly paid
to his predecessors. His own necessities were often grievous,
although the legend—for which his first biographer, Murphy,
was largely responsible—that he kept up until middle age the
self-indulgent and spendthrift habits of his youth, and during
his latter days was in a state of chronic impecuniosity, has been
demolished. But Fielding was sometimes reckless in his generosity, almost as recklessly impulsive as the Captain Booth of
his *Amelia*; and there is evidence that he was indebted to the
largess of two friends, Ralph Allen of Bath and the loyal and
generous Lyttelton, for relief in several monetary embarrassments.

CHAPTER VI

TOM JONES

SINCE *Joseph Andrews* and the *Miscellanies*, Fielding had made no contribution to literature beyond the preface to his sister's *David Simple* and some further items in a series of *Familiar Letters* which she published as a sequel to that novel. He probably started work upon *Tom Jones* in 1746, and continued steadily at it in the intervals of journalism for the next three years. As he had been running a sort of newspaper during the troubles with the Jacobites, and had taken a leading part in keeping his readers posted about the movements of the rebels and in warning the public against the treasonable influences that were still active after " The Forty-Five," it is not strange that the Jacobites and the excursions and alarums that agitated the country in this fateful time should bulk large in a novel giving a panorama of contemporary life in London and the provinces. Squire Western is a specimen of the ignorant, hard-drinking Tory landowner, half-a-century or more behind the times, whose dangerous vagaries Fielding had diagnosed in *The True Patriot* and *The Jacobite's Journal*. Partridge is a foolish Jacobite. The panic of some and the disaffection or indifference of others come into the picture. So also do the movements of the troops. And the fugitive Sophia is actually mistaken by an innkeeper, anxious not to fall out with the winning side, for Prince Charlie's handsome mistress, Jenny Cameron.[1] *Tom Jones* is a document for the history of the period in a way that Richardson's *Clarissa*, which was finished only a year earlier, is not. This results from the different outlook and opposite methods of the two writers.

Fielding had described *Joseph Andrews* in his preface as an

---

[1] For reflections on Fielding's anti-Jacobite journalism, see Cross, ii. 100-102 Other contributions from or references to items in his journals, incidentally throwing light on his rate of progress with *Tom Jones*, are dealt with in the succeeding pages.

A comic epic in prose

example of something new in fiction, the comic epic in prose. But *Joseph Andrews* was too slight a piece, too purely tentative, too much the result of a happy accident improved upon by genius, to bear the full weight of such an appellation. Presumably, he called it an epic merely as the prose correlative to a narrative poem, thinking of the structure rather than the content. But the word may be applied to *Tom Jones* with admirable propriety. It is a word, as Fielding remarks, implying some amplitude of scale, an action " extended and comprehensive," a great variety of characters. Fiction that is of epical scope will afford a panoramic view of a given epoch ; it will endeavour to bring out the general tendencies of that epoch by means of a scheme or plot showing events working out naturally to a decisive issue, and of a group of representative characters, implicated together, and standing out clearly from the random concourse of humanity in the background. That which is comic or absurd will be presented ironically ; in other words, the author will stand calmly aloof, never taking sides, smiling at the vagaries and affectations of all alike. By the delicate balancing of opposites he will bring about that equilibrium which is the end of disinterested comedy.

Both *Joseph Andrews* and *Jonathan Wild* had been provided with a plot that artificially reduced to an intelligible order the fortuitous incidents of life ; but the one, which began in burlesque, was light comedy, tending to farce ; the other, having a satirical motive, was not disinterested comedy at all. In spirit *Tom Jones* is a close analogue to the grave philosophic comedy of Molière. It is, however, to a large extent epical in structure, or rather an alternation of epical and dramatic, the narrative complicating itself so as to bring various conflicting interests and rival intrigues to a close encounter, and then, by means of a sudden disclosure, unravelling the complication. In common with epic and with the higher comedy, it is distinguished by the rigorous linkage of cause and effect, the agency of causation residing in the characters, in whom the play of motive is clearly exposed.

Fielding's intellectual realism

" The provision, then, which we have here made," says Fielding's preface, " is no other than Human Nature." It is as if he had combined, without betraying any joints or incongruities, two different kinds of fiction. On the one hand, his men and women, so many and so various, act so entirely in obedience to their temperaments, exist so much for themselves rather than for the sake of the story, that the novelist would seem to have yielded the reins to them, instead of making them subservient to any pre-conceived design. On the other hand, he has set forth a definite view of life, illustrated every side of it, and left the reader convinced that it is a very strong case. Fielding's introductory chapters to the successive books are not the principal means by which this view is enunciated. Take these away, and, though some luminous pages of critical dialectic would be missed, the meaning would still be perfectly plain. What this doctrine is comes out clearly even in a brief outline of the story.[1]

Its general trend is indicated in the title, *The History of Tom Jones, a Foundling.* Tom Jones, a young fellow of good disposition and a full allowance of natural appetites, is the adopted son of a great squire, the rich Mr Allworthy, a man of almost superhuman virtues, who might stand in a didactic story for justice and benevolence incarnate, or the divinity whose business it is to see everything righted in mundane affairs. Tom is what, for lack of a more sensible term, is called the hero, although his rôle is remarkably passive. The villain is Blifil. Blifil, Squire Allworthy's nephew and legitimate heir, is the orphan son of Allworthy's sister, Bridget, a spinster courted and won, when she was " somewhat passed the age of thirty," by a fortune-hunting Captain Blifil, who died. Blifil and Tom, brought up together, stand in precise antithesis to each other. Jones has an open, honest, and kindly disposition, which circumstances and evil communications can never entirely mar ; Blifil is one of those who would have no personality at all were not a sort of imitation character provided by self-interest and convention. Selfish in a mean, servile way he learns piety and good behaviour by rote,

Outline of the plot— the first two volumes

---

[1] The grandmotherly author of *Novels and Novelists of the Nineteenth Century*, William Forsyth, Q.C., writes : " The truth is, that it would be impossible to give an analysis of the novel, or even describe the plot except in the most meagre terms, without offending against the respect due to female delicacy now " (1871). This same writer talks about " the maudlin sentimentality of Richardson and the coarseness of Fielding and Sterne," and seems to have been unable to perceive anything in those novelists but the indelicacy which obsessed his mind (see pp 259 and 305). It was characteristic of that prurient age.

and affects love and admiration for Mr Allworthy, on whose good opinion his fortunes depend, without a grain of sympathy or even comprehension for the virtues he defers to.

Tom and Master Blifil are much of their time in company with Sophia Western, only daughter of the neighbouring squire, and she falls in love unawares with the debonair Tom, who is the soul of chivalry and has risked life and limb more than once for her sake. Tom might have responded, but his heart is elsewhere. He is entangled with a country wench, Molly Seagrim, daughter of a poaching gamekeeper who had ruined himself by abetting Tom in one of his escapades. Tom finds later on that Moll was the seducer rather than the seduced; but having got her into trouble he stands to his bargain, and even resigns himself to the prospect of marrying her if need be. But, even when his conscience is cleared in regard to Molly, and Sophia's obvious preference awakens an answering passion in himself, he will not wrong his benefactors by pursuing one so much above him.

Mr Jones had somewhat about him, which, though I think writers are not thoroughly agreed in its name, doth certainly inhabit some human breasts ; whose use is not so properly to distinguish right from wrong, as to prompt and incite them to the former, and to restrain and withhold them from the latter . . . though he did not always act rightly, yet he never did otherwise without feeling and suffering for it.[1]

The two families, it appears, have other designs; and, when Sophia's aunt, the redoubtable Miss Western, surprises the young lady's secret, a match between her and the odious Blifil, which had been vaguely contemplated as a means of uniting the two estates, is pressed forward, despite Sophia's stubborn resistance. Those critics who think that Fielding, all the while he was writing *Tom Jones*, had before his eye the main situation in Richardson's *Clarissa*, about which he is supposed to have known through his sister Sarah,[2] find here the counterpart to Clarissa's position when she is being pushed by her family into the arms of Mr Solmes

[1] Book IV., c. 6.
[2] Digeon, 163-164; for an elaborate argument that Fielding was deliberately writing against Richardson, see pp. 161-182. See also Cross, ii. 126-127 and 159.

and hopes for deliverance by Lovelace, with whom she is half in love. The situations are parallel and in contrast. But all that is probable is that Fielding was perfectly aware of the complete opposition between his view of life, of conduct, of character, and Richardson's view, and, without any particular rivalry, felt all the more assured that his own view was right and true. At any rate, this coincidence in the plots of the two novelists, and the absolutely different way in which the characters work out their destinies, are a luminous illustration of the fundamental antagonism of the two men's genius.

Tom quits the field. Traduced by Blifil, who, along with the time-serving Square and the spiteful Thwackum, who had tutored the lads, maliciously misinterprets everything he has done or said, he is cast off by Allworthy; and, caring little what becomes of himself, takes to the highway. He is all but penniless, for in the abandonment of despair he has carelessly lost the bill for five hundred pounds given him by Allworthy at his dismissal. But Sophia, hearing that her lover has been turned out naked into the world, sends him all her ready money, and shortly after, to escape a forced marriage with Blifil, takes flight herself. Tom tramps aimlessly on, and, falling in with a troop of soldiers marching to join the forces against the Pretender, is easily induced to join them. But various accidents intervene. Tom comes across Partridge, the village schoolmaster, who had been suspected by Allworthy of being the lad's father and had been turned away. He has the fortune to rescue from robbery and assault a Mrs Waters, who had been travelling with the soldiers and is supposed to be the captain's lady. This fair adventuress turns out in the sequel to be the identical Jenny Jones who had been saddled with the guilt of bringing Tom into the world, and, like Partridge, had been obliged to flee the neighbourhood. The present position of affairs, with these three thrown together, is ironical enough; but the consequences, as yet unforeseen, are more poignantly ironical.

The little party make their way to Upton-on-Severn and install themselves at the best inn, where a series of ludicrous, surprising, and pregnant incidents begins with a furious battle, before the dishevelled Mrs Waters can be safely established in her bedroom.

This is indeed the crisis of the story. Before our travellers get away next day a runaway wife, Squire Western's niece, Mrs Fitzpatrick, stops at the inn for rest and fresh horses, and is hardly gone before her husband arrives in hot pursuit. More momentous for Jones, Sophia with her maid, Mrs Honour, on her way to London to seek refuge with her cousin Lady Bellaston, also reaches Upton in the dead of night, and learns that her lover is in the same house. But, alas for Tom ! That frail and ill-starred hero has succumbed to the attractions of Mrs Waters, and the fact is discovered by Mrs Honour and reported to Sophia. She can think of no fitter reproach than to leave in his empty bed a certain muff that he used to fondle, pinning her name to it on a piece of paper. She then sets out again for London. Her father is close behind. Hardly has Jones had time to digest his remorse and shame at the sight of the muff when this pursuer arrives and there is another scene. But the squire does not overtake his daughter. A pack of hounds in full cry, a few miles farther on, is enough to divert him from his quarry; he gallops after and is in at the death, and, meeting with a cordial invitation to stay with his fellow-sportsman, gives up the chase.

The second pair of volumes   Fielding's first two volumes deal with country life, the next two with adventures on the road, the last two with town life. All three sections are full of incident. Even in the first part, which is the most epical, painting life and character in a broad and racy style, the narrative, going forward with a steady movement, breaks from time to time into lively, dramatic scenes. The second part is much more dramatic, a swift succession of adventures in which the different threads are hurried across the loom for the final entanglement. In the third part the story reaches a complexity that seems to defy all hope of a fortunate solution; and then, in the last chapters, by the time-honoured device of revelation and recognition, an issue is triumphantly provided. Thus the tale which began with epical narration terminates in an exciting drama of intrigue. This is complicated and rich in surprises, but probability is never outraged. With deep-laid cunning everything has been prepared far ahead. All is foreseen, nothing left to chance. One must read the story backwards, so to speak, to appreciate the beauty and precision of Fielding's plot, in which every character has an essential part to fulfil, and there is hardly an incident, no matter how insignificant, but contributes to the intended result. Little indeed is accidental, or could be omitted without detriment to the inner and outer symmetry.

This last portion of the novel, in which the soundness of the *The last* substructure is tested, is too intricate to be analysed in detail *two* except at inordinate length. Let us note some of the critical *volumes* points. Tom and Sophia are now in London. He is near the end of his money and in a state of desperation. She is safe for the moment in the house of her cousin, Lady Bellaston, who presently, however, hatches a scheme to match the heiress to a man of her own dissipated world, Lord Fellamar. Tom knows nothing of this; but, having by chance become possessed of a pocket-book belonging to Sophia and containing a hundred-pound note, he tries to find her out. But his luck is still against him. With " never less inclination to an amour " he becomes involved, by his " gallantry to the ladies," in an affair with Lady Bellaston, and receiving a present from this dangerous person, finds himself in a ticklish position. Going to her house one night to an appoint-ment, he is met, not by her, but by Sophia. They are interrupted by Lady Bellaston, and the ensuing scenes are comedy of the finest order. To free himself from the clutches of the demirep, Jones writes her a letter, formally offering marriage, which he is certain will secure a contemptuous refusal and his dismissal. But he reckons without his host, for the incriminating letter is after-wards produced as evidence of his treachery to Sophia. To get rid of this rival Lady Bellaston advises Fellamar to have Jones seized by a press-gang. At the critical moment, Jones is attacked by the jealous husband of Mrs Fitzpatrick, and runs him through the body in self-defence. The officers at once arrest him.

Tom Jones is now at the crisis of his misfortunes. He lies in prison, charged with murder; he has ruined himself irretrievably with Sophia ; he is finally disgraced with Allworthy, and Squire Western is beside himself with glee at the prospect of seeing him hanged. In this predicament he now learns something that adds horror to the tragedy. Mrs Waters has been identified as Jenny Jones, and he believes that Jenny Jones is his own mother. He has unwittingly incurred the guilt of Œdipus.

*The dé-
nouement*   But events, for which his generosity towards others is in
no small part responsible, are working in his favour, and a few
loyal friends are striving against long odds to right him.   In a
few more chapters the revolution in his fortunes is ushered in
with a naturalness and a show of probability beyond all praise.
Coincidences there are, but not of the sort that excite derision.
By chance, Mr Allworthy hears that Black George, who picked
up and appropriated the five hundred pounds which he gave
Jones, is trying to invest exactly that sum.   The theft is discovered, and Allworthy put on the track of Tom's other mishaps.
A letter is received from Square, who on his death-bed confesses
how iniquitously he had slandered Jones, and exonerates him from
the accusations that led to his dismissal.   Mr Fitzpatrick recovers,
and Jones is relieved from the guilt of murder.   On the collapse
of this charge, Dowling, the lawyer, is detected in suborning
witnesses against Jones, and taxed with the offence divulges that
he was commissioned by Blifil.   One thing leads to another.
Partridge makes it clear that he is not Tom's father.   Mrs Waters
lets out the secret.   Tom Jones is the son of Allworthy's own sister,
who at the point of death had confessed to Dowling and bidden him
inform her brother.   Blifil intercepted the message, and is even
now plotting to remove his half-brother out of the world.   The
revelation that Tom is Allworthy's nephew, and the exposure of
Blifil, whose villainy earns him his repudiation by Allworthy,
reverse the state of affairs.   Tom is now the recognized heir to
his uncle.   Squire Western, who an hour ago had sworn that if his
daughter refused to marry Blifil she should be turned out without
a rag to cover her, now is wild to see her marry Tom.

That young gentleman has still to make his peace with Sophia,
who has been wounded to the heart by the Bellaston intrigue.
This, in truth, is the most heinous of his offences, and has been
brought up against Fielding and his hero by generations of critics.
Fielding, whose ethics were in advance of his time, in this case
was only too true to its prevailing standards.   Moralists have
exaggerated the obliquity, and talked as if Jones had gone on
deliberately earning the wages of sin, whereas Fielding's account is very different.   Jones, in the course of his baffling search
for Sophia, fell into the Bellaston's snares.   On the spur of the

moment, when he believed that all worth living for was lost, he
accepted a challenge of gallantry, like the typical young man of
his day.   But he quickly realized the pitfall into which he had
tumbled, and struggled to get clear.   And he got clear before
many days were past.   If he had known more of life, if he had
been as wise as his author, Jones would have expressed his shame
and humiliation more feelingly.   But he was only a raw country
lad, learning by experience in a world that was not our world.[1]

Such is the story of *Tom Jones* and the plot in its main lines. *Excellence*
More complicated, but less arbitrary and artificial than the change *of the*
of names and the cross-identifications in Congreve's *Incognita,* *plot*
it is fertile in riddles and surprising solutions, yet puts hardly
any strain on the reader's faith.   The fastenings and hinges
of the mechanism are so discreetly counter-sunk that it is only
in the final chapters any of them attract attention.   Perhaps the
number of unexpected encounters at Upton is rather excessive,
though Fielding thought " the sagacious readers " would not be
surprised so much as those concerned.   But, on the whole, the
improbabilities and coincidences are not so many more than we
expect to meet with in the ups and downs of life as to call for
protest.[2]   An odd incident here and there may be superfluous
except for its own sake ; but there is only one large episode
which sticklers for artistic economy regard as an excrescence.
And for the story of the Man of the Hill, as for Mr Wilson's
story in *Joseph Andrews*, Fielding had precedents in *Don Quixote*
and other accepted models.   It was held perfectly legitimate to
fill a pause in the action with an entertaining story; and, more
scrupulously than most authors, Fielding inserted one that was

[1] Professor Cross (ii. 215-220) discusses the various judgments that have
been passed upon this episode.   As others have pointed out, Marivaux had
put his Jacob in a similar position in *Le Paysan Parvenu*, a story with which
Fielding must have been familiar.

[2] A significant tribute to the thought and trouble which Fielding applied
to working out the plot of *Tom Jones* is the minute analysis of the time-scheme
of which Dr F. S. Dickson gives an account in "The Chronology of *Tom
Jones*" (*The Library*, July 1917; see synopsis in Cross, ii. 188-196).   The
time-keeping in the main was very accurate—*e.g.* there certainly was a full
moon when Miss Waters started from Worcester with Ensign Northerton, as
related in Book IX., c. 6.   There are, however, a few slips—as Sophia's
wedding happening to fall on a Sunday, and Garrick appearing in London
when he was actually at Dublin.   The topographical details will also stand
very strict examination (see Cross, ii. 179-187).

not quite away from the point. The Timon of Mazard Hill met with his instructive misfortunes through squandering his affections on one who afterwards betrayed him. His indiscretion and the mess it made of his life are a parable to Jones, who for his part finds that natural sagacity and regard for the lessons of experience are a better guide than credulous reliance on the goodness of others.

The part played by mere accident

Fielding is always the comic novelist; and where tragedy seems imminent and almost unescapable—as in divers scenes in *Tom Jones* and the more poignant crises of *Amelia*—he habitually staves off the expected issue by means of some happy accident. We would like to expunge from memory one in especial. Only pious believers in a vigilant Providence can feel very comfortable about Sophia's too narrow escape from the blackguardly violence of Lord Fellamar, from a fate, that is to say, not less revolting and still more undeserved than Clarissa's, through the chance arrival of Squire Western at the crucial moment. Had the event been what the probabilities indicated, had the young lord's design, which Lady Bellaston had instigated and paved the way for, been successful, the subsequent proceedings would indeed have had little interest—the whole story of Tom Jones would have gone to pieces. It is more like melodrama than the higher comedy to represent ruin suspended over us by such a very slender thread.[1]

The implied philosophy of life

It would be absurd to try to put the whole meaning of *Tom Jones* into a few abstract terms. Fielding required nearly two thousand pages to express it, and those pages contain, not merely a story, but as comprehensive a portrayal of a world as could be brought within the unity of a book. The story, the general picture of life, the rich constellation of diversified characters, and the comments and explanations interspersed through the narrative or prefixed to the main groups of chapters, form a treatise on the art of life. The general drift of the lesson to be conveyed is plain from the foregoing summary. It is that the

---

[1] Fielding frankly confesses the hazardous nature of the situation and the accidental nature of Sophia's deliverance. "How miserable must have been the condition of poor Sophia when the enraged voice of her father was welcome to her ears! Welcome indeed it was, and luckily did he come, for it was the only accident upon earth which could have preserved the peace of her mind from being for ever destroyed" (Book XV., c. 5).

best qualifications for making a success of life are goodness of heart, charity rather than any theory of virtue, prudence, and a willingness to learn by experience, even at the cost of suffering for our mistakes. By acquiring wisdom and a better knowledge of mankind, Tom Jones, who has the right personal endowment, learns how to live and how to be happy. It is his nature to be open and unsuspicious. He falls an easy prey to temptation and quickly repents. He becomes a sinner, but never a villain. Villainy is so foreign to his character that he never suspects it in others, and no one was ever more forgiving: the incomparable Mr Allworthy chides him for excess of mercy to those who have basely wronged him. Fielding's attitude is one of indulgence to mere frailties and of reproof for blindness to the snares and stumbling-blocks that environ our path. Good impulses are nature's best gift, but they must be trained and controlled, else we shall be at the mercy of our own infirmities and of the evil machinations of others.

Prudence and circumspection are necessary even to the best of men. They are indeed as it were a guard to virtue, without which she can never be safe. It is not enough that your designs, nay that your actions, are intrinsically good, you must take care they shall appear so. If your inside be never so beautiful, you must preserve a fair outside also. This must be constantly looked to, or malice and envy will take care to blacken it so, that the sagacity and goodness of an Allworthy will not be able to see through it, and to discern the beauties within.[1]

Both in the general plan and in the smallest details, Fielding relied on the method of antithesis and contrast, whether to define his philosophic meaning or to bring out the latent comedy in

---

[1] Book III., c. 7. Fielding's ethical teaching agrees in general with Bishop Butler's—*e.g.* in such principles as the rightness of a rational self-love and the duty of prudence. He shows the working of the social impulses and affections which Shaftesbury regarded as innate, and like him would recognize " a public interest " in the normal individual's mind. Hutcheson was preaching at Glasgow, though his *System of Moral Philosophy* was yet unpublished, on the beauty of virtue and the moral life, on benevolence as the main incentive to good conduct. Fielding would have agreed with Hume that an enlightened combination of benevolence and self-love is the right foundation for our rules of conduct. Adam Smith, Tucker, and other exponents of the theory of moral sentiments, might have illustrated their doctrines from incidents in *Tom Jones* and *Amelia.*

The method of ironic antithesis and contrast

what was going on. In *Tom Jones*, and it is the same in *Amelia*, the more representative figures fall into sets of contrasted pairs, though the opposition is disguised by the multitude and diversity of the minor characters and the faults and imprudences of their betters. There is a subtle balancing of motives and moral peculiarities. The method is also seen at work in those turns of events that suddenly negative what seems inevitable, and likewise in such frequent instances of self-refutation as when Tom Jones vows the chastest constancy to his Sophia and the next instant falls an ignominious prey to the liquorish Molly.[1]

The most obvious contrast is that drawn between those two inmates of Mr Allworthy's household, representative of opposite schools of thought and morality, both equally objects of Fielding's satire, the philosopher Square and the irascible Parson Thwackum, tutor to Jones and Blifil.

In morals he [Square] was a professed Platonist, and in religion he inclined to be an Aristotelian. But though he had, as we have said, formed his morals on the Platonic model, yet he perfectly agreed with the opinion of Aristotle, in considering that great man rather in the quality of a philosopher or a speculatist, than as a legislator. This sentiment he carried a great way, indeed so far as to regard all virtue as matter of theory only. . . . This gentleman and Mr Thwackum scarce ever met without disputation ; for their tenets were indeed diametrically opposite to each other. Square held human nature to be the perfection of all virtue, and that vice was a deviation from our nature in the same manner as deformity of body is. Thwackum, on the contrary, maintained that the human mind, since the fall, was nothing but a sink of iniquity, till purified and redeemed by grace. In one point only they agreed, which was, in all their discourses on morality never to mention the word goodness. The favourite phrase of the former was, " the natural beauty of virtue " ; that of the latter was, the " divine power of grace." The former measured all actions by the unalterable rule of right, and the eternal fitness of things ; the latter decided all matters by authority ; but, in doing this, he always used the Scriptures and their commentators as the lawyer does his " Coke upon Littleton," where the comment is of equal authority with the text.[2]

[1] Book V., c. 10.   [2] Book III., c. 3.

All through the earlier chapters, the incessant squabbles of Thwackum and Square help to make clearer the intellectual position of the author. Square stands for abstract ethics, Thwackum for slavish and unenlightened respect for authority and reliance on the doctrine of salvation by faith. Thwackum is cruel, malicious, and selfish; but honestly believes himself a devout Christian and an infallible instructor of youth, though his precepts only furnish a pragmatical support for Blifil's sordid self-interest, and his bloodthirsty discipline only excites Tom's pugnacity.

Square and Thwackum are both essential to Fielding's scheme. *Square v.* Neither pietistic dogma nor the cut-and-dried maxims of an ab- *Thwackum* stract moral philosophy are of much avail without openness of disposition, generosity, and feeling for others. On the contrary, they are apt to breed hypocrisy. There had been something of Square and something of Thwackum in Richardson's edifying preachments. The ill-conditioned Thwackum remains Blifil's ally and Jones's bitter foe right to the end. Hoping to marry Sophia, and thus gratify both his own covetousness and his hatred for Tom Jones, Blifil " availed himself of the piety of Thwackum, who held that if the end proposed was religious (as surely matrimony is) it mattered not how wicked were the means. As to other occasions, he used to apply the philosophy of Square, which taught that the end was immaterial, so that the means were fair and consistent with moral rectitude. To say truth, there were few occurrences in life on which he could not draw advantage from the precepts of one or other of these great masters." [1] It is by the instrumentality of Square, who becomes a Christian— not of Parson Thwackum's persuasion—before he dies, that Tom is righted in the esteem of Mr Allworthy. Thwackum's bigotry and self-righteousness eventually deprive him of what he regards as his right, the favour and bounty of that great man.

There are other traces of an intellectual scheme, other con- *Other* trasts, that may have been the original factors in the equation as *antitheses* Fielding first envisaged the problem. The antithesis of Jones and Blifil was fundamental, but it is strained to such a degree that Master Blifil becomes a mere puppet. Over against the man of good impulses, hasty but open to correction, whose

[1] Book VII., c. 6.

nature is disciplined by bitter experience, it was necessary to place his opposite, the mean, self-centred being, on whom the only effect of Square's and Thwackum's exercises in casuistry is to make his selfishness more calculating.   A man may yield to his weaknesses, but must not become a slave to vice.   If he yields, let him take the consequences cheerfully; and if he shows regard for his fellows, much will be forgiven him.   Let him acquire prudence and knowledge of evil, whose snares are set for him on every side; without such knowledge he will never prosper, or even be secure.   But should he employ this worldly wisdom for base personal ends, and not as a safeguard against the short-comings of the flesh, then will he become a hypocrite and a villain, and a clear-sighted girl like Sophia will see through and detest him.   It is a minor ill to miss the material rewards held out to the virtuous by Richardson; the penalty that matters is the loss of a quiet conscience, and the contempt of those whose esteem is worth having.   Such is the moral of the contrasted careers of Tom Jones and Blifil.[1]

Allworthy and Squire Western   The philanthropic Allworthy is an essential figure in the scheme, and there may have been from the outset an intention of contrasting him with Squire Western, the man of reason with the man of instinct—culture, philosophy, civilization, with the natural man in his natural environment, the stupid, ignorant Tory squire, such as Fielding had already depicted in several of his plays and in the caustic pages of *The True Patriot*.   Fielding himself declares that Allworthy, with his preternatural goodness, was meant to typify the virtues of three benevolent friends, Ralph Allen of Bath, the almost brotherly Lyttelton, and the munificent Duke of Bedford.[2]   Tradition has it that Allen was the true original of the portrait.   He was the benefactor of Fielding and of several other literary men, whom he delighted to entertain at his new mansion of Prior Park, and to assist if need were out of his colossal fortune.

Let humble Allen, with an awkward shame,
Do good by stealth, and blush to find it Fame,

---

[1] Thackeray's Blifil was Barnes Newcome, who in his latter days takes to lecturing on the domestic virtues, after so flagrantly violating them.   Blifil afterwards turns Methodist, with a view to marrying a wealthy widow of that persuasion.   [2] Preface to *Tom Jones*.

Pope wrote of his unobtrusive charities, not entirely to the satisfaction of the doer.[1] But Allworthy is too much of a composite image of all the virtues to be a living person, and is handled with such deference that his mistakes of judgment do not come in for that measure of comic irony which is faithfully dealt out to every other person, not excluding the hero. Squire Western, on the other hand, as he gradually takes a larger part in the action, develops into one of the giants of lifelike characterization, and among the numerous scenes in which he fumes and blusters, or coos like any sucking dove at Sophia's caresses, there is not one to which his vitality and entirely unconscious humour do not give inexhaustible zest.

Other contrasts that strike the eye are of a more accidental kind. Thus, in Miss Western, the prim feminism of the blue-stocking regime is a foil to the she-libertine, Lady Bellaston, typifying the profligacy of a certain aristocratic set. But the more telling antithesis is between this " perfect mistress of manners, customs, ceremonies, and fashions," with her formidable literary and political erudition, and her brother, the gross, prejudiced, and blundering squire. These two never meet without some battle of temperaments that is infinitely amusing for the spectators. *Squire Western and his sister*

And the everlasting opposition between high people and low people, on which Fielding holds forth so wittily in *Joseph Andrews*,[2] is never far out of sight in *Tom Jones*. In the course of his ups and downs, the hero continually slips out of one sphere into the other, and it is in the lower that his adventures provide the highest comedy. " I will venture to say," Fielding observes, " the highest life is much the dullest, and affords very little humour or entertainment. The various callings in lower spheres produce the greater variety of humorous character; whereas here, except among the few who are engaged in the pursuit of ambition, and the fewer still who have a relish for pleasure, all is vanity and servile imitation. Dressing and cards, eating and drinking, bowing and curtsying, make up the business of their lives." But in the introduction to the fourteenth book, where he lets fall these sage remarks, Fielding has Richardson in mind, *High people v. low people*

[1] Epilogue to *Satire* I. 135-136.   [2] See above, p. 96.

who was one of the many English writers who "have totally failed in describing the manners of upper life," and "in reality know nothing of it." Richardson was further at fault in representing his persons of quality as vowed to the pursuit of erotic adventure. Lady Bellaston, as Fielding shows, stands for only a small class, those people of rank "upon whom passion exercises its tyranny," and who are distinguished by "their noble intrepidity and a certain superior contempt of reputation." The majority of women in her rank of life are taught by their mothers to despise the pleasures of love, and "being afterwards, by the care of such mothers, married without having husbands, they seem pretty well confirmed in the justness of those sentiments; whence they content themselves, for the dull remainder of life, with the pursuit of more innocent, but I am afraid more childish amusements. Folly rather than vice is the characteristic of the present beau monde, and the only epithet which it deserves is that of frivolous."

Ironical contrasts in the story   Closely allied to this balancing of characters or of groups or classes of people is Fielding's favourite way of showing what a person, or an act or impulse, or a demonstration of feeling, is really worth by the ironical apposition of contradictory facts—such as the inglorious overthrow of the enamoured Jones already cited. The evidence for is immediately followed by the counter-evidence, the climax by anticlimax. Western's anxious tenderness for Sophia, when he thinks that she and Blifil are going to make a match of it, his extravagant raptures and protests that she was his only joy on earth, are changed in an instant to oaths and threats when she tells him he is mistaken, and that to marry one she hates and detests would be worse than death.

"If you detest un never so much," cries Western, "you shall ha'un." This he bound by an oath too shocking to repeat, and after many violent asseverations, concluded in these words, "I am resolved upon the match, and unless you consent to it, I will not give you a groat, not a single farthing; no, though I saw you expiring with famine in the street, I would not relieve you with a morsel of bread."

Is this not a parallel to Parson Adams, preaching resignation, and then driven frantic by the report that his little boy is drowned;

or denouncing vanity, and extolling his famous sermon on the subject? Not less comic is the discomfiture of the master of the puppet-show, who has been denouncing the idle trumpery and low stuff that merely make people laugh, and enlarging on the good and instructive lesson conveyed by his own entertainment, and is suddenly confounded by the scandalous behaviour of his merry-andrew. The landlady accuses him of bringing in a parcel of puppets dressed up like lords and ladies, and turning the servants' heads. " I will tolerate no more such doings. It is only the way to teach our servants idleness and nonsense : for to be sure nothing better can be learned by such idle shows as these. I remember when puppet-shows were made of good Scripture stories, as Jephtha's Rash Vow, and such good things, and when wicked people were carried away by the devil. There was some sense in those matters; but as the parson told us last Sunday, nobody believes in the devil nowadays."

Nothing indeed could have happened so very inopportune as this accident ; the most wanton malice of fortune could not have contrived such another stratagem to confound the poor fellow, while he was so triumphantly descanting on the good morals inculcated by his exhibitions. His mouth was now as effectually stopped, as that of a quack must be, if, in the midst of a declamation on the great virtues of his pills and powders, the corpse of one of his martyrs should be brought forth, and deposited before the stage, as a testimony of his skill.[1]

The ingenuity of fortune is always providing these ironical *Contrasts* contrasts. In *Amelia* we shall have the scene where Booth is *of appear-* drinking and carousing and gaming his money away, whilst his *ance and* wife at home goes without her half-pint of wine to save sixpence. *reality* In the same spirit are the sharp transitions of mood in one and the same person, and the assurances and protests belying what that person really feels. Sophia, learning of Tom's intrigue with Mrs Waters, and believing all she has been told of his bandying her own name about, tries to console herself with the conviction that he is only a low despicable wretch, and that she can easily subdue her affection for one who is beneath contempt. " Yes,

[1] Book XII., c. 5-6.

Honour," she cries to her waiting-maid, " I am now easy. I am, indeed, I am very easy." And then she burst into a flood of tears.

Miss Western's fatal knowing-ness

There is irony upon irony in the account of Miss Western's conceited perspicacity when she imparts to her brother the news that Sophia is in love with Blifil, and proceeds to assure the young lady that there is no need for concealment since her father and Squire Allworthy wish for nothing better than such an alliance, Sophia believing all the while that it is Tom Jones her aunt refers to. Her sagacity was so wonderful, " no species of disguise or affectation had escaped her notice; but as to the plain simple workings of honest nature, as she had never seen any such, she could know but little of them." Squire Western is not so confident that Allworthy will be moved by worldly considerations: " Money hath no effect o' un." " Brother," said the lady, " your politics astonish me. Are you really imposed on by professions? Do you think Mr Allworthy hath more contempt for money than other men, because he professes more. Such credulity would better become one of us weak women than that wise sex which Heaven hath formed for politicians." Nevertheless, the lady is further at sea than her brother, whom she calls clown and blockhead, when he proves insensible to sarcasm.

His violent mutations from delight to rage are incomparable. The sapient aunt opens the subject gingerly by asking him if he has noticed anything extraordinary in her niece lately, and he takes instant alarm. It can't be the smallpox; she has had that. But Miss Western hints that there are worse things than the smallpox.

Here Western interrupted her with much earnestness, and begged her, if anything ailed his daughter, to acquaint him immediately, adding, she knew he loved her more than his own soul, and that he would send to the world's end for the best physician to her. " Nay, nay," answered she, smiling, " the distemper is not so terrible ; but I believe, brother, you are convinced I know the world, and I promise you I was never more deceived in my life, if my niece be not most desperately in love."—" How ! in love," cries Western, in a passion ; " in love, without acquainting me ! I'll disinherit her ; I'll turn her out of doors stark naked, without a farthing. Is all my kindness vor 'ur, and vondness o' ur come to this, to fall in love without asking me leave ? " " But you will not," answered Miss Western, " turn this daughter, whom you love better than your own soul, out of doors, before you know whether you shall approve her choice. Suppose she should have fixed on the very person whom you yourself would wish, I hope you would not be angry then."—" No, no," cries Western, " that would make a difference. If she marries the man I would ha' her, she may love whom she pleases, I shan't trouble my head about that."

Sophia jumps to the conclusion that her aunt has detected her fondness for Jones, and tries to put her off the scent by showing the utmost sprightliness toward Blifil. The squire was delighted; the aunt was not altogether so pleased. For " Sophia so greatly overacted her part, that her aunt was at first staggered, and began to suspect some affectation in her niece; but as she was herself a person of great art, so she soon attributed this to extreme art in Sophia." She tackles the coy maiden herself. " Did you think, child, because you have been able to impose upon your father, that you could impose upon me ? Do you imagine I did not know the reason of your overacting all that friendship of Mr Blifil yesterday ? I have seen a little too much of the world, to be so deceived. Nay, nay, do not blush again. I tell you it is a passion you need not be ashamed of." So she dexterously wheedles a frank avowal out of Sophia, and to their mutual consternation the lynx-eyed aunt finds that her niece meant Jones, and the niece that her aunt meant Blifil. The thrice-refined irony of these misconstructions reminds us that a dozen years ago the author had been adapting Molière to the English stage.

Of like nature at bottom are the dramatic ironies of many *Ironies of* other incidents, paradoxical situations, misunderstandings, mental *situation* somersaults. By exposing self-contradictions and self-pretences, and in all manner of ways confronting appearances with the reality, Fielding makes us see what his people are actually thinking and feeling and doing, and the reason, usually not apparent even to themselves, why they do that and not something else. This ironical attitude is of the very essence of his art, and presupposes a complete mastery over his characters and their interrelations. Enough to recall some crucial examples. Jones's good-natured landlady, Mrs Miller, gently but firmly insists on his having no more ladies to visit him, at the very moment that he receives a note from Lady Bellaston positively engaging him to see her alone in his lodgings. The subsequent dilemma, when he is surprised by the arrival of Lady Bellaston in the middle of his private conversation with Mrs Honour, is more comic even than the famous discovery of the moralist Square behind the screen in Molly Seagrim's chamber. He hides the waiting-woman behind the bed-curtains, where she hears every word of the compromising dialogue which he strives vainly to turn in a harmless direction. Suddenly they are interrupted by the drunken invasion of young Nightingale. The lady seeks the same place of refuge, and finds Honour there. To use a homely expression, the fat is in the fire with a vengeance.

Tom's offer of marriage, a risky but successful device to get rid of the demirep, used however against him afterwards as a proof of his faithlessness to Sophia, is another admirable stroke of irony. And the catalogue might be lengthened with instances from any of Fielding's books. Thus Nightingale's avaricious uncle plots craftily to separate his nephew from Miss Nancy, and just as he thinks he has won the victory is thunderstruck by the news that his own daughter has seized the opportunity of his absence to run away with an impecunious clergyman. Whilst the stupefied parent rushes off to see if he can retrieve the consequences of one ill-assorted match, the other which he has been trying to prevent is consummated.

" Don't abuse my girl," he has just said to Nightingale, who pleads that she would be as ready as he to follow the inclinations of her heart, " don't abuse my Harriet. I have brought her up to have no inclination contrary to my own. By suffering her to do whatever she pleases, I have inured her to a habit of being pleased to do whatever I like."

The argument and its confutation by events are juxtaposed with Fielding's usual neatness. The arrival by the same post of the " two letters in very different styles," from the repentant

Square and the grasping and dictatorial Thwackum, is an event of the same character. Mr Allworthy has his eyes opened to the pardonable nature of Tom's offences by the one, and the malice and denunciations of the other serve to put in a clearer light the whole train of spite and misinterpretation that effected Tom's undoing.

Irony and unerring detection of the twists and sophistries of *Ironical* motive are combined in various mental soliloquies, such as Black *analysis of* George's wrestling - match with his conscience over the five *motive* hundred pounds lost by his benefactor, Tom Jones, and picked up by himself. Avarice easily has the best of it over Conscience regarding the larger sum; but why hand over the sixteen guineas entrusted to him by Mrs Honour, when he has already broken faith? " Having quietly acquiesced in what was of so much greater importance, it was absurd, if not downright hypocrisy, to affect any qualms at this trifle." But, eventually, Fear stepped in to assist Conscience, " and very strenuously urged, that the real distinction between the two actions, did not lie in the different degrees of honour, but of safety: for that the secreting the £500 was a matter of very little hazard; whereas the detaining the sixteen guineas was liable to the utmost danger of discovery." [1] This pleasant incident is of cardinal importance to the hero's fortunes, and the clearing up of the mystery of the lost sum is a chief event in his final rehabilitation.

Exactly similar is the struggle in Honour's mind when Sophia has enlisted her in the unwelcome adventure of running away from home to avoid a forced marriage with Blifil. It occurs to the worthy handmaid ",that by sacrificing Sophia and all her secrets to Mr Western, she might probably make her fortune."

The fair prospect of a handsome reward for so great and acceptable a service to the 'squire, tempted her avarice; and again, the danger of the enterprise she had undertaken; the uncertainty of its success; night, cold, robbers, ravishers, all alarmed her

---

[1] Black George is a signal illustration of Fielding's breadth of sympathy. He plays the villain towards his benefactor Tom, or at least behaves with outrageous ingratitude. But George Seagrim never evokes disgust, as the less lifelike Blifil does. We can understand and tolerate his philosophy of the fox and his cubs, his ethics of the den, which are human, if almost infra-human in the loyalty to his own.

fears. So forcibly did all these operate upon her, that she was almost determined to go directly to the 'squire, and to lay open the whole affair. She was, however, too upright a judge to decree on one side before she had heard the other. And here, first, a journey to London appeared very strongly in support of Sophia. She eagerly longed to see a place in which she fancied charms short only of those which a raptured saint imagines in heaven. In the next place, as she knew Sophia to have much more generosity than her master, so her fidelity promised her a greater reward than she could gain by treachery. She then cross-examined all the articles which had raised her fears on the other side, and found, on fairly sifting the matter, that there was very little in them. And now both scales being reduced to a pretty even balance, her love to her mistress being thrown into the scale of her integrity, made that rather preponderate, when a circumstance struck upon her imagination, which might have had a dangerous effect, had its whole weight been fairly put into the other scale. This was, the length of time which must intervene before Sophia would be able to fulfil her promises; for though she was entitled to her mother's fortune at the death of her father, and to the sum of £3000 left her by an uncle, when she came of age; yet these were distant days, and many accidents might prevent the intended generosity of the young lady, whereas the rewards she might expect from Mr Western were immediate. But while she was pursuing this thought, the good genius of Sophia, or that which presided over the integrity of Mrs Honour, or perhaps mere chance, sent an accident in her way, which at once preserved her fidelity, and even facilitated the intended business." [1]

The accident is Mrs Honour's quarrel with Miss Western's maid, who gives herself superior airs, her sauciness to the maid's mistress, and that lady's complaint to the squire, who turns Honour away. Honour is only too glad now to accompany her young mistress on their joint quest of new fortunes.

Fielding's theory of the novel   Along with the discussion in the preface to *Joseph Andrews* of the nature and function of the novel, the introductory chapters in *Tom Jones* must be studied to elucidate Fielding's mature theory. Richardson's ethical debates, his questions of practical expediency in the conduct of life, his grave judgments on the evils rampant in the society of his day, are an integral part of

[1] Book VII., c. 8.

his didactic scheme. The novel had absorbed charactery and the essay, both which had expressed a serious though unsystematized philosophy. Fielding to some extent keeps the fiction and the disquisition in separate compartments; but not entirely, for the discursive element is never altogether pretermitted; explanation of motive, discussion of the alternatives of conduct presented at any given moment, and overt or implicit indications of his own views, are sown broadcast throughout. Fiction approximates to science, first, in accepting the obligation of being true to life as it is, and, secondly, in asserting the right to theorize.

We are reminded of Bacon's account of poesy as " feigned history," when we hear Fielding deliberately speaking of his art as " this historic kind of writing," and desiring the reader to *"This* distinguish between what is true and genuine and what false *historic* and counterfeit. Since, he says, " we have good authority for all *kind of* our characters, no less indeed than Doomsday Book, or the vast *writing"* authentic book of nature, as is elsewhere hinted, our labours have sufficient title to the name of history." [1] The faculties required for success in " one of the most useful as well as entertaining of all kinds of writing " are " no other than invention and judgment." By invention he means, not a creative activity, but " discovery, or finding out . . . a quick and sagacious penetration into the true essence of all the objects of our contemplation." " This, I think, can rarely exist without the concomitancy of judgment; for how we can be said to have discovered the true essence of two things, without discerning their difference, seems to me hard to conceive." On what foundation of careful and indefatigable study the novelist must rear the fabric of his feigned history is brought out by his remarks on the need for wide and accurate learning, experience " with the tools of our profession," and, above all " conversation," or knowledge acquired by familiar intercourse with his fellows, which " in our historian must be universal, that is, with all ranks and degrees of men : for the knowledge of what is called high life, will not instruct him in low, nor *è converso,* will his being acquainted with the inferior part of mankind, teach him the manners of the superior." [2]

[1] Book IX., c. 1.   [2] *Ibid.*

Sensibility as well as penetration required

Nor will these qualities avail the historian, he continues, thus coming to grips with the artistic problem of not merely describing but of compelling the reader to experience what is presented as if it were enacted before his eyes, " unless he have what is generally meant by a good heart, and be capable of feeling. The author who will make me weep, says Horace, must first weep himself. . . . In the same manner it is with the ridiculous. I am convinced I never make my reader laugh heartily, but where I have laughed before him." [1] And he requires the same responsiveness in his readers. " Examine your heart, my good reader," he says elsewhere, " and resolve whether you do believe these matters with me. If you do, you may now proceed to their exemplification in the following pages; if you do not, you have, I assure you, already read more than you have understood; and it would be wiser to pursue your business, or your pleasures (such as they are) than to throw away any more of your time in reading what you can neither taste nor comprehend." [2]

The test of veri-similitude

The philosophic reflections and the comic irony are addressed to our intellect, the sentiment and pathos to the heart; our intuitive sense of what is like nature constitutes the test of his verisimilitude. Fielding continually appeals to us to confirm his observations. The reader, being in possession of so much more than is known to the characters in the story, since the novelist lets him share his own omniscience, is a better judge of the probabilities and has truer insight. Whilst Sophia's artless dissimulation takes in her father, the way she overacts her part awakens the suspicions of her aunt, whose mind has been sharpened by the air of Grosvenor Square. But even the astute aunt knows less than the reader, in spite of her experience of the world, and goes astray through excess of cunning. " To say the truth, in discovering the deceit of others, it matters much that our own art be wound up, if I may use the expression, in the same key with theirs: for very artful men sometimes miscarry by fancying others wiser, or in other words, greater knaves than they really are." [3] After discussing the distinction between the possible and the probable and their place in fiction, and endorsing the old saying, " That it is no excuse for a poet who relates what is

[1] Book IX., c. 1.   [2] Book VI., c. 1.   [3] Book VI., c. 3

incredible, that the thing related is matter of fact," Fielding points out that the need to keep within the bounds of probability weighs much more heavily on the novelist than on the historian.[1]

> We who deal in private characters, who search into the most retired recesses, and draw forth examples of virtue and vice, from holes and corners of the world, are in a more dangerous situation. As we have no public notoriety, no concurrent testimony, no records to support and corroborate what we deliver, it becomes us not only to keep within the limits of possibility, but of probability too ; and this more especially in painting what is greatly good and amiable. Knavery and folly, though never so exorbitant, will more easily meet with assent : for ill-nature adds great support and strength to faith.[2]

This last gibe is almost an echo of Swift's outburst against the nameless crowd, and tallies with the impression gathered from *Joseph Andrews* and *Jonathan Wild* that Fielding regarded mankind in the mass as a sorry lot.[3]

The historian is not a mere chronicler. He undertakes to interpret and usually to make his own comments upon the matter in hand. History is an intellectual account of the facts, a recapitulation putting them in a clearer light and revealing the intricate structure of cause and effect, motive and reaction, which in the hurry and confusion of events is hard to make out. Its counterpart in the realm of imaginative art is fiction, an ordered version of life in general rendering intelligible that which was confused and obscure. Being an intellectual interpretation, it must needs be comic, unless the historian is as dull as Richardson. So might Fielding have put it, had he as some maintain been competing with that solemn and ponderous writer in *Tom Jones* as he had rebutted him in *Joseph Andrews*.[4] Fielding's intellectual realism, which scrutinized the actualities of life and presented a general likeness in which everything was made coherent and the

In-tellectual realism, and its relations to history, science, etc.

---

[1] In his preface to the *Journey to Lisbon*, Fielding says he would " have honoured and loved Homer more had he written a true history of his own times in humble prose, than those noble poems that have so justly collected the praise of all ages." His preference for truth according to the prose canon leads him thus far astray. See also the *Voyage to Lisbon*, Wed., 26th June.

[2] Book VIII., c. 1. [3] See above, p. 95.

[4] *E.g.* Digeon, 166-167, 173.

whole could be understood, which had the same object, in short, as the most characteristic literature of the Augustan age, has a certain kinship to science or moral and social philosophy. But the man of imagination enjoys one precious advantage over the graver humanist. Fielding's comprehensive grasp, his catholicity of vision, enabled him to contemplate his subject, human life, in all its aspects, and thus to perceive the comic always latent somewhere. The comic being, to a mind such as his at the height of his powers, the aspect under which its values fall into the truest perspective, he dwelt mainly on that aspect in his greatest novel, *Tom Jones*. Here, as in *Jonathan Wild*, the appeal to the emotions is at a minimum. There was, on the other hand, sentiment as well as humour in the adventures of Parson Adams; and in his last novel, *Amelia*, irony was to be largely relinquished for a more direct appeal to the feelings, even his favourite device of the telling contrast being used chiefly for that purpose. The theory on which he wrought his masterpiece is exquisitely enunciated in the invocation to genius which precedes the thirteenth book:

Do thou kindly take me by the hand, and lead me through all the mazes, the winding labyrinths of nature. Initiate me into all those mysteries which profane eyes never beheld. Teach me, which to thee is no difficult task, to know mankind better than they know themselves. Remove that mist which dims the intellects of mortals, and causes them to adore men for their art, or to detest them for their cunning in deceiving others, when they are, in reality, the objects only of ridicule, for deceiving themselves. Strip off the thin disguise of wisdom from self-conceit, of plenty from avarice, and of glory from ambition. Come thou, that hast inspired thy Aristophanes, thy Lucian, thy Cervantes, thy Rabelais, thy Molière, thy Shakespeare, thy Swift, thy Marivaux, fill my pages with humour; till mankind learn the good-nature to laugh only at the follies of others, and the humility to grieve at their own.

Character and circumstance determine action   A novel may be analysed into characters, actions, and sentiments; but it is impossible to divide it into so much character-drawing, so much narrative, dialogue, comment or elucidation, and so on. Character is revealed, and characters are differentiated, not only by descriptive portraiture but also by action and dialogue. Sentiments may be expressed without a word of comment. The usual antithesis between novels of character and novels of action is fallacious, since action is simply the mode in which character manifests itself. It is the working of the will that matters, whether the outcome is a deed or a change of heart. The novel of action is the novel of motive; so it may as well be called the novel of character. There is a clear antithesis between it and that inferior type of fiction, the novel of incident, in which the things that take place are supposed to be so interesting in themselves that the motives which led to them, and consequently the characters of those engaged, may be safely neglected. Fielding's stories are all rich in incident; but most of the occurrences are properly accounted for: they are the outcome of natural conjunctions of character and circumstance. No doubt, if they were carefully sorted out, there would appear *The rôle of* a larger proportion of chance happenings than would be tolerable *chance* in the epic poetry to which Fielding regarded his fiction as analogous, or in the higher drama. Mere accident is hardly admissible in poetry, which strives to eliminate all irrational elements from its portrayal of life. But chance does play a part in existence; and an art which depends for its effect upon a recognizable likeness to everyday experience may be all the more lifelike for not ignoring it. This must not, however, be at the expense of the integrity of the characters. The coincidences and other surprising chances in *Tom Jones* are merely parts of the complex of circumstance to which the characters react, and thus reveal what they are made of as clearly as in their interplay with each other. All the incidents hingeing upon the coincidence of Jones' and Sophia's flight with the Jacobite scare are of this external and accidental nature, and there are others still more fortuitous. Where chance is out of place is in the drama of motive and conduct.[1]

Fielding's view of life, then, or of the life amid which his lot was cast, is set forth in certain characters reacting in a natural and intelligible manner to each other and to their surroundings.

[1] Conrad wrote a novel, one of his best, and called it *Chance*. It is an admirable study of causation, which confirms the view stated here.

Such were his breadth of vision and his choice of representative figures, that the result was equivalent to a view of human life everywhere and always.) One character, however, stands somewhat apart from the rest. Besides those who are the points round which everything revolves, there are a number of by-characters who play a necessary part in a story having such wide significance as has been indicated. Even such minor personages as Supple, Squire Western's led-curate, the irresponsible man of fashion, Lord Fellamar, who tries to win Sophia by force, the disreputable attorney, Lawyer Dowling, the rakish, easy-going Nightingale, and the nameless crowd of innkeepers and their shrewish wives, doctors, soldiers, rustics, gipsies, and nondescripts, have not only something to do in the complications of the story but are also essential to the completeness of the picture. But Partridge, though he plays a useful rôle, is scarcely so important as his prominence might betoken. True, he is Tom's supposed father, and he chances to become attached to Tom as a kind of Sancho Panza,[1] in a manner very common in humorous fiction about this time. But as a character, Partridge is, so to speak, too big for his shoes.[2] In fine, one of the most delightful beings in the whole gathering owes his existence, first to the tradition derived from Cervantes, and, next and chiefly, to Fielding's need for an outlet to his purely irrelevant and sportive humour. There might have been an indifferent substitute for him in the comic scheme; and, though the loss would have been ours, we should not have been conscious of it.[3]

Partridge exists in most memories as the hero of that great episode, "Partridge at the Play," when he pays unconscious tribute to consummate acting in his immortal sneer at Garrick's

---

[1] Professor Cross discerns quixotic predilections in Partridge (Cross, ii. 205).

[2] Partridge's addiction to classical tags is reminiscent of the Seigneur Thomas de la Fuente in *Gil Blas* (II., c. 9), with his *Finis coronat opus*, *Ut ita dicam*, etc. This worthy, note too, has no use for plays that are not blood-curdling. "Ah ! si je m'étais attaché au théâtre, je n'aurais jamais mis sur la scène, que des princes sanguinaires ; que des héros assassins : je me serais baigné dans le sang. On aurais toujours vu périr dans mes tragédies, non seulement les principaux personnages, mais les gardes mêmes ; j'aurais égorgé jusqu'au souffleur."

[3] Smollett absurdly contended that Roderick Random's Strap was the original of Partridge. His novel had appeared the year before (1748). The charge hardly needs refuting.

impersonation of Hamlet: " He the best actor! why I could act
as well as he myself. I am sure if I had seen a ghost, I should
have looked in the very same manner, and done just as he did."[1]
But Partridge is not quite supererogatory. He often drops admirable comments on his master's incomprehensible proceedings
—he never will, by the way, acknowledge that Tom is his master
or anything more than his obliged friend. The scrapes into
which he drags the hero through his weakness for boastful gossip
have their due place in the story. But usually when Partridge
takes a hand in what is going forward, it is only to retard it, as
when he drives Tom distracted by beating about the bush and
prattling of Black George, whilst Tom is trying anxiously to
extract news of Sophia. Mrs Honour is another oddity who
gives a fuller measure of entertainment than we are strictly
entitled to by the terms of the bond.

Some clues to the way Fielding used actual experience in *To what*
constructing his more general picture were cited in the case of *extent*
Joseph Andrews. Originals have also been pointed out for some *Fielding*
of the characters in *Tom Jones*. According to old tradition, *drew from actual*
Thwackum was drawn from a Richard Hele, vicar of a place *originals*
near Salisbury, a prebendary of the cathedral, and master of a
school in the close; Square from Thomas Chubb, a tradesman
in the same city and a zealous Deist; Dowling from a lawyer of
that neighbourhood named Stillingfleet.[2] He is his own witness
that he had his wife Charlotte before his mind's eye in portraying
the charming Sophia. He said that Allworthy was a likeness of
Ralph Allen, to whom he was to dedicate *Amelia*, and also of
his powerful friends, the Duke of Bedford and George, Lord
Lyttelton. The two latter he mentioned, it is probable, for
complimentary reasons, howbeit the portrait of Allen is generalized, and the historical particulars are very different. According
to contemporary gossip, Squire Western was suggested by a
worthy noted for his sporting exploits, who outlived Fielding by
some thirty years.[3] Lady Bellaston was said to be drawn from

[1] Though Thomas de la Fuente (see note on preceding page) with his Latin
tags and his naïve views on tragedy may have given hints for Partridge, this
great scene is of course mainly suggested by that of Sir Roger de Coverley at
the play (*Spectator*, No. 335).

[2] Dobson, 135 n.   [3] Cross, ii. 166-167.

the wife of Lord Townshend.[1]   And, no doubt, many of the minor characters were still more faithfully depicted from individuals known to Fielding but too obscure to be traceable by any other person.

The insinuation that Tom Jones and Captain Booth were Fielding himself

It has been persistently alleged, and this is a count in the long-standing indictment of Fielding's morals, that both Tom Jones and the more peccable Captain Booth in the later novel were reflections of himself. The amount of truth in such a statement makes the untruth of the deductions from it the more misleading. As riders to the general proposition, it has been asserted that Fielding was as bad as Tom Jones at his worst, in his discreditable transactions with Lady Bellaston, for instance; and that he behaved to his wife Charlotte as deplorably as Booth treated Amelia, the later novel being, in short, inspired by remorse for his wrongs towards the wife he had lost.[2]   All this, obviously, is to read a great deal more than mere self-portraiture into these two pieces of characterization. The damaging assumptions of contemporary gossip and contemporary malice, too readily accepted by Fielding's first biographer Murphy, and by critics such as Thackeray anxious to make didactic points, have been riddled through and through by later investigation.[3]   Tom Jones and Captain Booth are studies of himself only in the sense that any fiction of the biographical cast in which there is a prominent central figure of the same sex as the author is pretty sure to be based largely on self-observation, probably in the main unconscious. In this sense, Christian is a reflection of John Bunyan, Crusoe of Defoe, Gulliver of Swift, Pendennis of Thackeray, Elizabeth Bennet, Emma Woodhouse, or Anne Eliot, of Jane Austen, Jane Eyre of Charlotte Brontë. In each case, Fielding proposed to delineate, not a picturesque oddity or the representative of a class ridiculous for its foibles yet fundamentally

---

[1] Cross, ii. 171-172.

[2] *E.g.* Digeon (see his study, p. 255). Professor Cross (esp. ii. 328-335) concludes that there is a good deal of personal reminiscence in *Amelia*, but that he was thinking at least as much of his father, Edmund Fielding, the gentleman-farmer of East Stour, as of himself, in relating the history of Booth's foolishness (*cp*. Digeon, 247-248). The remorse theory was apparently started by Frederick Lawrence, in his *Life of Fielding* (1855). See Blanchard, 428-430.

[3] See especially Cross's biography and Blanchard's *Fielding, the Novelist, a Study in Literary Reputation*, 1926.

human, but the typical young man of his own or of any time
and place, tried by the typical temptations; and how was he
to trace the ups and downs of the conflict between good disposition and the weakness of the flesh but by imagining himself
in the same predicaments? In these two novels, it is on the
two young men that the lens of moral analysis is almost exclusively focussed. But to identify either with Fielding is more
than hazardous, even if it is safe to say that they had no other
original.

How did the world receive this unparalleled masterpiece? Did *How was*
anybody realize that the art of fiction had made an incredible *"Tom*
bound forward; in brief, that the time of experiment, misdirected *Jones"*
travail, and shots in the dark, was over, and fiction had now in *received*
truth become an art? Was Fielding read by as many thousands *by the*
as his rival Richardson; were his books even a commercial *public?*
success? The answer is by no means an unqualified affirmative.
Joseph Andrews in 1742 had been a popular success, though not
on the scale of *Pamela's*, much less of Richardson's second novel
in 1748. The *Miscellanies* published the following year had done
a little to extend his fame with the sort of readers who subscribed
for collections of essays and desultory literature. But the sentimentalists and moralizers who encored *Pamela* and found not a
page tedious in *Clarissa* were not the sort to admit a liking for
the merry and often indecorous humour of Richardson's opposite.
They were the superior people. To such as they, Fielding was
inelegant, unrefined, and his comedy mere buffoonery. And they
were the majority, at least among those whose approval was
held to confer literary fame. The rage for Richardson was
for the most part uncritical and unliterary. Deeper than the
impression due to his sterling merits was the response of the
sentimentalists and moralizers to his lessons from life, which they
accepted in a very different spirit from that of artistic appreciation. In these ruling circles, a taste for Fielding was regarded
as disreputable. And, besides this disapproval, which was steady
though passive, Fielding had to contend against the active hos-
tility of the swarms of foes he had stirred up by the political and
social satire in his plays and by his outspoken journalism. To
the subject of this unrelenting abuse and the libels that stuck

long after their victim was in his untimely grave, it will be
necessary to return later on.

Compare the reception of Richardson and Smollett   But neither the puritanical objectors nor the personal haters
were able to boycott *Joseph Andrews*, which went quickly into
three editions, about half as many copies being sold as of *Pamela*
in the same time.[1]   And the entertainment it provided for those
who professed no such scruples could not fail to raise pleasant
anticipations when the greater work was announced. Apparently,
even before the last volume of *Tom Jones* had issued from the
press, Fielding was at work on a revised edition; and before
the end of the year five had appeared, including one printed at
Dublin from the first and uncorrected text.[2] This time Fielding
got ahead of Richardson, whose *Clarissa* was twice as long going
into four editions.   He far outsped Smollett, whose *Roderick
Random*, published first in 1748, did not reach a second edition
till 1758. Clearly, Fielding had plenty of readers, who no doubt
enjoyed him; but he still failed to win the suffrages of those
who dictated in matters of taste.   One or two eminent persons
frankly avowed their admiration, some others seem to have
enjoyed the book under the rose; the great majority ignored or
condemned *Tom Jones*.   But all the time the book steadily made
its way. The unfriendly *Gentleman's Magazine* could not keep
a blind eye turned upon a novel talked about by everyone, and
inserted a review after a year's obstinate silence. Thus, when
in 1751 another novel was ready, the shorter and inferior *Amelia*,
Fielding, who had accepted six hundred pounds for *Tom Jones*,
was paid the comparatively handsome amount of eight hundred
pounds on expectations that were not to be entirely fulfilled.

[1] Cross, i. 357.   [2] *Ibid.*, ii. 121-123.

CHAPTER VII

AMELIA

THOSE who looked for another *Tom Jones* were doomed to *"Amelia"* disappointment. When he wrote *Amelia*, Fielding's view of life *conceived* had been, if not enlarged, at any rate deepened and darkened *in a* by several years' experience of a magistrate's work in London. *different* After this he could never have written a *Tom Jones*. He was *spirit* now a sadder and, as he believed, a wiser man. His spirit had received a shock, which did not embitter, but made him tenderer of heart, and less disposed than of yore to laugh at mankind's frailties and disillusionments. In *Amelia*, instead of irony playing like summer lightning over the pretences and absurdities of men, the prevailing attitude is one of discontent, impatience, and indignation, tempered with pity for the victims of selfishness and folly. The ugly truth is stated literally, not hinted with luminous and delightful indirectness; denounced, rather than held up to ridicule. Our heart-strings are wrung more often than our laughter is kindled by hilarious mockery. It is not a jovial picture that he displays before us; and many of Fielding's most devoted readers were not pleased with such Spartan entertainment.

Tom Jones was not yet out when, in October 1748, Fielding *Fielding* took up his duties as presiding magistrate for Westminster; the *as a* following January he enlarged the jurisdiction of his office *magistrate* by taking the oaths as Justice of the Peace for the county of Middlesex. For the next five years he devoted the best part of his mental and physical energy to the superhuman task of establishing order and security in a city where vice and profligacy had long had it all their own way, where the Bench was corrupt and there was no police force worthy of the name, and gangs of thieves as well organized as Jonathan Wild's ruffian army infested the streets by day as well as night. Fielding had sought his post at Bow Street in order to obtain a settled income for his growing family. He had long been a martyr to gout, and the uncertainties of literary earnings by a man liable at any moment to a breakdown in health gave him acute anxiety. But, as he points out in the introduction to his *Journey to Lisbon*, he would still have been very badly off if the Government had not made him an annual allowance out of the public service money—an allowance which would have been larger but for the belief of his superiors that he held a very lucrative office. As a dramatist and manager he had played the political game without fear or favour. As a magistrate he was not less ready to do and, if need be, to suffer. Fielding knew that his novels were an accurate picture of things as they were. Not one of the four, from *Joseph Andrews* to the last, is without value as a social document, or without instruction as a sociological treatise, if studied from that point of view. And Fielding was potentially a man of action as well as a man of letters. He was not only ready to stand to the general truth of the picture he had drawn, but also to sacrifice health and wealth in putting into effect in the unhappy world around him a wider poetic justice than he had imagined in his fictions. Fielding's part in the legal and administrative reforms that eventually suppressed street robberies, improved the prisons, and alleviated the social conditions which bred crime, gained him in his own time nothing but abuse, although it was these years of magisterial overwork in unhealthy surroundings that were mainly responsible for his death in the prime of manhood.

His "Charge to the Grand Jury"   Fielding was repeatedly elected Chairman of Quarter Sessions for the City of Westminster, and nothing could show better the magnitude of the task he had undertaken and the spirit in which he addressed himself to it than the *Charge to the Grand Jury*, which he delivered on 29th June 1749. It is a homily upon the duties of citizenship, directed, not only to the jurors, but also to the public at large, and all who by station and profession were their natural leaders. They, he said, were collectively responsible for the abominations and iniquities prevailing around them; and he summoned them personally to take each his share in exposing, punishing, and suppressing every instance of disorder that came to their notice. The town had gone mad in the pursuit of pleasure.

For the upper part of mankind, and in this town, there are many lawful amusements, abundantly sufficient for the recreation of any temperate and sober mind. But, gentlemen, so immoderate are the desires of many, so hungry is their appetite for pleasure, that they may be said to have a fury after it; and diversion is no longer the recreation or amusement, but the whole business of their lives. They are not content with three theatres, they must have a fourth; where the exhibitions are not only contrary to law, but contrary to good manners, and where the stage is reduced back again to that degree of licentiousness, which was too enormous for the corrupt state of Athens to tolerate; and which, as the Roman poet, rather, I think, in the spirit of a censor than a satyrist, tells us, those Athenians, who were not themselves abused, took care to abolish, from their concern for the public.

From the stage, where, surely, Fielding himself had not always kept clear of blame, he turned to the masquerades, balls, and other assemblies which were opportunities for extravagance and immorality.

This fury after licentiousness and luxurious pleasures is grown to so enormous a height, that it may be called the characteristic of the present age. And it is an evil, gentlemen, of which it is neither easy nor pleasant to foresee all the consequences. Many of them are obvious; and these are so dreadful, that they will, I doubt not, induce you to use your best endeavours to check the further increase of the growing mischief; for the rod of the law, gentlemen, must restrain those within the bounds of decency and sobriety, who are deaf to the voice of reason, and superior to the fear of shame.

He goes on to particularize. There are the gaming-houses, which are " nuisances in the eye of the common law," yet provide the sharper with a ready means to prey upon all classes, including the lower sort, who are the most useful, since the community could not exist without their labour. There is the offence of libelling, in mentioning which Fielding was again sailing near the wind. More pernicious even than the libeller of private persons is he who scatters his poison on public persons. " The higher and greater the magistrates be against whom such slanders are propagated, the greater is the danger to society." The brothels, the dancing-halls, the gaming-houses must be suppressed. The playhouses must be reduced in number, or at least kept under restraint.   Fielding announces that such sumptuary laws as exist—and there were several on the Statute Book which were systematically flouted—will henceforth be severely enforced; and he invites the active co-operation of all well-disposed men in detecting and prosecuting offenders.   The cure for the evils afflicting society was in the hands of the public themselves.   This famous charge arraigns, in the form of a magisterial indictment, the social demoralization amid which Booth and Amelia were to enact their pathetic drama.   In both the exhortation and the novel the theme is substantially the same; too often, in truth, the novelist forgets that he is not speaking as a Justice of the Peace or a sociologist, and discusses existing conditions in a matter-of-fact and prosy way that he was never guilty of in *Tom Jones*.

The terrorism of the gangs of ruffians who robbed and murdered in the streets of London and set the feeble guardians of the peace at defiance came at length to such a head that the Government had to take measures to abate it.   Fielding's strict administration of the law and strenuous support of the officers of justice paved the way for drastic reforms which were in preparation.   He drafted a Bill for putting down street robberies, which may or may not have been adopted by the Government as the basis of their own proposals.   In January 1751 he brought out *His* a pamphlet, *An Enquiry into the Causes of the Late Increase of* *"Enquiry Robbers*, which proceeded in the same manner as the *Charge* *into the* to diagnose existing maladies.   The most demoralizing vice of *Causes of* the present day, he contended, was drunkenness, especially that *the Late* *Increase of* caused by indulgence in spirituous liquors.   "The poison called *Robbers"* gin" was ruining the lower classes, as Fielding's friend Hogarth also warned the age a few weeks later in his terrible engraving, "Gin Lane."   Once more Fielding denounced the gaming-houses.   He drew attention to the corrupt and iniquitous administration of the Poor Law, to the evil state of the prisons—nurseries of a criminal population—to the facilities offered to theft by the connivance of receivers, who could rarely be brought to book, and to some of the legal anomalies shortly to be held up to scorn in *Amelia*. Fielding called for an active and aggressive policy against the banded forces of wickedness; he as a magistrate employed all the powers that were granted him to direct the campaign.

In these circumstances, at the end of the same year, 1751, Fielding's last novel, *Amelia*, appeared.[1] No wonder if it is a pamphlet, a sermon, an indictment, almost as much as a work of fiction. Apart from Mrs Behn's *Oroonoko*, which scarcely counts, it is the first English novel of social reform, the first earnest study of actual conditions, with a clear lesson to propound and definite reforms to offer as a logical inference.[2] It has a plot, or at any rate a complicated series of situations, the dilemmas of which are very arbitrarily solved by unexpected disclosures at the end. Certain motives and some typical social degenerates are transferred here from Fielding's abortive comedy, *The Modern Husband*; but the circumstances are drastically altered. All through the book a shining contrast is kept steadily in view. In the forefront stands the figure of Amelia, a more tender, more exquisite image of his dead Charlotte, who had been the original of Sophia. It is the touching portrait of a matchless wife rather than the lover's picture of a bewitching girl. She, simple but never shallow or insipid, the loyal, affectionate wife and mother, invincible in her constancy and unwearied in her tenderness, declines to question the certitude of her faith in goodness or to debate the reasons for her self-devotion, though the very bases of her trust seem to be cut away from under her feet. Over against this meek but indomitable creature, Fielding sets the contemporary world, frivolous, immoral, godless. On the one side an England which is not a Christian country, a very different scene from the jolly, disorderly, but not utterly vicious land depicted in *Tom Jones*; on the other, the pure domestic affections, the unsophisticated pleasures, and the perfect terrestrial happiness, which might be a cure for all the prevailing maladies. The frail and susceptible husband is necessary, not merely as a foil to Amelia's virtues, but as the involuntary agent of her trials; but he is entirely of secondary importance. Amelia is, indeed, the most real of all Fielding's characters, and the reason

Publication of "Amelia"

---

[1] A revised edition appeared posthumously in Murphy's collective edition of the works. For the extent of the revision, see Cross, ii. 351-356.

[2] Defoe's novels were studies of social conditions and their effects on character, but did not indicate reforms, even indirectly.

is that, moved by personal affection, he followed in this instance the Richardsonian method of living in the very soul of his creation. For once he changed his method, and produced a being that stands significantly apart from the others.

A study of the art of life

Fielding sets forth his subject in the exordium to the first book. He is going to relate the various accidents which befell a worthy couple after their marriage. Some of the distresses which they waded through were so exquisite that they seemed to betoken malice and design on the part of fortune. But he questions whether the triumphs of knavery, the calamities of fools, and the miseries in which men of sense sometimes involve themselves are not better accounted for by their forgetting prudence and following the blind guidance of a headstrong passion. " Life may as properly be called an art as any other ; and the great incidents in it are no more to be considered as mere accidents than the several members of a fine statue or a noble poem." Histories of this kind may be regarded as models of human life ; and by minutely studying their chief incidents and the minute causes whence those incidents are produced, " we shall best be instructed in this most useful of all arts, which I call the ART of LIFE."

The opening scene—a glimpse of the prevailing evils

With this frank admission of a practical aim, he goes on to paint a typical scene in a police court in his own district of Westminster, as a first glimpse of the disorderly state of the city, the incompetence and venality of the magistrates, the monstrous abuses flourishing in the houses of detention, and other evils that had been forced upon his attention during his service at Bow Street. Justice Thrasher, before whom Booth is brought as the sequel to a misadventure in which he had shown nothing worse than imprudence, is a sketch of one of those trading justices among whom his enemies pretended to number Fielding. Ignorant of the statutes, relying on his clerk to tip him the wink and save him from flagrant blundering, as well as to let him know which side it was advisable to take for the sake of what could be got out of it, he browbeats the needy, discharges those of genteel appearance, and commits to gaol divers harmless persons who have nothing but their innocence to defend them. The scene sparkles with vivacity ; but a change of tone from the pleasant irony of *Tom Jones* is soon apparent.

Fielding begins in a bantering way that is near enough to his earlier style. But the humorous hits at the decrepit watchmen, the mercenary justice, rogue lawyers, one-sided authorities, and the whole tribe of prison-keepers, bailiffs, quack physicians, touting authors, and the like, are gradually dropped for a more serious and anxious discussion of the evils and anomalies. Later in the book, there are formal dialogues on such problems, Dr Harrison canvassing the subject of duelling with that fire-eater Colonel Bath, or, less comically, the religious question with Booth and his friends, or the injustice of promotion by purchase with his enlightened friend the peer. The worthy doctor, in spite of the wit and humour he displays on many occasions, grows more and more heavy and prosy, and ends in downright sermonizing. It is significant that instead of the pithy but genial and sprightly sallies with which the author of *Tom Jones* was wont to terminate his chapters, he usually winds up here with some such moral reflection as this :

Irony relinquished for a more earnest love

> There is, I believe, something so outrageously suspicious in the nature of all vice, especially when joined with any great degree of pride, that the eyes of those whom we imagine privy to our failings are intolerable to us, and we are apt to aggravate their opinions to our disadvantage far beyond the reality.[1]

Tom Jones was well-nigh all comedy; even the darker spots were irradiated with beams of Fielding's humour. Comedy is not totally lacking in the graver novel, but it is confined to the sayings and doings of a few oddities. For, although the author calls this a study in the art of life, it is not to be compared with *Tom Jones* in breadth and catholicity either of subject or of spirit. The focus is narrowed, the interest specialized. But that human nature is the same all through and one phase of life has a bearing on every other, it might be objected that *Amelia* is only a study of life in London at one exceptional period, and even so, mainly of life in the fast set. Most of the incidents take place within a very narrow radius, centring in the parish of St Martin's-in-the-Fields, with the playhouses and taverns close at hand, and

[1] Book VI., c. 10.

the parks, Ranelagh, Vauxhall, and other haunts of the idle and frivolous, on the circumference.

Summary
of the story
Very skilfully, however, in the first chapter or two, Fielding sets his stage with the proper surroundings for the drama to be enacted. Into the whirlpool of dissipation, the perils of which are revealed in the wrecks and strays thrown up at Justice Thrasher's court and the prison-house, Booth and his wife, like a couple of picaroons, of the unfortunate not the adventurous sort, are flung to sink or swim. Booth is a military officer out of employ, who married Amelia for love, and now, after failing as a farmer and exhibiting a singular lack of prudence or of common ability to look after his wife and children, is waiting for something to turn up. His appearance before the Justice and the consequent sojourn in gaol were the first of a long series of misadventures, in which the truth and stanchness of the fond couple are tried. Booth in the end comes off with divers overthrows that do not quite finish him, and do not exhaust the patience of his wife. She, to whom he is always loyal at heart however feebly he gives way to temptation, by her unexampled steadfastness foils all the conspiracies against her virtue, and forgives his lapses even when she has reason to believe him more to blame than he really is. But it is only through the intervention of an external providence, in the shape of their benefactor, Dr Harrison, and the sudden recovery of a fortune which Amelia did not know was hers, that they escape ruin.

Various
complica-
tions
This is the gist of their story. The main thread is ravelled up with subsidiary affairs; first, Booth's entanglement with Miss Matthews, an old flame whom he comes across again in the gaol. Thus thrown together, Booth and the gay lady yield to the seductions of the time and place, and when Booth is released she refuses to give him up. The remorseful husband is henceforth in a continual state of apprehension lest his wife should hear of his infidelity; and his wretchedness is redoubled when he learns that his friend and protector, Colonel James, is an unsuccessful rival for the person of his unintentional conquest. With the colonel only too certain to withdraw his support, and pretty sure to seek vengeance into the bargain, Booth sees ruin staring him in the face. This second thread, with the dangers and suspense

attending it, is bound in closely with another, and that with still fresh ones, till a number of different persons are implicated. Colonel James falls in love with Booth's charming wife, and now tries by fair means or foul to get her husband out of the way. The Miss Matthews affair has apparently blown over, Booth having promised to keep clear of the lady. The unsuspicious young fellow is the last person to be aware that his most influential and trusted friend is the secret enemy of his domestic happiness. And, likewise unknown to him, there is a still more dangerous plotter behind the scenes, in the person of a noble lord, an experienced hand at the seduction of young wives, whose salaried procuress is the Mrs Ellison in whose house the Booths are lodging. Amelia, not before it was time, is put on her guard against this villainous schemer, by a lady who had been entrapped by devices as abominable as those of Richardson's Lovelace.

The pair are wrapped in a web of intrigue, and Booth's impulsiveness and Amelia's innocence are poor safeguards against a host of snares. Husband and wife, unhappily, are not in each other's confidence. One thing or another prevents their opening their minds frankly. We watch them fencing in the dark. Amelia fears to let out all she knows lest her hot-headed husband should challenge the would-be seducer. When Booth's suspicions are at length awakened, first to the designs of the lecherous peer, and then to the treachery of his friend the colonel, he is paralysed by the consciousness of his own fault, and by the repeated threats of the infuriated Miss Matthews to betray him to his wife if he will not renew their intrigue. The mere dread of affronting Amelia's perfect loyalty is enough to make him shrink from warning her against attentions from James and the peer which outwardly appear so blameless. Thus, instead of the comic irony of the misunderstandings and reversals of situation in *Tom Jones*, Fielding here presents a more tragic irony—two souls fondly in love, yet working unconsciously against each other, cherishing baseless mistrusts and heart-burnings, and, on the husband's part at least, dealing unintended wrongs to his best and dearest.

The tragic irony of marital distrust

The climax is when the insidious peer, finding the well-worn stratagem of the masquerade ticket and subsequent surprise

The climax

abortive, employs his regular pimp, Captain Trent, to inveigle Booth. That ill-starred wretch is induced to play at cards, ends with a debt of honour to the captain, and a few days later is clapped into a sponging-house, where his other creditors seize the opportunity to load him with writs. Amelia had stripped herself and the children of their trinkets and everything except what they had on, and had managed to raise the fifty pounds owing to Trent. But in a fit of foolish optimism, Booth parted with the money to a certain great man who professed to be able by his influence to secure him an appointment. The same day, Booth received an urgent letter from Miss Matthews threatening to tell his wife everything if he did not call on her that evening. The bailiffs seize him at her door. And so Booth is back in his old quarters in the bailiff's castle, chewing the bitter cud of penitence and despair. That night, whilst Amelia is waiting for his return, she receives a note from Colonel James summoning him to a duel in the morning, for breaking his promise about Miss Matthews. It is followed by the news that her husband is arrested. For once she gives way. " 'Your papa [she cries to the affrighted children] is—indeed he is a wicked man—he cares not for any of us. O Heavens! is this the happiness I promised myself this evening?' At which words she fell into an agony, holding both her children in her arms." [1]

The dé-nouement   It is the midnight preceding daybreak. A long letter comes from Booth explaining and confessing everything. She visits him in the round-house next morning, and he begs her forgiveness. After a short silence she answers in the angelic words : " Indeed, I firmly believe every word you have said, but I cannot now forgive you the fault you have confessed; and my reason is—because I have forgiven it long ago." [2] Miss Matthews had carried out her threat to denounce Booth to his wife, and the violence of her resentment had betrayed how the land lay. Dr Harrison presently arrives, and bails out the prisoner. Then, with astonishing celerity, justice is done all round. It comes out that Amelia's sister and a rascally attorney had forged a will by which she had gained possession of their mother's property, left to Amelia. This scoundrel, Lawyer Murphy, who is Dr

[1] Book XI., c. 9.   [2] Book XII., c. 2.

Harrison's own confidential agent, plays a very similar game, it should be noted, to that of Squire Allworthy's solicitor Dowling in *Tom Jones*; indeed, matters are cleared up in a remarkably similar manner in both tales, if not quite so convincingly in the second. Dr Harrison loses no time in having Murphy apprehended, and hurries him before a magistrate, who, though he was just sitting down to his dinner, and he had been fatigued all the morning with public business, postpones all refreshment till he has heard the case. The delinquent is committed to Newgate, after which the magistrate, another Justice Fielding, invites the whole company to dine with him, and they spend the evening in merriment till the clock strikes eleven. Amelia is soon in possession of her fortune, and she and her husband spend the rest of their lives in perfect happiness.

In *Tom Jones*, as many have pointed out, Fielding followed the epical plan of the *Iliad*, whereas in *Amelia* he adopts the method of the *Odyssey* or the *Æneid*, and gives an account of past events in long conversations between Booth and Miss Matthews, who tell each other what has happened since they were young people together. All the antecedents to the existing situation being thus disposed of, the real business commences; the epical narration covering many years is followed by a swift drama of intrigue, which occupies no more than the six weeks taken up by the events after Tom's dismissal by Allworthy in the previous novel. In this drama of intrigue Fielding makes use of various characters and motives adapted from his old play, *The Modern Husband*—a rather clumsy attempt at candid realism which had been hissed off the stage. The alterations are very judicious, whether they simplify the former plot or the reverse. Mr Modern, who sells his wife to Lord Richly, was the original of Captain Trent, who does as much for the unnamed lord in *Amelia* and also acts as regular minister to his pleasures. His wife Hillaria doubles the parts to be taken by Mrs Trent and Miss Matthews, since she is not only one of Richly's mistresses, but also the former mistress of Bellamant, whose fair wife is now the object of Lord Richly's pursuit. There is no Colonel James, the aristocratic debauchee filling the parts of both characters as regards the machinations against the honour of the beautiful heroine. Mrs Modern at once

A different plan from the epical manner of "Tom Jones"

Material utilized from "The Modern Husband"

embarrasses the unfortunate Bellamant, who wants to be faithful to his wife, and acts as Lord Richly's tool in trying to inveigle her. Bellamant has a scapegrace son, Captain Bellamant, whose reckless, spendthrift ways anticipate one side of Captain Booth's characteristics, and a daughter Emilia, who expresses, crudely enough, the sentiments afterwards put in action by her namesake. She is disgusted with town life. " I am far from thinking any of its pleasures worth too eager a wish," she declares ; " the woman who has with her, in the country, the man she loves, must be a very ridiculous creature to pine after the town." [1] Bellamant, unable to get quit of Hillaria, and not very eager to do so, as he thinks he can square the possession of a mistress with unimpaired affection for his wife, is suddenly shocked out of this ignoble dalliance with evil by receiving from his wife's hands the hundred-pound note that he had given shortly before to Hillaria. What does it mean ? Has Lord Richly triumphed over his paragon of a wife, and are these the wages of her dishonour ? His feelings are much the same as Booth's on a similar occasion. Mrs Bellamant is as true, however, as Amelia ; but her magnanimous reply to her penitent husband is feeble in comparison with Amelia's great speech : " As you are your own accuser, be your own judge ; you can inflict no punishment on yourself equal to what I feel."

Fielding's "Modern Glossary" —a comment on the same theme The scabrous theme of *The Modern Husband* falls into a subordinate place in *Amelia*, and without losing its dreadfulness serves to throw the unswerving constancy of the poor officer's wife into higher relief. Fielding had written a number of comedies and farces making game of the follies and immoralities of the town, and he now used up a good deal of this old material, and used it to good purpose. That which had once provoked laughter now gave point to stern invective. [2] Fielding's irony, at this season of his life, is bitter and envenomed. The " Modern Glossary," which he inserted next year in *The Covent Garden Journal*, [3] gives a quizzical exegesis to several words that occur pretty often in the small talk of his latest novel. " Fine " is " an

---

[1] Act ii., scene 1.
[2] Cross, ii. 324-326 ; *The Justice caught in his own Trap*, with its similar criminal background, was one of these ; whilst Justice Squeezum, in *The Coffee-House Politicians*, is a first sketch for Justice Thrasher.
[3] No. 4, 14th January 1752.

adjective of a very peculiar kind, destroying, or at least lessening, the force of the substantive to which it is joined; as fine gentleman, fine lady, fine house, fine clothes, fine taste — in all which Fine is to be understood in a sense of synonymous with Useless." " Great. Applied to a thing, signifies bigness; when to a man, often littleness, or meanness." " Gallantry " is simply " fornication and adultery." The definition of " No body " is an amusing gloss on his favourite distinction between low people and high people : " All the people in Great Britain, except about 1200."

Some of the moral oppositions evident in the general scheme *Traces* of *Tom Jones* are traceable again in *Amelia*. Booth is a weaker *of an* and unwiser Jones, considerably older, old enough, indeed, to have *intellectual* learned experience, but still a prey to impulse; he, likewise, is *scheme in* good at heart and has a healthy conscience; but his ingrained *"Amelia"* faults yield only to a long course of drastic treatment. Like Jones, he is beset with temptations and plots against his integrity. But Booth, as was said before, is not the central figure. It is his wife Amelia who draws the enemy's fire. Her beauty and charm make her the mark of the profligate; and Booth's unhappy part is to tremble for his honour and writhe with anguish at the knowledge that he himself is the person mainly responsible for her distresses. Dr Harrison and Colonel Bath are roughly parallel to the contrasted pair, Mr Allworthy and Squire Western. Dr Harrison, the experienced clergyman, fatherly, but severe in the reprobation of faults, is less of an idealization than Allworthy; and, besides being truer to life, he has more wit and humour, in spite of his fondness for improving the occasion. Unfortunately for him, he has to officiate as chief spokesman in the discussions that take the place of Fielding's introductory essays in *Tom Jones*. Allworthy was popular with all who knew him or had heard of his philanthropy. Dr Harrison's virtues shine out in a less charitable world; and how he strikes the average sordid observer appears in the lecture of a father to his son, a young clergyman who had argued somewhat too cavalierly with the venerable doctor :

" I never told you he was a wise man, nor did I ever think him so. If he had any understanding, he would have been a bishop long ago, to my certain knowledge. But, indeed, he hath been always a fool in private life; for I question whether he is worth £100 in the world, more than his annual income. He hath given away above half his fortune to the Lord knows who. I believe I have had above £200 of him, first and last; and would you lose such a milch-cow as this for want of a few compliments? Indeed, Tom, thou art as great a simpleton as himself. How do you expect to rise in the church if you cannot temporize and give in to the opinions of your superiors? "

Char-
acters:
Colonel
Bath

Colonel Bath is like Western only in being a compound of ludicrous idiosyncrasies, in antithesis to Booth's more reliable friend, the man of intellect and ripe experience. He is one of Fielding's most charming eccentrics. There are two whimsical incidents that the name of Colonel Bath always brings up. The first is Booth's finding the dignified old soldier, in a grotesque deshabille, warming a posset for his invalid sister.

The major started from his seat at my entering into the room, and, with much emotion, and a great oath, cried out, " Is it you, sir? " I then inquired after his and his sister's health. He answered, that his sister was better, and he was very well, " though I did not expect, sir," cried he, with not a little confusion, " to be seen by you in this situation." I told him I thought it impossible he could appear in a situation more becoming his character. " You do not? " answered he. " By G—— I am very much obliged to you for that opinion; but, I believe, sir, however my weakness may prevail on me to descend from it, no man can be more conscious of his own dignity than myself."

He uttered these words " with great majesty, or, as he called it, dignity." Next morning he came very early to Booth's chamber, and told him he had not been able to sleep a wink after what had passed between them.

" There were some words of yours," says he, " which must be further explained before we part. You told me, sir, when you found me in that situation, which I cannot bear to recollect, that you thought I could not appear in one more becoming my char- acter; these were the words—I shall never forget them. Do you imagine that there is any of the dignity of a man wanting in my character? Do you think that I have, during my sister's illness, behaved with a weakness that savours too much of effeminacy? "

Booth has much ado to assure the major that he had meant to pay him a compliment, and succeeds only by citing such flattering examples of martial prowess, combined with softness of heart, as Brutus and the king of Sweden. Mention of the king of Sweden and his inconsolable grief for a favourite sister is too much for the major's feelings. He runs on about his Betsey, till the tears begin to overflow and he is unable to go on.

After a short silence, however, having wiped his eyes with his handkerchief, he fetched a deep sigh, and cried, " I am ashamed you should see this, Mr Booth; but d—n me, nature will get the better of dignity." I now comforted him with the example of Xerxes, as I had before done with that of the king of Sweden; and soon after we sat down to breakfast together with much cordial friendship; for I assure you, with all his oddity, there is not a better-natured man in the world than the major.[1]

This is the blend of comic and sentimental that answers exactly to the classic definition of humour. More purely comic is the episode of the duel forced on Booth by the great champion of the dignity of man, to enable him to retrieve his honour, which had been jeopardized by the innuendoes of Colonel James. Booth hardly knows what it is all about; but they engage with great fury, and he runs his punctilious antagonist through the body.

As soon as the colonel was become master of his speech, he called out to Booth in a very kind voice, and said, " You have done my business, and satisfied me that you are a man of honour, and that my brother James must have been mistaken; for I am convinced that no man who will draw his sword in so gallant a manner is capable of being a rascal. D—n me, give me a buss, my dear boy; I ask your pardon for that infamous appellation I dishonoured your dignity with; but, d—n me if it was not purely out of love, and to give you an opportunity of doing yourself justice, which I own you have done like a man of honour.[2]

Colonel James, the brother-in-law of the amiable fire-eater, *Gradual* challenges comparison on the score of lifelikeness with Richard- *revelation* son's Lovelace. He has many estimable qualities, and shows *of* himself so stanch a friend when Booth lies wounded and at *character*

[1] Book III., c. 8.   [2] Book V., c. 5.

death's door that he appears in himself an adequate proof of that young man's pet doctrine, " that all men act entirely from their passions; for Bob James can never be supposed to act from any motives of virtue or religion, since he constantly laughs at both." Fielding had now perfected the art of letting the reader gradually make out for himself what each character really is at bottom, instead of explaining the more abstruse twists and permutations of motive. Long before Booth sees through the colonel's double-dealing we are familiar with the ins and outs of the confirmed woman-hunter's nature; and even when his behaviour puzzles us for the moment and completely mystifies Booth we feel in the end that it is exactly what we should have predicted. This is a novel packed with cross-intrigues, misunderstandings, enigmatic situations, and surprising discoveries; and the clue to the labyrinth is a right estimate of the characters engaged. The art with which Fielding puts the reader bit by bit in possession of that clue, in its sure control of the subtle mechanism of motive, is beyond anything in *Tom Jones*.

Miss Matthews an example of this   His study of Miss Matthews illustrates the perfection and finish of his realism with the same clearness. The reluctant mistress of Colonel James, in love with Amelia's husband because he has in his breast that rare organ, a sensitive heart, is a piece of breathing humanity compared with which Lady Bellaston was but a stage figure, and Lady Booby only a puppet. Instead of fidgeting with her conscience, as Defoe's Moll Flanders and even Roxana used to do when they gave way to temptation, she manages to keep her high spirits and something of her girlish freshness, in spite of a close acquaintance with the wickedness of a cynical world. She knows the colonel inside and out, and many of Booth's early friends; hence her remarks as he proceeds with his narrative make any comment from the author superfluous. The obvious comparison with Defoe's two courtesans brings out the whole difference between the realism that watches the doings of human creatures from somewhere in the heavens and that which plods conscientiously along, registering every fact. Miss Matthews grows upon the reader in clearness and completeness, touch by touch, line by line, in the same gradual way as the rest of the characters that matter. When she rounds on Booth we are in no way surprised nor our sympathies outraged: we see the position so well from the woman's point of view.[1]

A minor figure, who becomes more important as we know him better, is Sergeant Atkinson, who has been compared to Partridge and even to Parson Adams, though there is little resemblance except in his being the traditional devoted squire to the adventurous hero. The historical interest of this character is that he forms a link between Fielding's comic realism and the sentimental fiction which was already in the ascendant with readers and was to extend its popularity after his death. It comes out that Atkinson's devotion has all along been accepted at the wrong address. He has watched over Booth with tireless solicitude; but the reason is that Booth is Amelia's husband, and he has loved her with a dog-like affection from childhood up. For once in her life Amelia feels a tenderness towards someone else than her husband and children, and realizes that Billy Booth is not the only man in the world with a sensitive soul and the capacity for a sterling affection.

Sergeant Atkinson, a link with the novel of sentiment

To say the truth, without any injury to her chastity, that heart, which had stood firm as a rock to all the attacks of title and equipage, of finery and flattery, and which all the treasures of the universe could not have purchased, was yet a little softened by the plain, honest, modest, involuntary, delicate, heroic passion of this poor and humble swain; for whom, in spite of herself, she felt a momentary tenderness and complacence, at which Booth, if he had known it, would perhaps have been displeased.[2]

Atkinson, as the modern pyschologist would say, has as much of the woman in his constitution as of the man; he mothers Booth and pets the children; hence the response of Amelia, whose dominant trait is her motherliness, whether husband or children are in question.

Is that side of her overdone, as it was by Thackeray, who fell

[1] The subject is one that has fascinated the most accomplished novelists; but probably Flaubert's Maréchale, in *L'Education Sentimentale*, is the only study better than Fielding's, and that mainly because done on a fuller scale. La Maréchale is drawn with her feminine singularities accentuated; Miss Matthews, in comparison, is more generalized—in short, as much a type as an individual.
[2] Book XI., c. 6.

*Further
instances
of senti-
mentalism*

so far short of Fielding when he tried to imitate the clear-headed,
critical, and ironical realism of his great predecessor? The
trials, the bitter disappointments and disillusionments, so sharply
contrasted with the weakness and remissness of her husband,
often provoke our impatience, not merely with him but also with
her. Why should she be so forgiving? Surely Booth's folly
deserved a smarter chastisement. He got some of his deserts,
but not enough, and never at the hands of his wife. Fielding is
unsparing in the contrasts he draws. He shows Booth losing his
money at the gaming-table, the money Amelia has been at her
wits' end to scrape together for a very different object. Amelia
puts the children to bed, and busies herself in cooking a little
supper for her husband, this being his favourite meal, and she
looks forward to a pleasant hour in oblivion of all their troubles.
But no Booth appears, and at ten she sits down by herself. Then
comes the famous incident of the half-pint of wine that was never
sent for.

Having sat some time alone, reflecting on their distressed
situation, her spirits grew very low; and she was once or twice
going to ring to send her maid for half-a-pint of white wine, but
checked her inclination in order to save the little sum of sixpence,
which she did the more resolutely as she had before refused to
gratify her children with tarts for their supper from the same
motive. And this self-denial she was very probably practising to
save sixpence, while her husband was paying a debt of several
guineas incurred by the ace of trumps being in the hands of his
adversary.[1]

The same contrast is emphasized in the incident of the sum
raised by Amelia to save her husband from the embarrassments
caused by his imprudence, and foolishly handed over to the great
man who is to do such wonderful things for Booth. It is made
the text for a sermon on this abominable practice of " touching,"
giving a bribe to an influential person who pretends to be able
to get the applicant employment.

Here I shall stop one moment, and so, perhaps, will my good-
natured reader; for surely it must be a hard heart which is not

[1] Book X., c. 5.

affected with reflecting on the manner in which this poor little sum was raised, and on the manner in which it was bestowed. A worthy family, the wife and children of a man who had lost his blood abroad in the service of his country, parting with their little all, and exposed to cold and hunger, to pamper such a fellow as this!

And if any such reader as I mention should happen to be in reality a great man, and in power, perhaps the horror of this picture may induce him to put a final end to this abominable practice of touching, as it is called; by which, indeed, a set of leeches are permitted to suck the blood of the brave and indigent, of the widow and the orphan.[1]

This is not the Fielding who once stood for the classical ideal of reason and even-handed justice, serenity and restraint; who saw the comedy from both sides, and maintained a healthy scepticism regarding the perfect whiteness or the absolute blackness of any individual. It is not the Fielding whose mockery was dealt out impartially, and could smile even at the superiority of Mr Allworthy to every human peccadillo.[2] The times had changed, and Fielding was a different man. Sentiment was gaining the upper hand with the majority of readers, and after his harsh experience at Bow Street he himself could not resume his old impassiveness. He seldom now has the heart to sport ironically with the shams and hypocrisies of life, but uses downright plain speaking in the denunciation of vice and evil.[3]

I must inform, therefore, all such readers (those who wonder why Amelia failed to see the object of Colonel James's attentions), that it is not because innocence is more blind than guilt that the former often overlooks and tumbles into the pit which the latter foresees and avoids. The truth is, that it is almost impossible

[1] Book XI., c. 5.
[2] Digeon 227-228.
[3] The Fielding of *Tom Jones*, however, still came to life occasionally. An instance is Booth's conversation with Mr Bondman the bailiff, in chapter two. Mr Bondman is all for liberty. "Is that so consistent with your calling?" cries Booth. "Methought, my friend, you had lived by depriving men of their liberty." "That's another matter," cries the bailiff; "that's all according to law, and in the way of business. To be sure, men must be obliged to pay their debts, or else there would be an end of everything." Booth eggs him on, and Bondman ties himself up in a knot in trying to reconcile liberty with the obvious right of every Englishman "to arrest another for a just and lawful debt."

guilt should miss the discovering of all the snares in its way, as it is constantly prying closely into every corner in order to lay snares for others. Whereas innocence, having no such purpose, walks fearlessly and carelessly through life, and is consequently liable to tread on the gins which cunning hath laid to entrap it. To speak plainly and without allegory or figure, it is not want of sense, but want of suspicion, by which innocence is often betrayed. Again, we often admire at the folly of the dupe, when we should transfer our whole surprise to the astonishing guilt of the betrayer. In a word, many an innocent person hath owed his ruin to this circumstance alone, that the degree of villainy was such as must have exceeded the faith of every man who was not himself a villain.[1]

Detection of legal and social absurdities   The keen eye of the magistrate had laid bare innumerable legal anomalies and injustices; hence many incidents that are clearly intended to indicate various urgent reforms. The servant-maid who robbed her kind-hearted mistress cannot be convicted of theft because it is shown by the defence that she was entrusted with the goods, and breach of trust is not a felony unless the goods be worth forty shillings. If the goods were not stolen, it is useless to prosecute the dishonest pawnbroker for receiving.[2] A ragged young woman and her starving father are committed to gaol for purloining a loaf, whilst a well-dressed fellow indicted for perjury, against a person whose life was at stake, secures bail. The one offence, " being felony, is held to be not bailable at law; whereas perjury is a misdemeanour only," and those charged are capable of being bailed. The villainous attorney who ruined Trent's father-in-law, and broke his heart, gets off scot-free by a quibble, though his offence was forgery, which had just then been made capital by Act of Parliament. He was acquitted, " by not admitting the proof of the party, who was to avoid his own deed by his evidence, and therefore no witness, according to those excellent rules called the laws of evidence; a law very excellently calculated for the preservation of the lives of his majesty's roguish subjects, and most notably used for that purpose." [3] The greediness of bailiffs and turnkeys, and the iniquity of immuring untried persons and even retaining the

[1] Final sentence of chapter ix., in Book VIII.
[2] Book XI., c. 7.   [3] Book X., c. 3.

acquitted until they had paid the customary prison dues and garnish, are a subject continually drummed into our heads.

In spite of his change from mockery to earnestness, Fielding does not appear to have altered his views on the basic problems of conduct. To the end he was lenient, culpably lenient, his enemies said, towards the frailties and misdemeanours chargeable to the nature of man. The moral philosophy of *Tom Jones* satisfied him to the last. Fraud, malevolence, and heartlessness he always hated, and sins of that description are much more prominent in *Amelia* than in any of his previous novels, except *Jonathan Wild*, which can hardly be regarded as an impartial survey of human life. But towards the question of men's religion a decided change of front is evident in Fielding's last novel, the main exponent of which is Dr Harrison, who here takes the place that Allworthy occupied in *Tom Jones*.[1] The dispassionate patron of Square and Thwackum held the scales unswervingly between the ethical geometry of the one and the bloodthirsty penal code of the other. Acknowledging the rule of right, he was prepared to temper it with mercy, but only after calm consideration. Allworthy was a graver and more deliberate Fielding who invested the author's verdicts with the authority and majesty of the judgment-seat. Dr Harrison is neither a greater sage nor more benevolent; but he is drawn with a warmer sympathy, and his character has a poise and a gracious bonhomie not to be found in the more stilted Allworthy.

Allworthy's was what has been termed the religion of every educated man; it was an attitude rather than a philosophy, the wisdom and serenity of one who had read and thought, had lived and observed, was benevolently inclined towards all men, and harboured no morbid fears regarding the hereafter. Cicero or Virgil or Seneca might have owned him as a disciple, nor would he have been repudiated by the contemporary deist. The difference between Allworthy and Harrison is that the latter has impregnated this broad-minded and tolerant philosophy of life with Christian sentiment, and preaches his sermons from Bible texts. When Fielding created Squire Allworthy, the accepted religion sat lightly on him, as on the shoulders of any man of

Fielding's altered attitude towards religion— Dr Harrison the chief exponent

[1] See Digeon (pp. 260 *et seq.*) on Fielding's later Christianism.

a worldly but not a frivolous mind, with inherited feelings of respect but no deep interest in spiritual concerns. But with a fuller and sadder knowledge of the social demoralization prevalent around him, he realized also his own responsibility as a potential teacher. He had shown his contemporaries what they were like; he had traced actions to their motives and motives to their roots in men's inveterate habits; he had demonstrated and explained, criticized and moralized, held the foolish and vicious up to ridicule or contumely. But neither friendly exposure nor good-tempered satire had availed to change the world, and it was doubtful whether the most luminous and irrefutable maxims ever penned would turn the average man from his heedless pursuit of pleasure. A new spirit must be infused and people's consciences awakened, and the only agency that would rouse the majority out of their selfish torpor was a revival of religion.

Amelia and Booth exponents also There are no more gibes at the Methodists, though it is not to be supposed that Fielding recanted his antipathy to the doctrine of faith not works. Dr Harrison is liberal enough to accept all forms of Christianity if they co-operated in the moral reformation that was the crying need of his day. In the homilies of the venerable doctor, his discussions of the state of England with various interlocutors, and his remarks on duelling and other uncivilized customs, Fielding continues the good work which began with the showing up of legal nuisances. *Amelia* is literature and also something more practical. Fielding was looking for results, as in his *Charge to the Grand Jury*, his *Enquiry into the Increase of Robbers*, and his subsequent war on the strongholds of crime. And for the sake of results, if the intellectual appeal hung fire, he was ready to invoke an enlightened self-interest or the religious conscience. Amelia is represented throughout as a firm believer, a faithful pupil of Dr Harrison; her convictions are as steady as her loyalty to her husband. Booth's scepticism is a perpetual grief to her. Her cup of happiness grows full when, in addition to their restoration to fortune at the end, Booth announces that he has at length been converted to the true faith, as the result of reading Barrow's sermons during his last sojourn in the round-house. " I shall," he says, " I believe, be the better man for them as long as I live." His chief doubt had been founded on this, "that, as men appeared to me to act entirely from their passions, their actions could have neither merit nor demerit." "A very worthy conclusion truly ! " cries the doctor; "but if men act, as I believe they do, from their passions, it would be fair to conclude that religion to be true which applies to the strongest of these passions, hope and fear; choosing rather to rely on its rewards and punishments than on that native beauty of virtue which some of the ancient philosophers thought proper to recommend to their disciples." [1]

[1] Book XII., c. 5.

CHAPTER VIII

FIELDING'S LAST WRITINGS AND HIS INFLUENCE

Fielding's change of views on the writers who had influenced him AN interesting gloss on the passages last quoted is furnished by an article in *The Covent Garden Journal*, two months after the publication of *Amelia*. Fielding compares the great wits and humorists who have written for the entertainment of men, and also to expose vices and follies.[1] Foremost he places " that great triumvirate, Lucian, Cervantes, and Swift," adding, " I would not be thought to confine wit and humour to these writers. Shakespeare and Molière and some other authors have been blessed with the same talents, and have employed them to the same purposes." Then he proceeds to condemn two writers who once admittedly exercised a powerful influence over himself.

There are some, however, who, though not void of these talents, have made so wretched a use of them, that, had the consecration of their labours been committed to the hands of the hangman, no good man would have regretted their loss : nor am I afraid to mention Rabelais, and Aristophanes himself, in this number. For, if I may speak my opinion freely of these two last writers, and of their works, their design appears to me very plainly to have been to ridicule all sobriety, modesty, decency, virtue, and religion, out of the world. Now whoever reads over the five great writers first mentioned above, must either have a very bad head, or a very bad heart, if he doth not become both a wiser and a better man.

Lucian, Cervantes, Swift, Shake- speare, Molière still ac- knowledged The imprint of the five authors thus honourably mentioned may without difficulty be traced on Fielding's mind and art, both in general and in certain characters and stories or episodes in particular. Trace is hardly the word, for he himself was neither too proud nor too modest to point them out. The earliest in- fluence and the most lasting was probably that of Lucian, whose

[1] No. 10, 4th February 1752.

spirit and style dominate *A Journey from this World to the Next.*
More of the ruthless sarcasm of Swift than of the refined irony of
Lucian is discernible in *Jonathan Wild.* Cervantes is frankly
acknowledged as Fielding's master in *Joseph Andrews*; and of
all the figures that novelists have endeavoured to cast in the
quixotic mould, Parson Adams is perhaps the only one that
stands out as a great creation of genius. But Fielding's spiritual
fellowship with Cervantes did not end with *Joseph Andrews,*
though he came to believe that Don Quixote himself was too
extravagant a figure, and that Sancho Panza was the true masterpiece of humorous characterization.[1] As the knight and his
esquire mark the two poles of idealistic imagination and sober
realism in the Spaniard's presentiment of human nature, so in *Tom
Jones* and *Amelia* there is a wide range between the idealism and
optimism embodied in such characters as Allworthy, Dr Harrison,
and Mrs Booth, on the one side, and the close facsimiles of the
common herd, gross, material, sordid, on the other. How much
Fielding learned from Shakespeare it would be difficult to define,
though of all our novelists, not excepting even Jane Austen, the
author of *Tom Jones* comes nearest to the dramatist in his catholic
and unruffled contemplation of mankind, his understanding of
motive, and his sleepless humour. The identity of his whole
conception and treatment of the comic with Molière's is easier
to substantiate.

Aristophanes and Rabelais, whom he now abjures, were by *Aris-*
no means always his antipathy. Some critics would attribute *tophanes*
the burlesque passages in *Joseph Andrews* and *Tom Jones* to *and*
Fielding's admiration for Scarron, author of *Le Roman Comique.*[2] *Rabelais*
But he was treading in the footsteps of older and weightier pre- *rejected*
decessors, the two giants of comic extravaganza whom he was
in gloomier days to repudiate. There was a seriousness implicit
in his wildest ebullitions of humour, even in the drollery of his
mock-heroics, much nearer to the fundamental gravity of the
mighty Greek and Gallic satirists than to the clever parodist of
the romancers.

Fielding has also left on record his appreciation of Marivaux,

---

[1] Cross, ii. 414, 433-434.
[2] *E.g.* Professor G. H. Maynadier (Introduction to *Joseph Andrews*, i., p. xix.).

to the hero of whose *Paysan Parvenu* his own Joseph Andrews
has some superficial resemblances,[1] and his revelation of half-
realized motive still more to the story of Marianne. But although
Marivaux and Fielding were comic novelists, and thus nearer
akin than either of them was to Richardson, the kinship was of a
general kind, and it would be as hard to produce definite evidences
of Fielding's discipleship as to agree with him in putting Marivaux
side by side with Molière, Shakespeare, Aristophanes, Rabelais,
and the great triumvirate. But the case is different with another
French novelist, cited once, and then not by name, in the picaresque
Joseph Andrews, as " the inimitable biographer " of *Gil Blas*.[2]
No mention There is no mention of Le Sage in those passages in which Fielding
here of indicates the writers, ancient or modern, who had helped to
Le Sage shape him; yet one could find a number of incidents and, what
is more, a number of ironical turns and tricks of mental analysis,
in *Tom Jones* and elsewhere, betokening a very lively recollection
of that author's works. M. Digeon observes that Fielding must
have had in mind the adventures of Blandine, wife of Don
Cherubin's valet, Toston, in *Le Bachelier de Salamanque*, when
he wrote Mrs Heartfree's account of her perils and escapes to
her husband, in *Jonathan Wild*.[3] Probably, also, Thomas de la
Fuente, with his scraps from the Latin gradus and his crude
taste for blood-curdling realism on the stage, in *Gil Blas*, gave
Fielding some suggestions for the much more elaborate character
of Partridge.[4]

It has been stated that the Universal Register Office, run by
Fielding and his half-brother, John, in the Strand, " had been

---

[1] *Joseph Andrews*, iii., c. 1, and *Tom Jones*, xiii., c. 1.

[2] *Joseph Andrews*, iii., c. 1.

[3] Digeon, 156-157, n. Blandine, like the later heroine, had been carried
off on shipboard, and her virtue assailed when she was in the most defenceless
condition. She tells her husband, just as Mrs Heartfree was to do in *Jonathan
Wild*, how resolutely and successfully she had withstood the advances of
Captain Cope, who had kidnapped her. The husband in each case is on
thorns at the risks his wife's virtue has run. The Frenchman accepts her
story with reserves. " I must admit," he says, " excuse my candour, that I
should not have expected so much resistance on your part. But, between you
and me, I am astonished at Cope's delicacy; and you won't mind my saying
that if your account is true, it doesn't sound very probable " (*Le Bachelier
de Salamanque*, c. 76). The situations are indeed remarkably similar, and
Fielding's tone just here is more slyly ironical than in the rest of the Heartfree
business.

[4] See above, 150, n.

suggested to 'Messires Fielding & Company' by a passage in *Possible*
Montaigne." [1] But there was a nearer literary source than *suggestions*
Montaigne, if such a one is to be looked for, in the general registry *from*
and *bureau d'adresse* conducted at Valladolid by Seigneur Arias *Le Sage*
de Londona, in *Gil Blas*.[2] Still, there is probably no more in this
than in the coincidence that Le Sage, in the same novel, alludes
to the tale of Caligula's horse, which his master lodged in a
luxurious house and proposed to make a consul, a legend on which
Fielding dilates in *The Covent Garden Journal*.[3] Perhaps, also,
it would be a mistake to attach much weight to the fact that
the rapacity of the magistrates and gaolers in *Amelia* remind the
reader irresistibly of their brother functionaries at Astorga and
Valladolid, who picked Gil Blas and his mate so clean before
setting them at large.[4] But, at any rate, the portrait of the affable
corregidor of Astorga, examining the unfortunate rescuer of
Doña Mencia with a benevolent and jovial air, and gently emptying his pockets and saddlebags, stripping him to see if there was
anything between his shirt and his skin, and finally leaving him
naked on the straw, is done in the very manner of which Fielding
was to be a supreme exponent.[5]

Gil Blas was the ultimate and finest embodiment of the

---

[1] Cross, ii. 226.

[2] Livre I., c. 17.

[3] No. 17, 29th February.

[4] Mais nous ne sortîmes point de ce lieu-là comme nous y étions entrés : le
flambeau, le collier, les pendants, ma bague et les rubies, tout y resta. Cela
me fit souvenir de ces vers de Virgile, qui commencent par *Sic vos non vobis*
(*Gil Blas*, ii. 5).

[5] Ce juge n'étoit pas de ceux qui ont le regard terrible ; il avoit l'air doux
et riant. Dieu sait s'il valoit mieux pour cela ! Sitôt que je fus en prison, il
y vint avec ses deux furets, c'est-à-dire ses deux alguazils. Ils n'oublièrent pas
leur bonne coutume : ils commencèrent par me fouiller. Quelle aubaine pour
ces messieurs ! Ils n'avoient jamais peut-être fait un si bon coup. A chaque
poignée de pistoles qu'ils priroient, je voyois leurs yeux étinceller de joie.
Le corrégidor surtout paroissoit hors de lui-même. Mon enfant, me disoit-il
d'un ton de voix plein de douceur, nous faisons notre charge ; mais ne crains
rien : si tu n'es pas coupable, on ne te fera point de mal. Cependant ils
vidèrent tout doucement mes poches, ils prirent ce que les voleurs mêmes
avoient respecté, je veux dire les quarante ducats de mon oncle. Ils n'en
demeurèrent pas là : leurs mains avides et infatigables me parcoururent depuis
la tête jusqu'aux pieds ; ils me tournèrent de tous côtés, et me dépouillèrent
pour voir si je n'avois point d'argent entre la peau et la chemise. Après
qu'ils eurent si bien fait leur charge, le corrégidor, m'interrogea. Je lui
contai ingénument tout ce qui m'étoit arrivé. Il fit écrire ma déposition ;
puis il sortit avec ses gens et mes espèces, et me laissa tout nu sur la paille
(*Gil Blas*, i. 12).

Fielding probably influenced by the earlier books of "Gil Blas" picaresque idea, but the book is not perfectly homogeneous. A change gradually occurs from the irony and Lucianic raillery of the earlier portion to the plain terms of a moralizing story-teller more disposed to teach and correct than to ridicule—a similar change, in short, to that observable between Fielding's earlier novels and his last. The young picaro, burdened with no superfluity of conscience or of common sense, is imperceptibly converted into a well-meaning person, chastened by experience, worried with scruples, but, on the whole, to be relied upon for straightforward dealings. It is, of course, not the young Gil Blas who is the ironist, but Le Sage whose eye-twinkle we catch as we study the ingenuousness, the optimism, and the self-complacency of the supposed autobiographer. It was these earlier books that fascinated the author of *Joseph Andrews* and *Tom Jones*, who delighted in the ironical surprises and reversals of expectation, and continually showed his own heroes likewise tumbling into Charybdis in their efforts to avoid Scylla. To say this is the regular trick of picaresque romancers hardly suffices. Often we find Fielding using exactly the same technical device that Le Sage used over and over again, in the parts of *Gil Blas* first published. Thus the mental conflicts of Black George and Mrs Honour on two famous occasions when they were confronted with opposite lines of action,[1] cannot but recall such a dilemma as when Gil had to decide whether he should help the perfidious Eufrasie to deceive his master, Don Gonzale, or endeavour to detach that senile lover from his mistress.

Conscience, however, seemed to have some little concern in the determination; it was quite ridiculous to choose the by-path of villainy when there was a better toll to be taken on the highway of honesty. Besides, Euphrasia had dealt too much in generals; an arithmetical definition of so much for so much has more meaning in it than " all the wealth of the Indies "; and to this shrewd reflection, perhaps, was owing my uncorrupted probity. Thus did I resolve to signalize my zeal in the service of Don Gonzales, in the persuasion that if I was lucky enough to disgust the worshipper by befouling his idol, it would turn to very good account. On a statement of debtor and creditor between the right and the

[1] See above, pp. 143-144.

wrong side of the action, the money balance was visibly in favour of virtue, not to mention the delights of a fair and irreproachable character.[1]

Gil, accordingly, let the amorous don know that he had seen a strange man concealed in the lady's chamber, and volunteered the addition that she had tried to lead himself, the incorruptible valet, into crooked ways. The upshot is in keeping with the rest. Gonzale believes Gil, and has it out with the courtesan, who, however, easily gulls him into mistrust of Gil's story, and the conscientious valet gets the sack.

Many such ironies enliven the course of the love episode of *Other* Aurore and Don Luis Pacheco. Fatuously misinterpreting her *ironical* affabilities, Gil Blas jumps to the conclusion that Aurore is *surprises* enamoured of himself, the modest but deserving footman, and hastens to spare her the embarrassment of making the first advances. He is crestfallen to find that she has sent for him in private merely to further her amour with Don Luis. A more celebrated instance is Gil's discomfiture when he summons up courage to warn his patron, the archbishop, who, before he fell ill, had earnestly enjoined this duty upon his faithful servant and confidant, that the eloquence with which the great prelate had enthralled his hearers was at length beginning to fail.

" To cut it short, you think it is time to think about retiring? "
" I would not have ventured," said I, " to speak so freely, had not your grace commanded it. I am only obeying your strict injunctions, and I humbly beg your grace not to take offence at my boldness." " God grant," he hastily interrupted, " God grant that I may never reproach you ! It would be a rank injustice. I am not in the least offended at your telling me your opinion. It is only your opinion that I find fault with. I have been completely taken in by your lack of judgment." [2]

The rogue's march is accelerated with the parting salute : "Adieu, Monsieur Gil Blas, je vous souhaite toutes sortes de prospérités, avec un peu plus de goût."

It is easy enough to multiply examples of this sardonic humour, corresponding closely with those already quoted from Fielding,

Book IV. 7, Smollett's translation.   [2] Book VII. 4.

The canon and Dr Sangrado especially from *Tom Jones*.[1] Who could forget Gil Blas' zeal in fetching the notary to make sure that his dying master, the canon, executes his last will and testament before Dr Sangrado has had time to do his deadly work, and his precautions that his own services should not be forgotten? When the will is read, Gil is taken aback to hear that the canon has left him his library and manuscripts, " for that he is a youth with a taste for literature, and this will enable him to continue his education." He is still more disconcerted when the supposed library turns out to be an old cookery book and a few odd volumes, and the collection of manuscripts some notes on a lawsuit. Sangrado, " who used his patients as a vintner doth his wine-vessels, by letting out their blood, and filling them up with water," [2] and who was " so expeditious, that he gave his patients no time to call in a notary," [3] and so was said to have forestalled many a testament, found a warm place in Fielding's heart, who rarely missed an opportunity of ridiculing the pretentious jargon and the quackery of the medical profession.

Le Sage and Fielding on affectation and hypocrisy   The introductory essays in *Tom Jones*, again, contain many remarks like the advice of Gil's colleague :

I perceive that you have wit at will, if you did but know how to draw upon it. The fear of talking absurdly prevents you from throwing out at all; and yet it is only by a bold push that a thousand people nowadays set themselves up for good companions. Do you wish to be bright? You have only to give the reins to your loquacity, and to venture indiscriminately on whatever comes uppermost; your blunders will pass for the eccentricities of genius. Though you should utter an hundred extravagancies, let but a single good joke be packed up in the bundle, the nonsense shall be all forgotten, the witticism bandied about, and your talent be puffed into high repute. This is the happy method our masters have devised, and it ought to be adopted by all new candidates.[4]

Lastly, compare Fielding's treatment of affectation and hypocrisy, in the preface to *Joseph Andrews* and in numerous other

---

[1] See above, especially pp. 138-144.
[2] *Joseph Andrews*, iii. 1.
[3] *Gil Blas*, ii. 2.
[4] *Ibid.*, iii. 4, Smollett's translation.

places, with the cynicism of Doña Melancia, the austere-looking duenna with the soul of a procuress:

It's a long time since I learned the great art of wearing a mask; and I consider myself doubly happy, in enjoying at once the pleasures of vice and the reputation of virtue. Between ourselves, this is about the only virtue there is in the world. To acquire the real thing is too expensive; most people nowadays are content with appearances.[1]

Fielding's approximations to the thought and artistic methods of Le Sage are worth stressing, inasmuch as this is the one of his sources that is usually overlooked and that he himself did not particularize. Nevertheless, he far surpassed Le Sage, as he surpassed Scarron and Marivaux, particularly in that wider sympathy and keener perception which saw how virtues and weakness inhabited the same individual, and how easy and treacherous was the descent into vice and folly.

Fielding had not yet done with journalism. Barely had *Amelia* reached the hands of the public when he was busy with *The Covent Garden Journal*, another periodical in the style of *The Tatler* and *The Spectator*, with features of the news-sheet as well as the literary magazine, which ran from January to August 1752. He had some assistants, but wrote by far the larger part himself. The journal is most interesting for its occasional discourses on points of æsthetics, and for such sidelights on his own fiction as the passage already quoted on his great predecessors. In another paper [2] he deals waggishly with the thesis that people accept as quite ordinary occurrences of their own time what, if related of some remote period, they would scout as incredible. Then he supposes an account discovered in the fortieth century of what was going on daily in the reign of George II., and asks whether the reader in that distant future would give a moment's credence to such allegations of folly and barbarism among the upper classes and depravity among the lower. The satire, which was then a novelty, does not cut very deep, but it shows what subject was chiefly weighing upon his mind in these latter years.

On the Bench, despite the alarming state of his health, Fielding's

"The Covent Garden Journal"

---

[1] Book II. 7.   [2] No. 17, 29th February.

*Fielding's
break-
down
in health*
activity had scarcely relaxed. He himself directed the operations of the constables, who raided the gambling-houses, and other irregular places of amusement, suppressed houses of ill-fame, and tried to cope with the armed gangs of burglars and footpads. Supplied with a fund of six hundred pounds to be used at his own discretion, Fielding organized a body of thief-takers, and in a surprisingly brief space of time " almost entirely extirpated " these gentry, and made the streets safe for peaceful citizens. But he was obviously breaking up. Early in 1754, his brother John finally took office as his successor at Bow Street, and the sick man went into the country to seek a change of air and try various drastic remedies for a complication of disorders. That summer was exceptionally cold and wet, and at last Fielding yielded to advice and went abroad. He sailed for Lisbon early in June, and arrived there at the beginning of August. He arrived only to die.

*"The
Journal of
a Voyage
to Lisbon"*
He began his last work, *The Journal of a Voyage to Lisbon*, to beguile the tedium of a long wait in the Downs for a favourable wind. " Some of the most amusing passages, if, indeed, there be any which deserve the name, were possibly the production of the most disagreeable hours which ever haunted the author." Thus modestly Fielding speaks of one of his most charming works, a work that none but a practised delineator of his species could have written. It is only with certain touches of that art, or with his reflections upon it, that we are concerned here. One playful sentence in the preface, while urging that the book is worth reading for its public utility, lets us see clearly what were his views on the need to be entertaining even when an author writes to instruct.

If entertainment, as Mr Richardson observes, be but a secondary consideration in a romance ; with which Mr Addison I think agrees, affirming the use of the pastry-cook to be the first; if this, I say, be true of a mere work of invention, sure it may well be so considered in a work founded, like this, on truth; and where the political reflections form so distinguishing a part.

The criticism concealed in this ironical apology shows how clearly Fielding was aware of his great rival's principal failing, the inability to distinguish between a treatise on human nature

and a work of art. Fielding, on the contrary, even in this diary
of casual observations, used his materials as the potter uses his
clay, and gave such a transparency to actualities as he had previously done to fictitious matters that we participate in his own
broad, kindly, amused survey of things human.

When Fielding comes to close quarters with anyone long *His low*
enough to know him thoroughly, his sympathy and understanding *esteem for*
are never in default. Thus the captain of the ship, who exasper- *the vulgar*
ated his invalid guest so much by his insensibility and bad manners, *rabble*
has justice done in the long run to his courage and seamanship.
But for the mob, regarded not as individuals but collectively,
Fielding had as little respect as Swift, or, for the matter of that,
as Shakespeare. There are few uglier pictures of man's in-
humanity to man than that of the paralysed and suffering author,
so ghastly with disease that timorous women with child shunned
to look at him, running the gauntlet of jeering rows of sailors and
watermen as he was carried on board ship.

It may be said, that this barbarous custom is peculiar to the
English, and of them only to the lowest degree; that it is an
excrescence of an uncontrolled licentiousness mistaken for liberty,
and never shows itself in men who are polished and refined, in
such manner as human nature requires, to produce that perfection
of which it is susceptible, and to purge away that malevolence of
disposition, of which, at our birth, we partake in common with
the savage creation.[1]

He wrote this when the incident was still rankling, and goes on
to speculate on the nature of " those who, while they boast of
being made after God's own image, seem to bear in their minds
a resemblance of the vilest species of brutes, or rather, indeed,
of our idea of devils: for I don't know that any brutes can be
taxed with such malevolence."

More memorable than Captain Veal perhaps is another character, Mrs Francis, the landlady at Ryde who fleeced and
maltreated her guests at the same time.[2] Before executing her

---

[1] *Voyage to Lisbon*, Wednesday, 26th June.

[2] Fielding's experience of bad inns charging at the same rate as the best
is summed up in an earlier sentence, still not out of date: " The difference
between the best house and the worst is, that at the former you pay largely
for luxury, at the latter for nothing " (Wednesday, 26th January).

portrait, he sets forth the whole theory justifying the ruthless
pictures of hideous exteriors occasionally painted by himself and
at every few pages by Smollett. After recalling Quin's exclamation about another player, " If that fellow be not a rogue, God
Almighty doth not write a legible hand," he observes, "in favour
of the physiognomist, though the law has made him a rogue and
vagabond, that nature is seldom curious in her works within,
without employing some little pains on the outside; and this
more particularly in mischievous characters, in forming which,
as Mr Derham observes in venomous insects, as the sting or saw
of a wasp, she is sometimes wonderfully industrious." Then
comes his pendant to the portrait of Beau Didapper or Mrs
Tow-wouse.

A tyrant, a trickster, and a bully, generally wear the marks of
their several dispositions in their countenances; so do the vixen,
the shrew, the scold, and all other females of the like kind. But,
perhaps, nature had never afforded a stronger example of all this,
than in the case of Mrs Francis. She was a short, squat woman;
her head was closely joined to her shoulders, where it was fixed
somewhat awry; every feature of her countenance was sharp and
pointed; her face was furrowed with the small-pox; and her
complexion, which seemed to be able to turn milk to curds, not a
little resembled in colour such milk as had already undergone that
operation. She appeared, indeed, to have many symptoms of a
deep jaundice in her look; but the strength and firmness of her
voice overbalanced them all; the tone of this was a sharp treble
at a distance, for I seldom heard it on the same floor, but was
usually waked with it in the morning, and entertained with it
almost continually through the whole day.[1]

One passage shows Fielding not so insensible to the glories of
external nature as the strict frugality of setting in his novels
might suggest. The family party were sitting one serene evening
on deck.

Not a single cloud presented itself to our view, and the sun
himself was the only object which engrossed our whole attention.
He did indeed set with a majesty which is incapable of description,
with which, while the horizon was yet blazing with glory, our
eyes were called off to the opposite part, to survey the moon,

[1] Sunday, 19th July.

which was then at full, and which in rising presented us with the second object that this world hath offered to our vision. Compared to these, the pageantry of theatres, or splendour of courts, are sights almost below the regard of children.

Fielding was at that moment not far from his end, and was probably not very sanguine about the curative results of the new climate. But there is no brooding sadness about these final pages, and it is characteristic of his sturdy manhood, his love of good living combined with a cheerful readiness to submit to the call of duty, that the very last job which he busied himself about and left on record was the bespeaking of a good dinner for the party.

Fielding, though his death was untimely, had done his work; *Fielding's* he left nothing unfinished except his trifling reply to Lord *achieve-* Bolingbroke. There is no room to believe that he would have *ment* written any more great novels had he lived longer. *Tom Jones* is incontestably his masterpiece; *Amelia* shows distinct signs of decline. *Tom Jones* is the most important landmark in the whole history of English fiction; Fielding's, in that one book, was the most important work ever done for the development of the novel. This will appear still more clearly as we pursue our history, and see how even those who ranged afar into spaces that Fielding never entered could not emancipate themselves from those canons the rightness of which he made manifest both by precept and by shining example. If the scope of his fiction was limited—more limited on one side even than Richardson's—it was by the limitations of his day and of the finest minds of his day. This man of large physique and bodily prowess, with the soul of a hero, held the balance even between the animal nature of man and a healthy and active intellect guiding the impulses of a tender heart. The powerful mind animating that ample frame did not launch out on speculations foreign to his age. Fielding was no mystic. He was simply one who trusted the dictates of his heart, and contentedly accepted a gospel which he daily saw helping to make men better. He rejected negative philosophies, not on any metaphysical grounds, but, without being afraid of begging the question, because they tended to show " that there were no such things as virtue or goodness really existing in human nature." [1]

[1] *Tom Jones*, vi. 1.

*His
realism
is not
without
ulterior
vision*

The task he undertook was to depict the age as he saw it, not to evolve a superior and more refined world, as was the half-conscious aim of Richardson in his last novel. But it is obvious that, all the while he was painting from life, he had before him the vision of a better state of things which was not too remote for mankind to attain to, were there the will. Among his characters are some, and they not the least lifelike, of as lofty a pitch as could possibly be imagined living sociably with their fellows in the world of that time. With these creations may well be compared the character of an actual person drawn so feelingly in the introduction to the eighth book of *Tom Jones*. The person is evidently Ralph Allen. Now Allen was an admirable and, in his sphere, perhaps a great man. But the sketch of Fielding the man which goes with the present account of Fielding the writer is sadly at fault if it does not exhibit a greater, morally as well as intellectually. Fielding was, not merely one of the finest and worthiest representatives of the age of common sense, but a man with moral convictions and a social outlook very far in advance of his time. That was why, then and for more than a century after his death, only the far-sighted were able to perceive his greatness.

*The
art-form
established
in "Tom
Jones"*

Without any prejudice to Fielding, it may then be granted that his masterpiece is no more than a true, sane, and exquisitely finished picture of his own time, and one that delights all beholders. But this art-form which he established was capable of indefinite expansion. Others would explore the debatable land of the conscious and the unconscious, pursue ideals of superhuman perfection, give body to the spirit of romance, and still work within the framework he had provided. It has often been noticed that his novels contain the germs of every kind of fiction that has come to maturity since. The novel of character, of situation, of plot, the novel of intrigue, the novel of adventure, however they may be differentiated according to the leading characteristic of each, all are there, complete or in embryo, not to mention "the slice of life," the problem novel, or the comic medley typified by *Joseph Andrews* and the sentimental novel by *Amelia*.

To Fielding is due the credit of establishing what may be regarded as the standard form, and of making the variations

possible. Defoe's patient realism had shown how far delineation *Compari-*
of outward and visible things could go, in a hybrid form without *son with*
either the seal of history or the authentication of pure art: he *Defoe and*
had displayed the whole economy of certain sections of life, and *Richardson*
produced a likeness apparently as inexhaustible in its details as
reality itself. Richardson had applied an analogous method to
the inner world of feeling and motive and the cultivation of self-
hood. But fiction that was afraid to call itself fiction, and had
to rely for support on anything extraneous to itself, was obviously
incomplete and unsatisfactory. Defoe and Richardson had merely
got together the materials, provided the stuff out of which the
autonomous work of art might be made; they had not realized
what further industry was demanded of the artist. Fielding took
the material, and cast it into new and fully coherent shapes,
without any distortion of the essential truth. He is the Shakespeare
of English fiction.

Yet hardly any in his own time, certainly not the majority of
those who read him with delight, were aware of the importance
of what had arrived. His case is an exception to the general rule
—that a writer's greatness is fully appreciated by the few in his *The*
own day and not till afterwards by the many, that the verdict of *attitude*
educated readers is more just than that of the multitude. Though *of his*
the vogue he had secured with *Joseph Andrews* and *Tom Jones* *poraries*
lost more than it gained with *Amelia*, it remained so considerable
that his works, singly or collectively, went into edition after
edition during the next two decades. Yet Fielding's greatness
remained without recognition by anyone of eminence in the
world of letters. When Gibbon spoke of *Tom Jones* in the lofty
phrase already quoted,[1] he gave utterance to a conviction that to
his contemporaries sounded monstrous and inexplicable. Only in
very recent times has Fielding met with his deserts; only after
many irrelevant controversies have the rival claims of Fielding's
admirers and Richardson's come to an equilibrium.[2]

[1] See above, p. 77.

[2] The strange vicissitudes of Fielding's fame are recorded with praiseworthy
fullness in Professor F. T. Blanchard's *Fielding the Novelist : A Study in Historical
Criticism* (1926). This "singular story of antagonism and misconception"
is an illuminating chapter in the history of criticism. Only the salient points
are summarized here.

Hostile prejudices   Fielding's intrepid career in drama, in journalism, and latterly on the magisterial bench, had mustered enemies around him from the time when he first came to London till his death, and after his death; his entry into fiction had exasperated one jealous rival who was answerable for another large body of detractors. When he should have been the figure in highest esteem in the world of letters, Fielding, from political animosity, personal malice, or professional spite, was either ignored or vilified in the leading reviews.   The scurrilous *Old England*, organ of the opposite party, left no stone and no garbage unturned to blacken his personal character.   The hidebound *Gentleman's Magazine* sought to crush him with contempt or innuendo.   Pope, Gray, Young, Horace Walpole, Dr Johnson, Bishop Hurd, Chesterfield, all those whose names would exert an authoritative influence upon a writer's prestige, " had either ill words for him or practically none." [1]   Smollett libelled him grossly, although he afterwards tried to make amends.   Fielding's cousin, Lady Mary Wortley Montagu, gave the warrant of a relative to the rumour that he was a debauchee and a spendthrift, that he spent his time as a magistrate " raking in the lowest sinks of vice and misery," and that his books were hastily put together to get him a disreputable living.   These and like unsavoury reports were given a further currency by Walpole and other influential writers, including Dr Johnson.   But perhaps the worst of Fielding's misfortunes was that they were accepted with a great deal more of the same stamp by his supposed friend Arthur Murphy, to whom was entrusted the memoir prefixed to the first collective edition of his works.   Murphy was probably the author of the patronizing and apologetic introduction to *The Journal of a Voyage to Lisbon*. At any rate, he gave the sanction of an intimate friend to scandals that originated in Grub Street libels or in the assumption that Fielding could not have told the stories of Jones and Booth so vividly unless he were retailing his own history.

Richardson's enmity and that of   The author of *Pamela* never forgave the satire in *Joseph Andrews*.   Fielding's popularity was gall and wormwood to his rival; any syllable of praise for *Tom Jones* or *Amelia* was a blow at the creator of Clarissa.   He described Fielding's characters

[1] Blanchard, 126.

and situations as " wretchedly low and dirty," convinced himself *Richard-* that the two blackguards, Jones and Booth, were impersonations *son's* of Fielding himself, and never ceased to traduce his enemy, *friends* together with his works, his wife, and everything that belonged to him, even when that magnanimous enemy lay in the grave. Richardson was the truly representative novelist of that age—the age of sentimentalism rather than of reason; he was the centre of a cult, and his insinuations against the man who represented the modern spirit met with no remonstrance from his adherents and no refutation from Fielding's friends. Dr Johnson, who was under personal obligations to Richardson, loyally supported the author of *Clarissa*, and professed to believe him the greatest of novelists. His heavy declaration that Richardson " taught the passions to move at the command of virtue," and the critical dictum that " Richardson picked the kernel of life . . . while Fielding was contented with the husk," sound ludicrous to-day. Boswell had the sense to rate Fielding more at his proper worth and took the arch-critic severely to task on the subject. It is, indeed, a question whether Johnson was quite honest with himself in his condemnation of Fielding. There is some evidence that he knew in his heart that Fielding was not merely great, but the very criterion by which greatness must be measured.[1] Taken off his guard, he acknowledged all this. " Harry Fielding never drew so good a character ! " he wrote, in congratulating Fanny Burney on *Evelina*. " Very well said ! " he cried, when somebody remarked that " Fielding, who was so admirable in novel-writing, never succeeded when he wrote for the stage." The fallacy on which the view of Johnson and other upholders of the dignity of literature was based—apart from the prejudice due to mendacious gossip—the fallacy that he who paints low life must necessarily himself be low, is now seen to be as illogical as the humorous adage, "Who drives fat oxen should himself be fat "—Dr Johnson's own witticism.

It was hardly to be expected that with so many respectable *Attitude* names against them the women novelists would avow themselves *of Jane* disciples of Fielding. Nevertheless, Maria Edgeworth and Jane *Austen* Austen had read him, and read him with more intelligence than *Edgeworth*

---

[1] Blanchard, 190-205, especially 200-202.

Fanny Burney displayed, and their finest work is essentially the comic realism of *Tom Jones*. Jane Austen, with perhaps the sole exception of Meredith, in spite of her narrower scope, is Fielding's closest parallel in English fiction. Maria Edgeworth thought herself a Richardsonian, and was in truth such in her didactic hours; but when she let her genius have its own way it speedily led her into the region opened up by Fielding. In *Ormond* (1817) she had Richardson's example in view. Harry Ormond came across a copy of *Tom Jones*, and was so enthralled that he " resolved to be what he admired—and if possible to shine forth an Irish Tom Jones." He thinks how pleasant it would be to enjoy life and be an accomplished " blackguard," and become moral after he has had his fling. " Blackguard is a harsh word," writes Miss Edgeworth, " but what other will express the idea? " Subsequently, he makes the acquaintance of Sir Charles Grandison, his feelings are touched, he is inspired with virtuous emulation, and becomes " ambitious to be a *gentleman* in the best and highest sense of the word." Richardson's novel entirely counteracts the effect of the other book, and Ormond " often declared that *Sir Charles Grandison* did him more good than any fiction he ever read in his life." [1] The lesson is a wholesome one and the end most edifying; but, although the history of Harry Ormond and his growth from an aimless youth into a man of high principles is the main theme of the book, the chapters that reveal the genius of Maria Edgeworth are those others in which King Corny and Sir Ulick O'Shane are the principal actors, and these are in the Fielding tradition.

Attitude of the Romantic age towards Fielding, and that of the Victorians   Another who owed far more to Fielding than he was ever conscious of was Sir Walter Scott, who in his faithful portraiture of the life he knew and in the comic delineation of his best characters, though not in the historical romanticism which his admirers overpraised, is in the direct line of descent, howbeit his realism was not an intellectual realism. In his short Life of Fielding he recapitulated the old slanders without taking the trouble to verify them. The first great critics to recognize Fielding's pre-eminence were Coleridge, Hazlitt, and Lamb, who have left some of the wisest observations on the nature of his genius. Leigh Hunt and

[1] *Ormond*, viii.

Byron also paid their tribute; but for the time being these unusual opinions attracted little notice, and the main body of intelligent readers remained indifferent, or clung to the established prejudice. It is amusing to read how the youthful Macaulay got into the wars with supporters of *The Christian Observer* by venturing to express his enthusiasm for *Joseph Andrews*.[1] For now, in the wane of romantic freedom, Malvolio, Tartuffe, and Pecksniff were reinstated in the censorial chair, and hardly budged till the latter part of the reign of Victoria. Cobbett, Miss Ferrier, Archbishop Whateley, and De Quincey could not abide Fielding, and, in the next generation, Carlyle, Tennyson, FitzGerald, Browning, and Charlotte Brontë condemned him. It is not very difficult to understand why the name of Fielding drove Charlotte Brontë into spasms of fury; it is strange, however, that Stevenson knew no better than to describe *Tom Jones* as " dirty, dull, and false." [2] But Stevenson was a romancer, and an historical romancer to boot; and the curious doctrine that historical fiction was more elevated than any other kind of fiction was accepted throughout the Victorian era. Dickens, however, paid due homage to Fielding, as might have been expected of the satirist of Pecksniff and Chadband; but his sanity was counterbalanced by the backsliding of Thackeray, who learned his art from Fielding and then libelled him more insidiously, in the name of a disciple, than Murphy had done in the name of friendship.[3] Ruskin, who apotheosized Sir Charles Grandison, was unable to see anything in Richardson's contemporary. Even Matthew Arnold had no good word for him. Verily, the attitude towards Fielding has been a touchstone for testing the imagination, the sense of humour, and the enlightenment of every period since his time.

George Eliot was the first eminent novelist to declare in unequivocal terms the supremacy of Fielding. But perhaps Meredith may prove to have done more than anyone else to reawaken the spirit of intellectual comedy which must prevail if Fielding is to be appreciated in all his richness. Meredith was an inheritor of Fielding's art who developed it on independent lines, and his *Beginnings of a change —George Eliot and Meredith; the modern view*

---

[1] Blanchard, 356-357.
[2] *Ibid.*, 372.
[3] " Thackeray really did more than any other man has done to stain the memory of Fielding " (Cross, iii. 225).

Essay on Comedy is a handbook to the comedy of *Joseph Andrews* and *Tom Jones*, as well as to that of Molière and Congreve. The researches of Keightley, Austin Dobson, and Mr de Castro, the monumental Life by Professor Cross, and the survey of the occultations of Fielding's fame from which many of these facts have been cited, enable the modern reader to push aside the slanders, contemplate the real man, and form an unprejudiced estimate of the greatness of his work.

CHAPTER IX

SMOLLETT

THE novelists competing for public favour at the middle of the *The three* century were three—Richardson, Fielding, and Smollett. So well *novelists* established by now was the new literary form that even writers *of the day* of such wide orbits as Johnson and Goldsmith availed themselves of it, and half the fun of Sterne's *Tristram Shandy* was in the way he turned the accepted structure upside down and inside out, or made the story go backwards instead of forward. Thus the obvious thing to do, when Smollett found it advisable to add to his income by turning his literary proclivities to account, was to write a novel. A somewhat unfeeling delight in satire, with the opportunities that would naturally arise for avenging miscellaneous grudges and animosities, had also something to do with his choice of an outlet.

Tobias George Smollett (1721-1771) came of a landed family *Smollett's* seated in the Leven valley between Loch Lomond and Dum- *early life* barton. He was the youngest child of the youngest son of Sir James Smollett, laird of Bonhill, and the offspring of an improvident match that had not met with his grandsire's approval. Born in the neighbouring house of Dalquhurn, where Sir James had furnished the pair with just enough to live on, Smollett soon lost his father, and, after receiving the good schooling which is the birthright of every Scotsman, was called upon to earn his own livelihood at the earliest possible moment. The boy was accordingly apprenticed to a Mr George Gordon, medical practitioner in Glasgow, and remained with him till he was eighteen, following the appropriate courses of study at the university. Gordon is supposed to be the man caricatured as Potion in *Roderick Random*; but it would be just as reasonable to identify him with Potion's rival, Crab. Smollett complimented him by name in *Humphry Clinker*,[1] and there are no grounds for believing that Gordon,

---

[1] See Letter of 28th August, from Matt. Bramble to Dr Lewis.

who had professional relations with Sir James of Bonhill, remained on any other than friendly terms with his quondam apprentice.

The Smollett legend

There is, in truth, a Smollett legend, which grew up, like the apocryphal life of Mrs Behn and the Fielding slanders, out of ingenious, or ingenuous, identifications of characters and incidents in *Roderick Random* with Smollett's personal history. As already noted, fiction in the autobiographical form always tempts to such confusions of subject and object; and in Smollett's case it is obvious, and there is no denial on his part or anyone else's, that in this first novel he did use actual occurrences as raw material. But, except for certain ill-considered sallies, he used them as a writer of picaresque fiction was entitled to do; and to try to construct a life of Smollett out of the transformed material is worse than hazardous. In a letter which his biographers have often quoted without taking it properly to heart, Smollett definitely states: "The only similitude between the circumstances of my own Fortune, and those I have attributed to Roderick Random, consists of my being of a reputable Family in Scotland, in my being bred a Surgeon, and having served as a Surgeon's mate on board of a man of war, during the Expedition to Carthagena. The low situations in which I have exhibited Roderick, I never experienced in my own Person." [1] The laird of Bonhill evidently was not over-generous towards the son who married without consulting him, or to that son's children. Smollett's cousins were probably not over-affectionate towards the witty young scapegrace who indited skits and seems to have behaved to them in the manner of a very young Peregrine Pickle. But that Smollett was at feud with the head of the house, at daggers drawn with his kinsmen, and estranged from his old acquaintances in Scotland, for most of his after-life, is disproved by his letters, and still more clearly refuted by the many allusions to actual persons which Smollett, as was his wont, inserted amidst the fiction in *Humphry Clinker*. Sir James was by no means so hard on his son Archibald and the poor cousin whom he married as Roderick's penurious grandfather shows himself in the novel. Yet Smollett felt his position as a moneyless relative acutely enough to be rather fond of portraying purse-proud fathers tyrannously thwarting the

[1] *Letters*, ed. E. S. Noyes, p. 80.

claims of young affection. As a romantic novelist he always took
the side of love, whatever its quality.

Nevertheless, the points of contact between Smollett's life and *Relation-*
his fiction are close and direct, wherefore it behoves us to review *ship of his*
briefly the salient episodes. In middle age he wrote in elegiac *life to his*
terms of his early days, and his could not have been altogether a *fiction.*
disgruntled boyhood, in spite of the satires recorded, on cousins,
fellow-students, and reputable townsfolk in Glasgow. The callow
youth found time, before he left Mr Gordon, to write a tragedy;
and the lamentable history of that tragedy, its intrinsic beauties,
the compliments, sincere or otherwise, which it won from those
he had sought as patrons, and the disappointments met with at
the hands of despotic theatrical managers, are recapitulated at
length in the story of the literary hack, Melopoyn, whom Roderick
Random encounters in the Marshalsea. When Smollett came to
London, in 1739, he brought his tragedy with him. His failure
to get it accepted was a grievance that rankled for years. It was
one of the motives that determined him to leave London and try
his luck in the navy; and as soon—ten years later—as a first
literary success gave the opportunity, he brought it out in print,
to confound the stupidity and malice of those who had banned it.

The play itself is a curiosity. Its subject is the same as that *"The*
of Rossetti's *King's Tragedy*, the murder of James the First of *Regicide"*
Scotland by Sir Robert Graham and Sir Robert Stewart. For
the historic Kate Barlass, who thrust her bare arm through the
staples to keep out the assassins, Smollett substituted the lofty
Eleonora, an inflated doll. Rivals for this lady's hand are the
treacherous Stewart and the loyal Dunbar. The latter dies upon
her corpse, exclaiming:

> O Eleonora! as my flowing blood
> Is mix'd with thine—so may our mingling souls
> To bliss supernal wing our happy—Oh!

Grime, as Smollett calls him, would be a peculiarly noisome
villain if he had any life in him at all. But this tragedy, or heroic
melodrama, is entirely mechanical; and the ranting speeches, in
faultless and charmless blank verse, with its reiterated " Ohs! "
excited the derision of Shebbeare and other unfriendly critics.

Disappointed in his poetic ambitions, Smollett fell back upon the profession to which he had been bred, and securing the post of surgeon's mate on a line-of-battle ship, probably the *Cumberland*, sailed in 1741, in Sir Chaloner Ogle's squadron, for the West Indies, to join Vernon's expedition against the Spaniards in Carthagena.

The Car-thagena Expedi-tion, and his return to England

Smollett long afterwards wrote a detailed historical account of this disastrous affair for his *Compendium of Voyages* (1766). But the classic memorial of the event is Roderick Random's narrative, in the novel published five years after his return to England. So long as this is not read as literal autobiography it can be accepted as an extremely vivid and probably an accurate report by an eye-witness. Vernon and Wentworth, the naval and the military chiefs, were mutually jealous and thwarted each other's orders, with the result that the fleet returned to Jamaica, repulsed, disgraced, and ravaged by disease. Smollett had had his fill of the navy. He stayed long enough in Jamaica to provide himself with a bride, in Miss Nancy Lascelles, a native of the island, by whom, he says, he enjoyed a comfortable though moderate estate, and then came back to England, late in 1742 or early in 1743.[1] He took a house in Downing Street and set up as a surgeon. It was his wife's money, apparently, that enabled him to live in this expensive quarter, where he neighboured the official residence of the Prime Minister; for Smollett never made much of an income from his practice, and he began to entertain a circle of friends, mostly his fellow-countrymen, thereby acquiring a reputation for lavish hospitality and sprightly conversation. One friend and frequent correspondent was the eminent Scottish minister, Dr Alexander Carlyle, who happened to be in Smollett's company when the town went mad with joy at the news of Culloden. Though neither a Tory nor a Jacobite, Smollett was so afflicted at the reports of Cumberland's atrocities after the battle that he composed his affecting poem, *The Tears of Scotland*—the most impassioned and the best-known of many occasional pieces of various date. No copy has been traced earlier than that in a collection of choice poems by various hands published in 1767; but there is some evidence that it went into print at once

1 S. H. Buck, *A Study of Smollett*, 59.

(1746). If so, it was the first work of Smollett's to achieve publication.[1]

This was quickly followed by two satires in Popian couplets, *His entry Advice*, in 1746, and *Reproof*, early in 1747. These are the same *into literature* sort of personal lampoon in the guise of a general reprobation of the vices of the age as Peregrine Pickle is represented as composing after he has lost his fortune and been snubbed by the Minister. The parties aimed at are indicated by initials or similar hints; but little room is left for any mistake, especially in such a case as that of General Cope, who was everybody's butt for running away at Prestonpans. Smollett missed no opportunity of trouncing military or naval commanders responsible for such humiliations. He had hawked *The Regicide* about till he had worked himself into a state of universal exasperation. Another dramatic effort, in the form of an opera, *Alceste*, the music for which was to have been provided by Handel, brought him another rebuff. Rich, of Covent Garden, pronounced it totally unfit for the stage. It was not until 1756 that Smollett at length succeeded in getting a farcical after-piece, *The Reprisal*, put upon the boards at Drury Lane—that is, not until he was the author of three successful novels.

The first of these, *Roderick Random*, appeared in 1748. *"Roderick Random"* Smollett began and finished it in eight months, broken by some long intervals,[2] and the book was none the worse for this rapidity of composition. Not one of the others shows the same dash and pungency of narrative and characterization. In the preface Smollett expounds his views on fiction. He praises Cervantes for curing romance of its vagaries, and converting it "to purposes far more useful and entertaining" than the glorification of chivalry, "by making it assume the sock, and point out the follies of ordinary life." But his own acknowledged model is Le Sage, whom, however, he somewhat unreasonably charges with extravagance, interests too local, and such quick transitions from distress to happiness as afford no time to indulge the pity or "that generous indignation which ought to animate the reader against the sordid and vicious disposition of the world." This last is a pregnant sentence. Smollett was not one of the novelists

[1] S. H. Buck, *Smollett as Poet*, 23-27. [2] *Letters*, 7.

who love their fellow-men.   On the contrary, except for some
mitigation in the last of his novels, he uniformly depicted a world
of spite and ill-nature, envy, conceit, and all uncharitableness.
Hardly anyone in his novels is set in a pleasing light, except at
someone else's expense.   Mutual suspicion and eagerness to take
one another off prevail even between friends.   It was in this
spirit that he set out in *Roderick Random* " to represent modest
merit struggling with every difficulty to which a friendless orphan
is exposed, from his own want of experience, as well as from the
selfishness, envy, malice, and base indifference of mankind."   In
this recital, he goes on, he has "not deviated from nature in the
facts, which are all true in the main, although the circumstances
are altered and disguised, to avoid personal satire." [1]

Smollett afterwards told us what he thought a novel ought to
be.   He conceived it as " a large diffused picture, comprehending
the characters of life, disposed in different groups, and exhibited
in various attitudes," each individual being subservient to the
general plan, which, however, requires one principal personage to
" attract the attention, unite the incidents, unwind the clue of
the labyrinth, and at last close the scene, by virtue of his own
importance." [2]   Thus, whilst the term "memoirs," which he
applied to his first novel, fits them all, and his central figures,
with the exception of Matthew Bramble, are all of them adventurers, he does not follow strictly the picaresque tradition.   It is
only now and then that his heroes turn rogue, or for the mere
fun of the thing make sport of the vices and follies of mankind.
But the structure, consisting in a string of episodes, with no
connection except that they happen to one personage, is of the
regular picaresque order.   After a sufficiency of incident, the
story comes to a huddled conclusion with the sudden enrichment
of the hero and his marriage to the lady whom the novelist had

---

[1] Some persons having been offended by various passages in *Roderick Random*
through supposing the hero to be Smollett himself, he wrote to Dr Carlyle:
"I take the opportunity of declaring to you, in all the sincerity of the most
unreserved friendship, that no person living is aimed at in all the first part of
the book, that is, while the scene is laid in Scotland ; and that (the account of
the expedition to Carthagena excepted) the whole is not so much a representation of my life as that of many other needy Scotch surgeons whom I have
known either personally or by report " (*Letters*, ed. E. S. Noyes, No. 5).
[2] Dedication to *Ferdinand Count Fathom.*

in an earlier chapter thoughtfully provided to be his reward in the last. From beginning to end, the incidents are the staple interest, the incidents for their own sake rather than as stages in a definite journey. And something of the same sort may be predicated of the characters, who come on and go off, displaying their peculiarities for our entertainment, but are all but destitute of any importance as part and parcel of the story: they might be re-sorted and reshuffled at haphazard without much effect upon the course of events. Fielding had dealt in character, as well as in characters. Smollett's concern was with the superficial features of temperament and mannerism in which men differ, not with the deeper human qualities that unite them.

Like his creator, Roderick is a Scot, and grandson of a well-to-do gentleman, who misliked the match between his youngest son and a penniless girl. But the behaviour of Roderick's grandfather towards the needy boy, whose father has disappeared, is unconscionable. The lad's uncle, Tom Bowling, comes to the rescue, but unfortunately soon disappears also, on one of his long voyages, and Roderick anon has to fend for himself. The first cycle of his adventures centres in his chequered journey to London, in search of fortune, in the company of his old schoolfellow Strap. Extraordinary mishaps and rencounters, nocturnal blunders at houses of entertainment, escapes from highwaymen, and other spicy or sensational incidents, succeed each other rapidly, very much in the style made classic by Scarron. Of the approved anti-romantic kind, and the best of that kind, are Strap and Roderick's experiences in London, where they fall victims to modern cony-catchers, and, after an interview with a magistrate who might be first cousin to Fielding's Justice Thrasher, have a narrow escape of Newgate. Roderick tries to enter the navy as a surgeon's assistant, but finds that medical qualifications are not enough without the wherewithal to bribe the underlings of the Navy Office. He takes a situation with a French apothecary, and meets with further ridiculous mishaps. Then, having the hard luck to be seized by a press-gang, he has the good luck to be recognized as a certified practitioner, and to be given the post of surgeon's mate on a man-of-war, which sails with the Carthagena squadron.

The fresh cycle that now begins is the most absorbing part of the story. Smollett confines himself in the main to what might be expected to come under the notice of a young man in Roderick's position, which is indeed an inside view of the filth, the horrors, the brutality and crass stupidity to which he and his shipmates were victims. Theirs, he lets it be assumed, was only the common lot of the rank and file at this period. For a pretended act of insubordination he is pinioned to the deck at the height of an engagement, and endures all the terrors without the relief of taking an active part in the fighting. But even a medical staff with a cargo of sick to look after have time to watch and criticize the tactics of the commanders. Roderick is sarcastic on the blunders committed, and on the alleged favouritism of the authorities at home, who allowed veteran regiments and their officers, who happened to have influence at Court, to remain inactive, whilst raw recruits were sent out as cannon-fodder.[1]

Smollett in this story discovered the sphere of character in which he was to be most at home, and in which his lead was to be followed most brilliantly by future novelists, the seafaring tribe. Lieutenant Bowling and Jack Rattlin, with Commodore Trunnion, Jack Hatchway, and Tom Pipes, from the succeeding novel, were to be the progenitors of a long and distinguished family of skippers and tarpaulins, owing their rank in literature to their genial humours and their picturesque lingo. Morgan the Welshman, descended in right line from Caractacus, was indebted to Shakespeare's Fluellen for his aphoristic Cambrian word-play, but has much about him that is original. Not less striking whilst they hold the deck, though it is the animus of wrath and caricature that vitalizes their features, are the brutal and overbearing Captain Oakum, who clears the sick-bay, as soon as he takes command, by the simple process of ordering the patients on duty; the ignorant sycophant, Dr Macshane, who certifies the invalids as fit; and the perfumed fop, Captain Whiffle, who succeeds Oakum, and comes aboard in a ten-oared barge, overshadowed by a vast umbrella, and is so overcome with the scent of the surgeon's first mate that he has to be plied by his valet with a

[1] Chapter xxiii. is history pure and simple.

smelling-bottle, whilst three footmen sprinkle him and cleanse the cabin of all trace of the intruder.

The third part of Roderick's adventures mixes romance with its direct opposite, and Smollett's brand of romance is crude and insipid. Coming home from the West Indies the hero is shipwrecked, robbed by his mates, and left naked on the shore. He takes service with a middle-aged lady who writes poetry and reads her compositions to the long-suffering footman. Roderick falls in love with her niece, the beautiful Narcissa; and, when it leaks out that he is a scholar and a linguist, the young lady scents a mystery and shows signs of responding. But these tender passages are cut short by a rival of her own class, and the helpless lover has to take flight. He is carried off by smugglers, lands in France, where he has further adventures, enlists, and goes to the wars, meets his old crony Strap, now Monsieur d'Estrapes, and the pair migrate to London, where Roderick enters the world of fashion and proposes to mend his fortunes by marrying an heiress. He makes his way into various sets, fine gentlemen at the ordinaries and coffee-houses, would-be men of letters, rival fortune-hunters— with whom he quarrels over their pretensions to the capricious belle, Melinda—gamesters, quacks, and other targets for Smollett's ridicule. After being fleeced by two noblemen, Strutwell and Straddle, who make a show of pushing his interests with the Ministry, his funds being exhausted, he repairs to Bath to reimburse himself at the card-table or by a lucky marriage. There he encounters Beau Nash, and meets Narcissa again. He wins a few days' fame by trouncing a bully; but in a penniless condition once more returns to London, and presently is arrested for debt and thrown into the Marshalsea. It is here that he comes across the unfortunate Melopoyn, who tells him all about the rejected tragedy, which is of course the story of Smollett's own disappointments.[1] But at the moment when Roderick is in the depths of despair, his uncle, Tom Bowling, hunts him out, secures his

---

[1] The actors, managers, and men of influence who had not Mæcenased Smollett, mentioned under pseudonyms in Melopoyn's story, are Charles Fleetwood of Drury Lane (Supple), Quin (Bellower), Rich, of Covent Garden (Vandal), Garrick (Marmoset), Chesterfield (Sheerwit), Lacy (Brayer). For a full account of Smollett's quarrels over the hapless *Regicide* and other matters see S. H. Buck, *A Study of Smollett*, iii.

release, and takes him abroad on a trading voyage. They fall in with a Spanish don, who turns out to be Roderick's long-lost father, now fabulously rich, and our hero returns in splendour to marry Narcissa, and Strap to wed Miss Williams—the erstwhile broken-down courtesan whom his master had befriended.

This is the briefest summary of a rapid succession of exciting, horrifying, or ludicrous incidents, all related with indefatigable vivacity. The scenes range from the broadest comedy and horse-play to the macabre realism of the carnage or of the medical horrors on shipboard and to the luscious sentiment of the love-business. By far the finest parts are the nautical chapters, in which sea-dogs of every picturesque breed perform their antics, humorous, grotesque, or lurid and blood-curdling. These figures are all outlandish, violent, exaggerated; in Fielding's phrase, they are caricatures, " monsters, not men "; yet they are obvi-ously animated with that life and vigour which comes of direct observation. It is as if Smollett had been in a fury of hatred, disgust, contempt, or derision when he observed them. It is not merely that the laughter provoked is the savage laughter of the satirist rather than the genial laughter of true comedy. Smollett had that peculiar touch of acrid Scottish humour to be recognized in his compatriots Hawes and Dunbar, in the past, and in Charles Johnstone, Burns, and Byron a little later. This was the first time that the real salt-water mariner had appeared in English literature, though often enough land-lubbers and colourless dolls had mas-queraded in seamen's clothes. Smollett heads a long and opulent chapter in English fiction, the novel of the sea, in which he has had such successors as Marryat, Fenimore Cooper, and Michael Scott, Dana and Herman Melville, Clark Russell, Conrad, and W. W. Jacobs, several of them greater than he, others inferior, some vastly different, but all indebted in one way or another to his example.

Little further need be said on the question how far he drew from actual originals. There were at least four claimants for the honour of having sat for Strap; but Smollett has settled that dispute by referring in one of his letters to " my neighbour John Lewis Bookbinder " of Chelsea, " alias Strap." [1] Many of the

---

[1] Noyes, 45 and 119.

nondescripts who put in fleeting appearances in the London
episodes and elsewhere give the impression of having been rapidly
sketched from life, several of the naval personages still more so.
But Smollett's disclaimers must be accorded due weight. As to
Roderick Random himself, in spite of these disclaimers and the
risk of mistaking fiction for history, we can but conclude that at
least as much of the author must have gone to his making as of
Fielding to Tom Jones or Captain Booth, and in the same unintentional way. Smollett would not have regarded young fellows
of the stamp of Roderick and Peregrine as heroes had he not
nursed a secret esteem for some of their least heroic traits, which
evidently did not offend him. If they were not reflections of
himself, they were reflections of what he admired and would have
liked to be.

Smollett is a prince among story-tellers. In sheer narrative
force he has never been beaten. Whether recounting some
sensational or laughable event that happened before his eyes, or
describing what might have happened were life as exciting and
amusing as it ought to be, he makes the reader visualize everything in the sharpest actuality. Pungency, and a knack for just
the right amount of telling detail, characterize the incidents that
rapidly succeed each other in *Roderick Random*; but not the
roguish irony of Le Sage or the more philosophic irony of Fielding.
He is always ready with the pithy phrase and the compulsive
adjective. Smollett's vigorous and incisive style, fluent, but
almost destitute of grace and elegance, was a style unexcelled for
the narration of exciting, extraordinary, or farcical occurrences,
and the portrayal of characters in keeping therewith. That
style is at its best in the dialogue of his salt-water originals,
whose humours vent themselves in a forcible sententiousness that
is nature accentuated. Lieutenant Bowling's passages with
Roderick's dying grandsire and the disappointed relatives round
his corpse after the reading of the will are a first-rate example.
He takes leave of the jubilant young heir, who regrets that he
cannot bait the clergyman with his dogs, since Bowling had
slaughtered the animals when they were baiting Roderick: " You
and your dogs may be damned; I suppose you'll find them with
your old dad, in the latitude of hell. Come, Rory—about ship,

my lad—we must steer another course." With those to whom
the lighter side of his great comic rival appealed, those who
had no taste whatever for the ponderous Richardson, Smollett's
brilliance matched Fielding's. Many readers thought they recognized the same pen, and *Roderick Random* was actually ascribed
to Fielding in the French translation.[1]

The success of this first novel decided Smollett to stick to
literature, or at any rate the manufacture of books, as his right
vocation, the one that was likely to pay, though he still hankered
after the more dignified calling, and tried by fits and starts to
make his mark as a physician. He took the degree of M.D.
at Marischal College, Aberdeen, in 1750, and two years later
published an *Essay on the External Use of Water, with particular
Remarks on the Mineral Waters of Bath.* Another professional
work in which he had some considerable though anonymous part,
either writing or revising it and being paid for the job, was a
treatise entitled *Cases of Midwifery*, published under the name of
a well-known specialist, Dr William Smellie (1753-1754).[2] This
was, however, only one of the miscellaneous pieces of book-
making to which Smollett was driven by his pecuniary needs.
The reputation of a wit which had militated against Fielding's
success in the law was no more helpful to a man intent on setting
up a medical practice. Further, Smollett's unorthodox views
on the Bath waters did not ingratiate him with his professional
brethren; and, popular as he was in his own circle, he failed
to attract patients. One of his translations of foreign classics, a
very liberal and full-flavoured paraphrase of *Gil Blas*, done partly
perhaps by other hands, came out in 1749. About the same time,
probably, he started on his next novel, *Peregrine Pickle*.[3]

The Adventures of Peregrine Pickle appeared in four volumes
in 1751. In 1750 Smollett had been to Paris with his friend
Dr John Moore, afterwards his editor and biographer, and author
of *Zeluco* and other novels, to gather material for his new venture
in fiction, so it has been repeatedly stated in various memoirs;
and, whether that was the actual object of his journey or not, the

---

[1] This *Histoire et Aventures de Roderik Random* was continually published as
a work by Fielding from 1761 onwards. It was included in Fielding's
Œuvres complettes (1804).

[2] Noyes, 135-137.　　　　　　　　　　　　　　　　[3] Buck, 1-2.

results were freely utilized in the second volume. But there is no evidence for the common assumption that he wrote the novel entirely after his return from France. On the contrary, the differ- ence of tone between the earlier chapters and the rest, and the abruptness of the change of scene, seem to indicate that he began it soon after finishing *Roderick Random*, when the spell of the nautical humours enlivening that book was still powerful. By far the best and freshest part of the new story is the business of the garrison and the doings of its inmates, Trunnion, Hatchway, and Pipes. The remainder is but a further instalment of the farcical adventures, practical jokes, and amorous escapades that formed the staple of Roderick's history ashore. The book might have been thrown together anyhow, and the insertion of the " Memoirs of a Lady of Quality " in the third volume severs the thread even of Peregrine's fortunes and exploits, which alone gives any connection to the rambling structure.

Peregrine is a cruder and more insufferable Roderick, though Smollett rarely betrays any suspicion that he is celebrating the deeds and misdeeds of an arrant young blackguard. Before blossoming out into a man of fashion and a callous young egotist, whilst still a mere lad, indeed, he becomes unnaturally and in- credibly an object of aversion to his own mother. He finds no protection from her malice in his weak-kneed father, Gamaliel, but ere long secures a foster-parent in Commodore Hawser Trunnion, and is able henceforth to snap his fingers at his un- friendly kinsfolk. Trunnion resides at the neighbouring garrison, where, defended by walls and moat, with drawbridge up at night and patereroes ready to salute distinguished visitors, he and his old comrade, Lieutenant Hatchway, and the boatswain, Tom Pipes, maintain the sort of life that they used to lead on shipboard, taking watch turn and turn about, and never allowing any member of the female sex to show her face there after dark. Hence uproarious comedy when the hard-bitten and woman-hating commodore is presently seduced, or hoaxed, or browbeaten, into matrimony, and Perry's aunt, Mrs Grizzle, takes up her quarters in the strange household.

The grotesque gambols of these sea-monsters on land is better fun even than the absurdities of their originals in *Roderick Random* on shipboard. Commodore Trunnion's wedding cavalcade sailing to church and delayed by contrary winds still raises a laugh, in spite of the extravagance. It would fall flat, however, without the preposterous dialogue and the briny lingo. To the messenger sent to inquire why they are so late, Mr Trunnion replies: " Hark ye, brother, don't you see we make all possible speed? Go back and tell those who sent you that the wind has shifted since we weighed anchor, and that we are obliged to make very short trips in tacking, by reason of the narrowness of the channel; and that as we lie within six points of the wind, they must make some allowance for variation and lee-way."—" Lord, sir ! " said the valet, " what occasion have you to go zigzag in that manner? Do but clap spurs to your horses, and ride straight forward, and I'll engage you shall be at the church porch in less than a quarter of an hour."—"What ! right in the wind's eye? " answered the commander; " ahey ! brother, where did you learn your navigation? Hawser Trunnion is not to be taught at this time of day how to lie his course, or keep his own reckoning. And as for you, brother, you best know the trim of your own frigate." The tomfoolery of the impish lieutenant and the artless boatswain, playing harlequin and clown, is a rude and boisterous but genuine humour, and even the ill-conditioned pranks of young Peregrine would not grate upon our nerves but for the reflection that the boy is the father of the man.

But Smollett, presumably when he resumed the story after his holiday in France, sent the young scapegrace abroad on the grand tour, and now his jaundiced view of the world got the better of him. His hero is ready to make a butt of anybody whom it is not dangerous to offend; he puts more malice and often enough sheer brutality into his practical jokes, and pursues his amours with cold-blooded indifference to the feelings of his victims and to the allegiance he professes to the distant Emilia. Smollett's caricatures of the ignorant painter whom he calls Pallet, and of the pedantic physician, meant for Akenside, though amusing to those who knew the originals, are the kind of fare that soon grows stale in a novel.[1] And the celebrated entertain-

---

[1] Smollett's conviction that most of the art criticism talked or written by those who had done the galleries on the Continent was either insincere

ment in the manner of the ancients—a scene at which Smollett took as much pains as his learned amphitryon took at the furniture and bill of fare—is a very tedious pleasantry.

Interest revives at the end of the second volume with the advent of the misanthropic Cadwallader Crabtree, who feigns deafness in order to confound those who make fun of him to his face, or who let out everything that they would keep most private, in the fond belief that he cannot hear a word. After having travelled over the greater part of Europe, " as a beggar, pilgrim, priest, soldier, gamester, and quack; and felt the extremes of indigence and opulence, with the inclemency of weather in all its vicissitudes," he has arrived at the same conclusion as Smollett: " that the characters of mankind are everywhere the same; that commonsense and honesty bear an infinitely small proportion to folly and vice; and that life is at best a paltry province." [1] The disillusioned rake and the sage who remains a reprobate at heart, in spite of having experienced the hollowness of pleasure, now join hands, and there is a change in the method of the hoaxes on all and sundry. The chief exploit of the two confederates is to pose as a fortune-teller and his servant, in a comic fashion which is an improvement on the old story of *The Man in the Moone telling Strange Fortunes* [2] and Defoe's semi-fictitious account of Duncan Campbell. [3] Cadwallader's pretended deafness, which enables him to overhear a thousand secrets, and the unsuspected complicity of Peregrine, provide such a stock of scandalous revelations that ladies who come to consult the oracle are dumbfounded to hear their hidden frailties brought up against

---

homage to celebrated names or pure affectation, which is the motive in the caricature of Pallet, was also a reason for his own downright and unorthodox judgments in his *Travels through France and Italy*, which provoked so much criticism from Sterne and others. He set the example of praising what appealed to himself, and many of his verdicts were not so far wrong as his contemporaries made out. Smollett's characterization of Akenside as " a mere index-hunter, who held the eel of science by the tail," may be compared with Sterne's sentence on Smollett, in *A Sentimental Journey* ("In the Street— Calais "): " The learned Smelfungus travelled from Boulogne to Paris—from Paris to Rome—and so on; but he set out with the spleen and jaundice; and every object he passed by was discoloured or distorted. He wrote an account of them; but 'twas nothing but the account of his miserable feelings." Smollett had no right to object to such animadversions of one traveller on another, since he had begun it by satirizing Akenside.

[1] C. lxxii.   [2] See Volume II., p. 233.   [3] Volume III., pp. 177-178.

them. Such omniscience must clearly be nothing less than super-
natural. All this is excellent satire. It is followed by more
buffoonery and picaresque adventure, not very different from
Random's, Peregrine likewise being arrested for debt and put
into the Fleet, as Roderick was into the Marshalsea, and then, in
a final reversal, securing a fortune and his bride.[1]

The best characters, of a different mintage from Cadwallader,
are Commodore Trunnion and Boatswain Pipes, between whom
most readers find it hard to fix their preference. Trunnion,
when Smollett has finished with him, is richer in quaint singularities and the nautical metaphors in which he expounds his
philosophy of life. But his character went through various
changes. At first only a butt, he wormed his way into his author's
affections, and was altered in the course of the story very much
for the better. Pipes remains the simple, loyal, imperturbable
creature he was at the beginning. He is a second Strap, with
the advantage that his oddities are admirably in tune with the
strange humours of Trunnion and Hatchway. What could be
more absurd than his ingenuous attempt to melt Emilia with
the fictitious news that his master has committed suicide in
despair at her rejection? He rushes in apparently speechless
with emotion.

When Pickle's name was mentioned, he seemed to make an
effort to speak, and in a bellowing tone pronounced, " Brought
himself up, split my top-sails ! " So saying, he pointed to his own
neck, and rose upon his tiptoes, by way of explaining the meaning
of his words.

Of a higher order is the commodore's death-scene, in which
Smollett surpassed himself. Here, absurdity and pathos melt into
each other, in a way that without impertinence recalls the death
of Falstaff.[2] And Hatchway's epitaph on his chief has a beauty
in its uncouthness that atones for this practical joker's former

---

[1] One farcical chapter, about the young beggar-woman whom Peregrine
takes home, washes, and dresses up like a lady, teaches how to behave in
polite society, and then introduces to his friends, and who then outrages all
decorum and disgraces her protector by letting fly a volley of oaths in the
drawing-room, strangely anticipates Mr Bernard Shaw's *Pygmalion*, without,
so we must believe, actually suggesting it (C. lxxxvii.).

[2] The comparison has already been made by S. H. Buck (*Smollett as Poet*, 82).

misdeeds. Pickle's father, Gamaliel, and his aunt Grizzle, the latter altered like Trunnion as the story goes on, hold their own as charming originals, even in competition with the Garrison trio.

The other characters are not so engaging. Smollett managed to do his worst with those that he obviously meant to make attractive. His heroines are all milliners' dummies: the heroes who marry them certainly do not deserve anything better. Repeatedly, both Random and Pickle treat their devoted squires with a callous ingratitude which does not seem to have irked their creator in the slightest. Hazlitt said there was " a rude conception of generosity in some of his characters, of which Fielding seems to have been incapable." This virtue, however, comes in, as it were, by a back-stroke; it appears only in such by-characters as Strap and Pipes, and is evidently meant to be relished as a foible, a quaint humour, a choice eccentricity. Peregrine's showy liberality is merely a part of the character he tries to assume as a dashing and open-handed man about town. His rascally attempt upon Emilia's virtue is almost a direct parody of Richardson's *Clarissa*, and in this episode he cuts a deplorable figure—that of a shabby and vulgarized Lovelace, who is spurned by the injured girl in a harangue echoing the very words and gestures of her prototype:

" Ruffian as you are, you durst not harbour one thought of executing your execrable scheme, while you knew my brother was near enough to revenge or prevent the insult; so that you must not only be a treacherous villain, but also a most despicable coward." Having expressed herself in this manner, with a most majestic severity of aspect, she opened the door, and walking downstairs with surprising resolution, committed herself to the care of a watchman, who accommodated her with a hackney-chair, in which she was safely conveyed to her uncle's house.[1]

Again there is the very echo of *Clarissa* in the letter sent by Emilia's mother, informing Peregrine that he has wounded her daughter to the quick and that she is determined not to entertain his offer of reparation:

[1] C. lxxvi. ; *cp.* above pp. 43-44.

My daughter was no upstart, without friends or education, but a young lady, as well bred, and better born, than most private gentlewomen in the kingdom.

And, while the mother hints that he may some day earn forgiveness by future good conduct, Emilia remains implacable long enough to give her lover some wholesome qualms.

Peregrine Pickle as it stands to-day is very much of a farrago; but only those who have examined the first edition of 1751 can appreciate its heterogeneousness to the full, for Smollett seized the opportunity to let fly at all his real or supposed enemies with unrestrained scurrility.   A second edition was not called for till 1758, by which time his feelings towards Garrick, Fielding, Lyttelton, and others whom he had savagely abused, were entirely altered.[1] Not only did he cut out these attacks, he also toned down many passages that offended by sheer grossness.   Thanks for the latter slight improvement are due rather to the rebukes of his critics than to Smollett's own good taste, for he was still to write the obscene and revolting *Adventures of an Atom*.   Along with the rest, the " Memoirs of a lady of quality ' were revised; but since this part of the work is only a certain amount of foreign matter which Smollett allowed to be inserted for a fee, its sole interest, except to those who are curious about ancient scandals, is in the anomalous case of literary ethics that it presents.[2]

[1] Dr H. S. Buck, in *A Study of Smollett, chiefly " Peregrine Pickle "* (1925), shows that there was no second edition in 1751, as has been assumed ever since Smollett's biographer, Anderson, affirmed it.   Dr Buck had the good luck to discover a copy of the actual second edition, of 1758, which had been hitherto overlooked, and of which he seems to think only one copy is extant. He gives a full account of Smollett's quarrels, and the libels they gave rise to in *Roderick Random* and *Peregrine Pickle*.   They hinged almost entirely on the real or imaginary rebuffs sustained in his pertinacious efforts to get *The Regicide* accepted by one or other of the London theatres.   Lyttelton may have offended him by his unwillingness to recommend another play of Smollett's of which only a single mention is known.   He was also Fielding's friend and patron, and Fielding was supposed to have been guilty of plagiarizing from Smollett's Strap and Miss Williams in the characters of Partridge and Miss Matthews.   Lyttelton and Fielding are clumsily satirized in Scrag and Spondy, who disappeared in 1758.   By that time Smollett had also repented of a still more brutal skit upon Fielding, his *Faithful Narrative of the Arts practised upon the brain of Habbakuk Hilding, Justice, Dealer, and Chapman* (1752).

[2] Dr Buck (*ibid.*) collates those passages in which the two editions are at variance; the collation is voluminous.   He also deals with the problem of the " Memoirs," which were the chief attraction of the book for the contemporary public.   Who wrote, and who revised, the " Memoirs "?   Some have asserted

Smollett had written himself out as a story-teller. He had no more yarns to spin of laughable accidents on the road or strange events aboard ship; his menagerie of ocean monsters had all been exhibited. He was now thrown back upon his powers of invention, which were mediocre, to contrive a story that would entertain and characters that would pass muster. But, though a first-class hand at recounting an incident, reproducing a scene, or evoking in colours more vivid than life such figures as had impressed themselves upon his vision, Smollett had little constructive and less creative ability. Within its limits his technique was masterly, but in the powers that make the artist he was singularly deficient. Left to his own resources, when he had exhausted the comedy of the Pickle and Trunnion households, he could only repeat in the second part of *Peregrine Pickle*, with perfunctory variations, the farcical business already employed in *Roderick Random*. With more extensive variations and permutations he now tried to follow up the brilliance of his first novel and the more doubtful success of his second in the laboured and jejune *Ferdinand Count Fathom*. Later he was to apply his talent for humorous characterization to an ill-advised attempt at rivalling the author of *Don Quixote*. And, last of all, in what is in many respects his finest novel, *Humphry Clinker*, he left story-telling alone, and gave a humorous portrayal of manners from the incompatible points of view of several correspondents writing down their private impressions of the same experiences.

He who had accused Fielding of making free with two of his own favourite characters now calmly appropriated from Fielding the idea of a scoundrel-hero. *The Adventures of Ferdinand*

that Smollett wrote them, from materials supplied by Lady Vane, others that she wrote them herself. Dr Shebbeare has also been credited with writing, or at least editing, the lady's story. A similar claim has been put forward for Dennis Mackercher, one of Lady Vane's lovers and also apparently a friend or esteemed acquaintance of Smollett's, to be identified with the magnanimous but not very level-headed gentleman described as Mr M—— in *Peregrine Pickle*. Dr Buck shows that there is no real evidence for Mackercher, whilst the feeble and colourless "elegance" of the style rules out Smollett as the original writer, though not as editor or reviser. Nor is it likely that Shebbeare wrote the "Memoirs." His style elsewhere shows him incapable of writing like this, whereas Smollett was far too capable a writer. Possibly, Shebbeare may have overlooked and corrected the narrative composed by the fair and frail autobiographer. The "Memoirs" must have been the work of Lady Vane, perhaps touched up by Shebbeare; and the revision was hers also, with a correction here and there by Smollett.

Count Fathom (1753) is not, however, written in a tone of ironical admiration. To sustain such an attitude through a long story would have been beyond the capacity of Smollett, who rarely succeeded in preserving the self-consistency of any but the simplest characters from start to finish, and failed badly in the case of this pseudo-hero. His object, he said in the preface, was to set up an evil character as a beacon to warn others from plunging into the gulf of perdition. But it is too evident that he revelled in the tale of misdeeds, as he had done in the misbehaviour of Roderick and Peregrine; and the sham indignation and solemn admonishment with which at intervals he pays obeisance to propriety are unconvincing.[1]

The same preface, as already noted,[2] declares that he regarded the novel as " a large diffused picture." But Smollett was neither a thinker on life and art nor a serious novelist, and this impromptu bit of theorizing need not be taken seriously. *Ferdinand Count Fathom* may be described as a sort of picaresque novel having a thorough-going miscreant instead of a genial rogue as its central figure, and an intricate plot superimposed, in order to produce a contrast with the behaviour and happier fortunes of the virtuous people, and to conduct the malefactor in the end to a most unforeseen state of penitence. Smollett committed the capital mistake of twisting to didactic purposes a story that should have been told either in the spirit of devil-may-care picaresque comedy or with the cool irony of Fielding's *Jonathan Wild*. A cynical beginning is a bad preparation for a sentimental ending. He was never quite sure whether the interest was to be in the exploits and narrow escapes of his adventurer, or in the unmerited sufferings and eventual deliverance of the persons victimized. He failed miserably to excite any interest in his villainous hero's reformation. A repentant picaro is a contradiction that ruins whatever irony there be. An outright rascal should end in the same way as Fielding's Jonathan. Smollett would have appealed to the example of his professed model, Le Sage. Gil Blas reforms when the chance is given him; but then Gil Blas is only half a

---

[1] Yet they satisfied some people—for instance, Smollett's biographer, Dr Robert Anderson (see Smollett's *Miscellaneous Works*, i., " Life," 38-39).
[2] Above, p. 202.

picaro—a rogue not by nature but by circumstance, and never
out and out a villain. And Le Sage did not try to convert his
easygoing scapegrace into a saint.

Smollett, in *Ferdinand Count Fathom*, falls between not two
but a whole row of stools. First, he confounds the tale of picaresque adventure with the criminal biography; then he changes
over to crude romance and the trials and betrayals of two fond
lovers, on to which, for our edification, he patches the absurd
conversion episode. According to his preface, he even mistook
the career of his monster of turpitude for a tragic theme. Howbeit, the only passages that cast any spell upon the modern reader
are of yet another category—those in which Smollett plays upon
our sense of terror and suspense and weaves an atmosphere of
gloom which gives a foretaste of the Gothic novel. The opening
scene is a sardonic tableau in the right picaresque vein. It is the
last scene in life of Ferdinand's mother—a wicked old camp-
follower who meets her death from a wounded officer whom she
is about to dispatch, as she wanders over a battlefield rifling the
fallen. Having kept open house to the regiment, she cannot
pitch on her offspring's individual father. Ferdinand is protected
and brought up by a Spanish count, whose generosity he repays
with the meanest treachery. In villainy he is as precocious as
Jonathan Wild. The duty of the strong and cunning is to prey
upon the rest of mankind, and he begins with his benefactors.
All his chief exploits indeed—his confidence tricks, his mercenary seductions, his elaborate swindles—are at the expense of
those who treat him with tenderness and trust. In the absence
of Fielding's strong intellectual appeal, the reader is revolted.
The narrow escapes alone excite a thrill; and these show a
presence of mind on Ferdinand's part and an audacity belying
the author's assurance that his hero is chicken-hearted.

Ferdinand, however, does not believe in risking his skin on
" the rough field of Mars." When, instead of the peaceful avocations of pilfering and card-sharping, he is invited to take his share
in the horrors of night alarms and skirmishes in the Thirty Years
War, he thinks it more sensible to desert, taking the precaution
beforehand to remove all the portable belongings of his friend,
Count Renaldo, son of his old protector. Here come in the

aforesaid passages of high romanticism. Pretending to be a man of family who has taken umbrage at his treatment by the Germans, Fathom receives a courteous welcome from the French and is enrolled as a volunteer. But nothing is farther from his intentions than to undergo more military service, and he soon contrives to slip off in the direction of Paris. He has good reason to suspect that his Tyrolese servant intends to rob him; so he robs the servant first and takes another road, only to discover that the wily Tyrolese has already emptied the saddle-bags and filled them up with rusty nails. Chagrined, but not yet beaten, our adventurer pursues his way; and late at night, deserted by the guide picked up at a village, he finds himself in the midst of a forest, far from the abodes of men. "The darkness of the night, the silence and solitude of the place, the indistinct images of the trees that appeared on every side, stretching their extravagant arms athwart the gloom, conspired, with the dejection of spirits occasioned by his loss, to disturb his fancy and raise strange phantoms in his imagination."

Mrs Radcliffe herself could not have improved upon the gloomy symphony of sights and sounds and mysterious apprehensions in the account of Ferdinand's night in the forest. Perchance the guide was a decoy, and had left him to give the signal to some gang of robbers. "Fathom halted in the middle of the road, and listened with the most fearful attention; but his sense of hearing was saluted with naught but the dismal sighings of the trees, that seemed to foretell an approaching storm. Accordingly, the heavens contracted a more dreary aspect, the lightning began to gleam, the thunder to roll, and the tempest, raising its voice to a tremendous roar, descended in a torrent of rain." There we have the emotional diction as well as the landscape-painting of the Radcliffe school, but a generation earlier. Striking at random into the forest, to throw the defaulting guide off the scent, Fathom at length discerns a distant light, and finds himself before a lonely cottage, where an old woman receives him with much hospitality. But he is by no means quit of his suspicions. Closely examining the garret to which the beldame has conducted him, he discovers, hid in the straw, the body of a man, still warm, and evidently recently stabbed. Terror gives the frightened man resolution.

He undresses the corpse, puts it in the bed, and takes its place in the straw. About midnight two men creep into the room, and one thrusts a poniard into the supposed sleeper. The compression of the windpipe produces a sort of groan, and, believing they have done his business, they retire, to strip their prey at leisure. Fathom overhears that they have other booty in view, and presently he hears them ride away. Seizing his chance, he faces the old woman, who takes him for the phantom of her murdered guest. He mounts her before him on his horse, and with a pistol at her ear compels her to lead him to a place of safety.

After this picturesque excursion the story reverts to the beaten track. Fathom, like Peregrine Pickle, but in a more professional manner, makes a precarious livelihood at the gaming-table, by predatory amours and by more dangerous frauds. Fleeced by two superior sharps at Paris he has a more successful run in England, but at last, like Random and Pickle, finds himself in gaol, and, like them, waiting for a rescuer. The rescuer arrives. It is none other than Count Renaldo, still under the delusion that Fathom's disappearance was due to his being captured by the enemy. He now empties his purse to set the unfortunate at large. At this point the mystifications and coincidences of the romantic plot are linked up with the other, in a fashion much admired by Smollett's contemporaries. Renaldo is in love with a beautiful stranger, and whilst he returns to Austria to prepare for their union he leaves her in his friend's custody. But Fathom has already determined to make this innocent creature his own prize. He tries every device to undermine her virtue, till, urged to desperation, she has no refuge but the grave. Too late, Renaldo becomes apprised of Fathom's real character, and hurries back. There is no need to be uneasy, however; all this is only in preparation for the two most romantic strokes of the whole intrigue. Renaldo determines to pay a nightly visit, whilst in England, to the tomb of the hapless Monimia. At midnight he is admitted to the church, and as he throws himself on the cold stones he hears solemn notes issue from the organ, played by an invisible hand. Suddenly a white shape appears; it is that of Monimia. In exalted tones he addresses the departed spirit. But the apparition starts away, and, sinking on a chair, sighs: " Indeed, this is too much ! " Renaldo catches in his arms, " not the shadow, but the warm substance of the all-accomplished Monimia." She had sought a refuge in the grave, but it had been a sham funeral. The other stroke is on a par with this: it is Ferdinand's sudden contrition and his forgiveness by those whom he had wronged. Smollett enjoyed this sentimentalism so much that he reintroduced the chief actors years later in *Humphry Clinker*, where Fathom is rediscovered as a village apothecary in Yorkshire and " a sincere convert to virtue." By a pleasing accident he becomes the rescuer of the count and countess from a murderous attack by highwaymen. In such a sequel and such a postscript Smollett fitted an anticlimax to what had gone before, and made romanticism absurd. His earlier effort in that vein, the adventure in the forest, had succeeded, because he did not push it too far. Somewhat in the manner of the contemporary graveyard poets, it conjured up an atmosphere of gloom and terror, to which Smollett, who in *Roderick Random* had painted some ghastly scenes from memory, knew how to impart a fearful actuality. *Ferdinand Count Fathom* is as much a farrago as the previous novel, and an awkward combination of old materials and new. The new features give it a curious historical interest.[1]

For the next few years Smollett gave novel-writing a rest; he was too busy with the wholesale production of a more sober kind of literature, from the establishment at Chelsea, where, according to a malicious rival, he had under him " several journeymen-authors," and was prepared to undertake " tragedy, comedy, farces, history, novels, voyages, treatises in midwifery, and in physic, and on all kinds of polite letters." [2] Malicious, but no exaggeration. He was already at work upon a translation of *Don Quixote*, which eventually appeared in 1755, and was alleged by the ill-disposed to be only a rehash of Jarvis's version of 1742.[3] Later on he put his name as editor or translator-in-chief to English editions of the works of Voltaire and of Fénelon's *Télémaque*,

---

1 For an identification of some of the loans from picaresque novelists, see F. W. Chandler, *The Literature of Roguery*, ii. 313-318.

2 Dr Shebbeare (see Smollett's *Letters*, ed. E. S. Noyes, 168).

3 The better-disposed could not but admit that it was "little else than an improved edition" of Jarvis (*e.g.* Anderson, in the Life prefaced to *Miscellaneous Works* of Smollett, i. 52).

the former in thirty-eight volumes. In 1756 he accepted the editorship of a new literary organ, *The Critical Review*. This gave him plenty of work, and also a platform for expressing his likes and dislikes with his customary force and frankness. By some judicious compliments he reingratiated himself with Garrick, one result of which was that his smart little naval extravaganza, *The Reprisal*, was accepted, and made a popular hit at Drury Lane in 1757. Equally ready to give or to take offence, Smollett quickly found himself embroiled with many enemies, old and new. The most troublesome quarrel was with Admiral Knowles, whose conduct during the Carthagena affair had not met with Smollett's approval, and who was now violently assailed for pusillanimous behaviour in an action off Rochefort. Knowles at last took legal proceedings and Smollett was fined and imprisoned for three months in the King's Bench (1759). He spent the time writing a short novel, *The Adventures of Sir Launcelot Greaves*, which appeared as a serial in a new periodical, *The British Magazine* (1760), of the management of which Smollett took charge, assisted by Goldsmith.

These were not all the undertakings with which his hands were full. The most formidable was his *History of England*, a mercenary venture intended to compete with Hume's, of which two volumes had already come out and the remainder were known to be in preparation. Smollett boasted that he read some three hundred books in the short time at his disposal if he was to forestall his rival, and he wrote at the same tremendous pressure. So far as his designs on the purchasing public were concerned, he was the winner. He brought out four volumes in 1757, and a continuation in five volumes in 1763-1765. For history of the old-fashioned kind, and a compilation at that, it was by no means bad ; Smollett's narrative power and vigorous style made it eminently readable, and it held its own until all old-fashioned histories came to be superseded. Another huge piece of book-making was *A Compendium of Authentic and Entertaining Voyages*, in seven volumes (1766), and yet another, a geographical, historical, and statistical work entitled *The Present State of all Nations*, in eight volumes (1768-1769). Smollett was employed as swashbuckler by Bute and the Tories in a newspaper, *The Briton* (1762-1763), although he had not yet cut his connection with *The Critical Review* and *The British Magazine*. The scurrilous war between this print and *The North Briton*, started in opposition by Wilkes, is a part of English history.[1]

" Launce-lot Greaves "   With the exception of such disjointed things as *The Coverley Papers*, *Launcelot Greaves* was the first novel to appear serially in English.[2] Smollett had finished his revised version of *Don Quixote* four or five years ago, and it was a cheap and easy pleasantry to take the superficial features of Cervantes' story and transfer them to eighteenth-century England. It was partly for the sake of the drollery, and partly as one way of relieving his irritability at political humbug, religious fanaticism, and the other annoyances that obstructed Smollett's vision. The satire is of a random and very miscellaneous kind. Smollett was not pleased with either Whigs or Tories. His redresser of grievances denounces both candidates in the scene at the hustings—a scene which may have given suggestions both to the author of *Melincourt* and to the author of *Pickwick*. Sir Valentine's speech to the " Gentlemen vreeholders of this county " is in the rustic style of Squire Western, but the different harangues point towards those addressed to Peacock's Mr Christopher Corporate in the great election for the borough of Onevote. There are other anticipations of things afterwards famous in fiction. Captain Crowe's brother-in-law in his mode of diction is a prototype of Mr Jingle.

" I'll tell you what, brother, you seem to be a—ship deep laden —rich cargo—current setting into the bay—hard gale—lee-shore —all hands in the boat—tow round the headland—self pulling for dear blood, against the whole crew. Snap go the finger-braces —crack went the eye-blocks—Bounce day-light—flash star-light —down I foundered, dark as hell—whizz went my ears, and my head spun like a whirligig."

The incident of the squire's being put in the stocks through the machinations of Ferret also makes one think of a similar incident

---

[1] Much new light on Smollett's quarrel with Wilkes and its consequences is provided by Dr Noyes's edition of the *Letters*.

[2] It appeared in *The British Magazine* (January 1760–December 1761). Goldsmith's *Citizen of the World* was coming out in *The Public Ledger* during 1760-1761, and was slightly later.

in *Pickwick*. Ferret, by the way, is a caricature of Smollett's enemy Shebbeare. One of Mrs Malaprop's many predecessors may be recognized, and also the voice of Bob Sawyer's landlady:

"Woman!" cried Mrs Gobble, impurpled with wrath, and fixing her hands on her sides, by way of defiance, "I scorn your words. Marry come up, woman! quotha; no more a woman than your worship." Then bursting into tears, "Husband," continued she, "if you had the soul of a louse, you would not suffer me to be abused at this rate; you would not sit still on the bench, and hear your spouse called such contemptible epitaphs."

Smollett tried to improve upon Cervantes by producing a pair of Quixotes. Sir Launcelot has his Sancho in Timothy Crabshaw, and a double in Captain Crowe — the sea-dog turned knight-errant. The combination of nautical and chevaleresque buffoonery is startling and rather amusing, but the salty lingo has by now become a mere mechanical trick. Crowe relates how

he descried five or six men on horseback, bearing up full in his teeth; upon which he threw his sails aback, and prepared for action—that he hailed them at a considerable distance, and bade them bring to; when they came alongside, notwithstanding his hail, he ordered them to clew up their courses, and furl their top-sails, otherwise he would be foul of their quarters—that hearing this salute, they luffed all at once, till their cloth shook in the wind; then he hallooed, in a loud voice, that his sweetheart, Besselia Mizzen, wore the broad pendant of beauty; to which they must strike their top-sails, on pain of being sent to the bottom —that after having eyed him for some time with astonishment, they clapped on all their sails, some of them running under his stern, and others athwart his forefoot, and got clear off—that, not satisfied with running ahead, they all of a sudden tacked about; and one of them boarding him on the lee-quarter, gave him such a drubbing about his upper-works, that the lights danced in his lanterns; that he returned the salute with his hop-pole so effectually, that his aggressor broached to in the twinkling of a handspike; and then he was engaged with all the rest of the enemy, except one, who sheered off, and soon returned with a mosquito fleet of small craft, who had done him considerable damage; and, in all probability, would have made a prize of him, hadn't he been brought off by the knight's gallantry.

But the peculiar interest of *Launcelot Greaves*, as of *Ferdinand Count Fathom*, lies in certain novelties that were afterwards to become regular form with many writers of fiction. Thus, at the outset, instead of a methodical introduction, Smollett paints a little tableau in the Scarron style. In the kitchen of the Black Lion—a hostelry on the road from York to London—a group of travellers and the landlady with her two daughters are found in very natural conversation; and at once we are plunged into the middle of things. Further, with no small skill, Smollett manages continually to carry the story forward by means of dialogue and by-play instead of regular narrative; in short, he provides something like a conversation novel, without, however, scanting incident. Unfortunately, he did not bestow half enough pains on the book, and so did not make much out of his departures from ordinary practice. The satire nearly always misses fire, and the work as a whole is hastily cobbled up and not worthy of an experienced novelist.

Smollett inserted in *Humphry Clinker* a fancy sketch of himself at home at Monmouth House, Chelsea, where he lived and worked from 1752 till his visit to Italy in 1763. Jerry Melford describes how he was taken down by Dick Ivy to see Mr S. and his "assembly of Grubs," and found him living on the skirts of the town, where "every Sunday his house is open to all unfortunate brothers of the quill, whom he treats with beef, pudding, and potatoes, port, punch, and Calvert's entire butt beer." "At two in the afternoon, I found myself one of ten messmates seated at table; and I question if the whole kingdom could produce such another assembly of originals." Mr S. gives this crew of oddities every chance of showing off their several talents; in short, he puts them through their paces, unperturbed by their lack of respect for himself. Dick explains to the bewildered Mr Melford that S. himself is an eccentric, who befriends these sorry creatures, though "he knows them to be bad men, as well as bad writers," and is likely to be disappointed if he thinks he can make them serve either his profit or his ambition. S., he goes on, brought a hornets' nest about his ears by assuming the editorship of a critical journal, and, strange to say, is perfectly aware that the persons whom he has just been entertaining are the authors of most of the abuse with which he has been assailed, in papers, poems, and pamphlets. He is a man who does not know the value of money, and whose pride is gratified by the homage of these literary retainers. Dick, however, cannot persuade his friend that this is a fair view of the case, and Mr Melford sums it up thus for the benefit of his correspondent: "By all accounts, S. is not without weakness and caprice; but he is certainly good-humoured and civilized: nor do I find that there is anything overbearing, cruel, or implacable in his disposition." [1] Dr Carlyle, however, bears witness that Smollett really was unkind enough to entertain himself and his friends with the queer foibles of his literary myrmidons. [2]

But Smollett's life during these years was not all idyll or all amusement. He was the slave of the booksellers, although the overseer of inferior slaves; and he had good reason for making the rich bookseller Birkin, otherwise not unkindly portrayed, in *Humphry Clinker*, threaten the joker at his expense with writs and indictments, since the poor devil was after all a writer in his own pay. That Smollett produced nothing of first-class quality between his first two novels and his last was due to the ever-lasting drudgery to which an irregular income and spendthrift habits condemned him. He is continually writing to his friends in some such phrase as: "I must infallibly find 50*l.* in a few days in order to maintain myself in any sort of tranquillity." [3] The value of his wife's West Indian property went steadily down, and the income was often behindhand. Smollett received two thousand pounds for his *History of England*; not bad pay, but subject to various deductions. His middleman profits, when he had paid his underlings and sold a work to the booksellers, could never have been princely. In 1763 things had reached a crisis. Smollett was labouring under misfortune and mortification. *The North Briton* had killed *The Briton*. He was in bad repute with all parties. Now his health broke down, and he received a blow from which he never recovered in the death of his daughter and only child. The stricken man " gave up all

---

[1] *Humphry Clinker*, letter to Sir Watkin Phillips, 10th June.
[2] *Autobiography* of Alexander Carlyle, ed. J. H. Burton (1910), 355-356.
[3] *Letters*, ed. E. S. Noyes, p. 49; and *passim* for other references to his pecuniary straits.

connexion with the *Critical Review*, and every other literary system," [1] and quitted England.

Smollett's His two volumes of *Travels through France and Italy* (1766)
"Travels" are a readable and characteristic book, and might have been a work of literature had it only occurred to Smollett to make over his experiences into fiction, as he afterwards did with similar materials. He adopted the attitude throughout of the critical and independent observer, who ridicules the hackneyed compliments and the hackneyed complaints of the conventional traveller, and is determined to say what he himself thinks, especially when it is the exact opposite to accepted opinion. As Sterne put it, in *A Sentimental Journey*: "The learned Smelfungus travelled from Boulogne to Paris—from Paris to Rome—and so on; but he set out with the spleen and jaundice; and every object he passed by was discoloured or distorted.—He wrote an account of them; but 'twas nothing but the account of his miserable feelings." That was the sneer of a rival. But there were misanthropic outbursts enough in the book to provoke it—such, for instance, as the sweeping reflection suggested by the tie between any rich devotee and her confessor:

> For my part, I never knew a fanatic that was not a hypocrite at bottom. Their pretensions to superior sanctity, and an absolute conquest over all the passions, which human nature was never yet able to subdue, introduce a habit of dissimulation, which, like all other habits, is confirmed by use, till at length they become adepts in the art and science of hypocrisy. Enthusiasm and hypocrisy are by no means incompatible. The wildest fanatics I ever knew, were real sensualists in their way of living, and cunning cheats in their dealings with mankind.[2]

His On his return to England in 1765 Smollett was better neither
journey to in health nor in temper. He went to Bath—a place that suited
Scotland him, in spite of many caustic diatribes at its expense. Then he made a long-contemplated journey to Scotland (1766), the tour which gave him the theme of *Humphry Clinker*, and in the course of it saw various friends with whom he had kept up a more or less desultory correspondence, and renewed some old and half-

---

[1] *Letters*, ed. E. S. Noyes, p. 96.
[2] *Travels*, Letter V.

forgotten acquaintances. But apparently it was not such a cheerful progress as Matthew Bramble's. He wrote, on returning to
Bath, where he experienced a surprising access of his old vigour:

Had I been as well in summer, I should have exquisitely enjoyed
my expedition to Scotland, which was productive to me of nothing
but misery and disgust. Between friends [he is writing to Dr
John Moore] I am now convinced that my brain was in some
measure affected, for I had a kind of coma upon me from April
to November without intermission.[1]

His recovery was in fact but short-lived. Smollett had a presentiment that he would be forced to return to Italy, and that
his next exile would be a final one. Before his journey to France
and Italy he had tried to obtain a consulship abroad. There
seems to have been talk of giving him a pension, no doubt in
recompense for his services to the Bute administration,[2] but he
patriotically urged his preference for a post that would enable
him to earn his salary. He now renewed his application for a
consulship; but Shelburne proved as unsympathetic as Pitt and
Bute had been previously. These disappointments help to explain
the rancour and violence of the personal satire in *The History
and Adventures of an Atom* (1769), published anonymously the
year before he again left England with his wife for Italy, where
in another year he was to die.

This elaborate skit on a host of enemies belongs to the same "*The Ad-
unsavoury order of secret histories as *The New Atalantis* and the *ventures of
History of the Court of Caramania*.[3] The idea of the inanimate *an Atom*"
object figuring as a spy had been used over and over again in all
sorts of scandalous chronicles, and only recently Charles Johnstone,
in *Chrysal, or the Adventures of a Guinea* (1760-1765), had
employed it in a satirical account of affairs at home and abroad
during the epoch of the Seven Years War, which is hardly less
scurrilous than Smollett's. Swift's *Gulliver* had not been without
some general influence on this class of satire, and it may be that
Smollett had read the spurious continuation of *Candide*, though he
disclaimed more than " a small part " in the English edition of

---

[1] *Letters*, ed. E. S. Noyes, p. 100.
[2] *Ibid.*, pp. 78-79 and 204-206.
[3] See Volume III., pp. 116-117.

Voltaire's works, which part included the notes historical and critical.[1] But in this lampoon he imitated nobody in particular; he simply varied a well-worn device in an ingenious way, and directed it against everyone he disliked with entire disregard for good feeling or natural squeamishness.

It is an allegorical history of British affairs, from 1754—the eve of the Seven Years War—to 1765, when the agitation against the Stamp Act drove Bute into retirement. The Wilkes business and the warfare between *The Briton* and *The North Briton* naturally take a prominent place in a perversion of history the main object of which was to stigmatize as scoundrels or nincompoops all the public men that Smollett hated, and his ferocity excepted no one. A purely fantastic Japan stands for Great Britain, the north island for Scotland and the south for England; the objects of his malice are distinguished by pseudo-Japanese names, many of them flavoured with obscene suggestion. Yakstrot (Bute), Orator Taycho (Chatham), Fika-kaka (Newcastle), and Jan-kidtzin (Wilkes) are held up to savage derision, and the hits at Got-hama-baba (George II.) would have been treasonable in the preceding reign. Smollett, at any rate, deserves credit for his intrepidity. His very foulness is in his case, as it was in Swift's, inseparable from a certain devastating power, though the perverse ingenuity and artificiality of the fable made it practically ineffectual. It was all too unreal to do much damage, except to Smollett's own reputation. His old resentment at the treatment of his native country after "The Forty-Five" is heard in the sarcastic allusion to the hero Qamba-cun-dono (Cumberland):

While the amiable Qamba-cun-dono was employed in the godlike office of gathering together and cherishing under his wings the poor, dispersed, forlorn widows and orphans, whom the savage hand of war had deprived of parent, husband, home, and sustenance; while he, in the north, gathered these miserable creatures, even as a hen gathereth her chickens; Sti-phi-rum-poo and other judges in the south were condemning such of their parents and husbands as survived the sword, to crucifixion, cauldrons of boiling oil, or exenteration; and the people were indulging their appetites by feasting on the viscera thus extracted.

[1] *Letters*, ed. E. S. Noyes, p. 82.

He continues, in the manner of Swift's *Modest Proposal*, to discuss the economic advantages that might have been secured by proper marketing of the butcher's meat and offal from Jacobite prisoners. More deadly is the contemptuous good nature with which he sums up Bute's merits and demerits, concluding :

It was here he over-rated his own importance. His virtue became the dupe of his vanity. Nature had denied him shining talents, as well as that easiness of deportment, that affability, liberal turn, and versatile genius, without which no man can ever figure at the head of an administration. Nothing could be more absurd than his being charged with want of parts and understanding to guide the helm of government, considering how happily it had been conducted for many years by Fika-kaka [Newcastle], whose natural genius would have been found unequal even to the art and mystery of wool-combing.[1]

When, at the end of 1768, Smollett left England he knew that he was going into " perpetual exile." He rusticated himself on the slopes of Monte Nero, four miles from Leghorn, in a delightful and salubrious spot overlooking the sea, and there, in spite of a jocular proposal to his friend, Dr John Hunter, that his body, now dry and emaciated, should be mummified and sent home for medical purposes, he seems to have recovered enough vigour to enjoy life, and certainly enough to have enjoyed writing his last novel, *The Expedition of Humphry Clinker* (1771).[2] To cast a novel into the form of a diary of a tour was decidedly heterodox. There had been nothing exactly like it since fiction had come of age; though in days of inexperience there had

---

[1] A very defective key to *The Adventures of an Atom* will be found in William Davis's *Second Journey round the Library of a Bibliomaniac* (1825), pp. 116-118. Other characters than those mentioned above are : Apothecary (Dr Hill), Bupo (George I.), Bihn-goh (Admiral Byng), Brut-an-tiffi (Frederick of Prussia), the Great Cham (the Emperor), Fokhsirokhu (Fox, afterwards Lord Holland), Fas-khan (Boscawen), Gotto-mio (Duke of Bedford), Gio-gio (George III.), Lhur-chir (Churchill, the poet), Mura-clami (Murray, afterwards Lord Mansfield), Praff-fog (Pratt, afterwards Lord Camden), Rhum-kikh (Lord Mayor Beckford), Thon-syn (Colonel George Townshend) ,Twitz-er (Grenville), Ya-loff (General Wolfe), Zan-ti-fic (Sandwich). China is France ; Corea, Spain ; Fakku-basi, the House of Hanover ; Fatsissio, America ; Meaco, London ; Pekin, Paris ; Ximo, Scotland ; Xicoco, Ireland ; Quib-quab, Quebec. The Shit-tilk-ums-heit, or " more fool than knave," are the Tories, the She-it-kums-hi-til, or " more knave than fool," the Whigs.

[2] See E. S. Noyes' notes to *Letters*, 232. No doubt *Humphry Clinker* was begun before Smollett left England.

been something of the sort, *The Unfortunate Traveller*, for instance, not to mention Defoe's travel-stories, which are not a very relevant comparison. But Sterne had published his *Sentimental Journey* (1768), which Smollett probably read, as he unquestionably had read *Tristram Shandy* (1759-1767). The immediate suggestion, however, came from Anstey's *New Bath Guide* (1766), a collection of letters in doggerel rhymes, supposed to be written by a family staying at Bath. Here is that fruitful idea, out of which Smollett drew such fresh and exhilarating comedy, of a batch of incongruous diarists chronicling the same occurrences. For this is not the epistolary method of Richardson, employed to record the successive phases of a mental and emotional history, but a new way of playing humours off one against another. Anstey provides the romantic young lady—inditing letters to her friends in verse more elegant and refined—the crusty old valetudinarian, the lady of fashion, the lady of no fashion, the medical fraternity, and the crowd at the Pump Room and the baths. There are also the raw maid-servant Tabitha, the preacher Nicodemus, and even the ghost of Mr Quin, whom Mr Bramble, in *Humphry Clinker*, meets in his mortal shape. Thus the correspondences in the personages between the poem and the novel are not slight or accidental. Incidents, also, are repeated; for instance, the noisy greeting from the town waits, which was received in as different a spirit by the various individuals in Anstey's lodging-house as by Mr Bramble and his retinue in *Humphry Clinker* :

> For when we arriv'd here at Bath t'other day,
> They came to our lodgings on purpose to play;
> And I thought it was right, as the music was come,
> To foot it a little, in Tabitha's room;
> For practice makes perfect, as often I've read,
> And to heels is of service as well as the head:
> But the lodgers were shock'd such a noise we should make,
> And the ladies declar'd that we kept them awake;
> Lord Ringbone, who lay in the parlour below,
> On account of the gout he had got in his toe,
> Began, on a sudden, to curse and to swear:
> I protest, my dear mother, 'twas shocking to hear
> The oaths of that reprobate gouty old peer.[1]

[1] *New Bath Guide*, Letter V.

It is a reasonable conjecture that Smollett saw what fun could be got out of a more elaborate story of a sojourn in Bath, and a tour, something like his own, to the north, whilst he was an invalid at this watering-place in 1767, when he no doubt read Anstey's recent effusion.

He had gone there on returning from Scotland. Matthew Bramble's peregrination is based on a real journey, and not all the incidents are transmuted into fiction. Along with the fictitious adventures which provide the entertainment numerous facts and observations of a prosy, statistical order are set down, as if Smollett were keeping a real diary of his travels. What the "Expedition" would have been without the fiction, the incentive to which came partly from Anstey and partly from Sterne, may be judged by the previous book of travels. His own tour had been disappointing, through the ill-health that dogged his footsteps. So Smollett solaced himself by describing the tour he would like it to have been, with the company and the casual encounters in which his soul would have delighted. Mr Bramble is not a portrait of himself, but the middle-aged and mellowed Smollett's idea of a shrewd, good-natured, highly temperamental gentleman, who, after many hard rubs with the world, has made up his mind to laugh at its incurable follies, or, if these are too much for his irascibility, to enjoy his own outbreaks of furious invective. Bramble is the author himself in the same sense and to the same extent as Roderick Random and Peregrine Pickle were his youthful self, no more. Naturally, Smollett puts into the mouth of this favourite character many of his own opinions, and always lets him have the last word on any disputatious topic. His Welshman's fierce tirades about the insanitary conditions at the fashionable health resort are an exaggerated version of his own professional criticisms. It is only one of Smollett's misanthropic outbursts when Mr Bramble exclaims:

There is another point, which I would much rather see determined; whether the world was always as contemptible as it appears to me at present? If the morals of mankind have not contracted an extraordinary degree of depravity within these thirty years, then must I be infected with the common vice of old men, "*difficilis, querulus, laudator temporis acti*"; or, which is more probable, the impetuous pursuits and avocations of youth have formerly hindered me from observing those rotten parts of human nature, which now appear so offensively to my observation.[1]

The rest of the party are rough-sketched by Matt. Bramble in an early letter to his old friend and correspondent, Dr Lewis, Liddy, his niece, coming first:

She is a poor good-natured simpleton, as soft as butter, and as easily melted: not that she is a fool; the girl's parts are not despicable, and her education has not been neglected; that is to say, she can write and spell, and speak French, and play upon the harpsichord; then she dances so finely, has a good figure, and is very well inclined; but she is deficient in spirit, and so susceptible, and so tender forsooth! Truly, she has got a languishing eye, and reads romances. Then there is her brother, Squire Jerry, a pert jackanapes, full of college petulance and self-conceit; proud as a German count, and as hot and hasty as a Welsh mountaineer. As for that fantastical animal, my sister Tabby, you are no stranger to her qualifications. I vow to God, she is sometimes so intolerable, that I almost think she is the devil incarnate come to torment me for my sins; and yet I am conscious of no sins that ought to entail such family-plagues upon me.[2]

The niece and her aunt have every appearance of being creations in the same two different veins as Smollett's earlier feminine characters. Miss Lydia is a somewhat less vapid young lady than Narcissa and Emilia. Tabitha Bramble is a superior article of the same manufacture as Peregrine's aunt, Grizzle Trunnion. She is drawn with the pen of a caricaturist, who seems to be

---

[1] Letter to Dr Lewis, 8th June. Just as in his *Travels*, Smollett, through Mr Bramble or ironically through the pedantic remarks of his young Oxonian, Mr Melford, delivers himself of heterodox opinions on all manner of subjects. Some of the most heterodox were not, however, so entirely his own as they may seem to the reader to-day. The theory that the Gothic style is Saracen, for example, and that it was imported into England from Spain, where it had been established by the Moors (see Mr Bramble's letter to Dr Lewis, 4th July), was accepted by a good many—by Thomas Warton, for instance, with whose hypothesis that the romances had a similar origin, or were at least profoundly influenced by Oriental fiction introduced through Spain, it was thoroughly in harmony.

[2] Letter to Dr Lewis, 17th April. In Galt's *Ayrshire Legatees*, which is closely modelled on *Humphry Clinker*, the romantic young lady and the ponderous and pompous young intellectual are reproduced in the brother and sister, Miss Rachel and Mr Andrew Pringle.

placidly emptying upon her all the vials of misogyny; she is a grotesque but perfectly natural mixture of stupidity, primitive cunning, and primitive rapacity. The workings of a dim intellect are admirably rendered in the way she identifies her private interests with the intentions of Providence and the moral welfare of the servants at home. It is many degrees below hypocrisy. " God forbid that I should lack Christian charity," she writes to the housekeeper at Brambleton Hall, " but charity begins at huom : and sure nothing can be a more charitable work than to rid the family of such vermine "—as idle and wasteful servants. " Pray order everything for the best, and be frugal, and keep the maids to their labour. If I had a private opportunity, I would send them some hymns to sing instead of profane ballads; but, as I can't, they and you must be contented with the prayers of your assured friend, T. BRAMBLE." [1]

Not so complete a grotesque, but of a similar make, is the hand-maid, Winifred Jenkins, a most lifelike blend of ignorance and simplicity, with shrewdness and cunning. When by her wedding with Humphry Clinker, who has been recognized as a by-blow of Matt. Bramble, she is " removed to a higher spear," and ex-cuses herself from " being familiar with the lower sarvants of the family," who are exhorted to " behave respectful and keep a proper distance," a hit at the classic ending of Pamela's story, with some reminiscence of Fielding's parody, is fairly obvious. Again, the workings of a muddled brain are accurately and delightfully shown, as in her account of the savage Highlanders, who " speak Velsh, but the words are different."

Humphry Clinker is a new version of the simple-minded faith-ful henchman, such as Strap or Tom Pipes. Smollett, like enough, had not thought of him when he began the story; Humphry probably came into his head as accidentally as he becomes attached to the party of travellers, at an advanced stage of the journey, when Mr Bramble suddenly befriends the poor waif who has just been dismissed by the inhuman innkeeper. Mr Bramble afterwards

---

[1] Letter to Mrs Gwyllim, Housekeeper at Brambleton Hall, 14th June. She reminds Mrs Gwyllim that she must render account " not only to your earthly master, but also to Him that is above; and if you are found a good and faithful sarvant, great will be your reward in haven. I hope there will be twenty stun of cheese ready for market by the time I get huom," etc.

seems to recollect that he felt some mysterious stirrings of the
heart towards him.   But Humphry's character and importance,
it is easy to see, develop through a series of afterthoughts, the
crowning one of which, evidently suggested by the plot of *Tom
Jones* and made the occasion for burlesquing the *dénouement* of
Joseph Andrews, was to discover him to be Mr Bramble's forgotten bastard.   Humphry's entry on the scene is the occasion
for a display of Matt's irony :

"You perceive," said the squire, "our landlord is a Christian
of bowels.   Who shall presume to censure the morals of the
age, when the very publicans exhibit such examples of humanity?
Hark ye, Clinker, you are a most notorious offender.   You stand
convicted of sickness, hunger, wretchedness, and want.   But, as it
does not belong to me to punish criminals, I will only take upon
me the task of giving you a word of advice: Get a shirt with all
convenient dispatch, that your nakedness may not henceforward
give offence to travelling gentlewomen, especially maidens in
years." [1]

In the recognition scene Humphry is unable to produce a
strawberry-mark like that of Joseph Andrews; but the old
wooden snuff-box, which he pulls out of his bosom, containing
the small cornelian seal and the two scraps of paper, is a satis-
factory substitute; the parody is complete.[2]   A further jocular
afterthought was to entitle the story Humphry Clinker's tour
instead of Matthew Bramble's.

Originals have been discovered for Jerry Melford and Lismahago.   Mr Melford is said to have been drawn from Smollett's
nephew, Alexander Telfer, rumoured to have been regarded by
the novelist as a possible husband for the daughter whom he lost.
He inherited the Bonhill estate (1789), Smollett, to whom it
would have come, having predeceased him.[3]   That much more
remarkable character, Lismahago, is supposed to have been suggested by a Captain Robert Stobo, who fell into the hands of the
Indians during the wars in America, and afterwards escaped to

[1] Mr Melford to Sir Watkin Phillips, 24th May.
[2] *Ibid.*, 8th October.
[3] *Letters*, ed. E. S. Noyes, 228 ; note on Letter 71, to Alexander Telfer of
Scotston, Esq.

England. Smollett mentions Stobo in a letter to David Hume as " a man of very extraordinary services and sufferings in America," and " not less modest and sensible in the conversation and occurrences of civil life than enterprising and indefatigable in his military capacity.[1] Whatever the starting-point, Smollett gave his humour free rein in evolving his Lieutenant Obadiah Lismahago, who is an odder mixture even than his friend and brother-in-law to be, Mr Matthew Bramble. Bramble is choleric, caustic, disillusioned, yet philanthropical, prickly as a hedgehog outside, warm-hearted, even tender, and a man of courage within. The contradictions in Lismahago's personality are more paradoxical. As in Mr Bramble's case, his absurdities precede the revelation of his merits. Jerry Melford announces his uncle as " an odd kind of humourist, always on the fret, and so unpleasant in his manner, that, rather than be obliged to keep him company, I'd resign all claim to the inheritance of his estate." Yet he thinks he may like him better on further acquaintance, and runs on: " Certain it is, all his servants and neighbours in the country are fond of him, even to a degree of enthusiasm ; the reason of which I cannot as yet comprehend."[2] He comprehends before long, and so does the reader. Lismahago's first appearance is more disconcerting still. He is meant to be grotesque, and a grotesque he remains : the wonder is how Smollett warms our hearts and wins our respect for a creature so ungainly. The tall, meagre figure, like Don Quixote on Rosinante, who introduces himself by falling off his horse in an attempt to dismount gracefully before the ladies, exposing the patched and plastered cranium which had been scalped by the Indians, maintains such a real dignity, in spite of his absurd efforts to stand upon it, preserves such a fund of sheer, hard sense, though it is revealed only through his itch for contradiction, and bears ridicule with such an imperturbable superiority, that it is not surprising that a judge of good company, such as Mr Bramble, should look on him as a valuable acquisition to the society at Brambleton Hall when he has settled down there with Tabitha. No one sees more clearly through the wiles of that desperate spinster than the stoical lieutenant, and no one is more

---

[1] *Letters*, 103, *cp.* notes, 223-224.
[2] Mr Melford to Sir Watkin Phillips, 2nd April.

certain to keep her peevishness under due restraint. He takes her with all her vagaries as an unexpected but welcome provision for his old age; and nothing could be more admirable than the quiet determination with which he secures her unattractive person and her compact little fortune, and the reserve and dry humour with which he stands the gibes of scoffers and the sentimentalism of the lady.   It has often been noticed that Tabitha's wooing of the canny lieutenant reads like a more grotesque version of the passages between the Widow Wadman and Uncle Toby. What hints Smollett may have taken from Sterne he turned to comic effects perhaps inferior, but at any rate extraordinarily different.[1]

A book which is partly the record of a real journey is bound to mingle some history with the fiction and to blend the historical with the fictive.   Real persons appear, some under their own names—for instance, the Duke of Newcastle and the elder Pitt, Smollett's uncle, the laird of Bonhill, Quin the actor, Dr Carlyle, and the literary magnates of Edinburgh to whom he introduces Mr Bramble. Others may be identified more or less conjecturally. Then there are some who seem as if they had come straight from Smollett's note-books, where he had jotted down anecdotes illustrating his peculiar views of human nature.   Such are the two Baynards, who furnish Mr Bramble with such a comprehensive exhibition of woman's folly and love of ostentation and of the weakness of an infatuated man.[2]   Such edifying incidents, and others that would not have been worth noting had they not happened, alternate with some that pass the bounds of farce. Clinker's arrest as a highwayman, his appearance before Mr Justice Buzzard, and his defence by the individual who had himself committed the robbery and was known to the magistrate to be the true culprit, reads like extravaganza, and comes poorly out of a comparison with the scene in Justice Thrasher's court, in *Amelia*. *Humphry Clinker* contains a full measure of violent satire, which is all the more piquant for the prevailing good temper, and for being put in the mouth of a person not incapable of urbanity.

[1] Scott, in his introduction to *A Legend of Montrose*, paying homage to the "master-hand" that delineated Lismahago, generously admits that this character "must deprive the present author of all claim to absolute originality in that of Captain Dalgetty."

[2] Mr Bramble to Dr Lewis, 30th September.

To make such a rambling story pass muster as a novel Smollett perfunctorily attached a plot, the slender affair of Lydia's mysterious lover, who eventually turns out to be the son of a well-to-do old college friend of her uncle. Thus, with the consummation of Aunt Tabitha and Lismahago's courtship, and that of Winifred Jenkins and Humphry Clinker—now old Matt's acknowledged son—there is a full allowance of marriages to end up with. By another concession to usage Smollett prefixes two letters, one from the depositary of the correspondence, the other from the publisher, speculating whether they may get into hot water through the liberties taken with such an awkward customer as Mr Lismahago, now a Justice of the Peace. The letters are, at any rate, very witty.

Smollett, like Fielding, finished novel-writing and died at the age when Richardson began. Unlike theirs, his last was his wittiest and mellowest, though in strength and go it was inferior to his first novel. If we compare the three writers in the way they dealt with character, we observe a transfer of attention from inside to outside, from the heart to the skin. Richardson kept his eye fixed upon the inner consciousness. Fielding was more interested in surface peculiarities. These latter were everything to Smollett. From the time when the younger exponents of charactery drifted into fiction, perhaps the majority of those English novelists who still count have made more out of the oddities and vagaries of the individual than out of a deeper interpretation of life: to adopt Johnson's phrase about Fanny Burney, they have been " character-mongers " first and foremost, whatever else they may have been next. Fielding recognized and tried to balance the two tendencies. In Smollett, serious criticism of life will be looked for in vain, though he probably thought he was dispensing it in some of his flashes of malign humour. He gets what amusement he can out of the human spectacle, and that is the whole extent of his philosophy.[1]

---

[1] He puts this fairly in a letter to Garrick : " I am old enough to have seen and observed that we are all playthings of fortune and that it depends upon something as insignificant and precarious as the tossing up of a halfpenny, whether a man rises to affluence and honours, or continues to his dying day struggling with the difficulties and disgraces of life. I desire to live quietly with all mankind, and, if possible, to be upon good terms with all those who have distinguished themselves by their merit " (*Letters*, 69-70).

The influence of his example on later fiction will continually appear in the following pages. The Smollett touch in portraiture and all that contributes to portraiture is, of course, chiefly recognizable in the novelists whose interest is monopolized by the diversities and picturesque anomalies of mankind, above all, in those who specialize in some province of human nature strongly marked with mannerisms of its own, nautical life, for instance. The natural tendency of such a passion for the twists and angularities of temperament and habits and manners, and their visible outward expression, is towards the grotesque. In the line of descent from Trunnion and Lismahago we may recognize, not only debonair eccentrics such as Uncle Toby and Dr Primrose, but also the grimmer progeny of Dickens's imagination, Quilp, Sally Brass, Noah Claypole, and Uriah Heep, as well as Tom Pinch and Tommy Traddles, who are of the family of Strap and Tom Pipes. Smollett's sprightly style, the comedy that sparkles in the very diction—likewise the immediate expression of his delight in externals—reappears in the work of his followers: Dickens had a style of his own from the very first, but he learned it from Smollett. Even a failure like *Launcelot Greaves* left its mark upon *Pickwick Papers*.

One of the paradoxes of Smollett is the apparent delight in sheer brutality which went side by side with a very sincere feeling for the pathetic. *Roderick Random* seems to show an absolute relish for horrors, and here and everywhere he appears to revel in mere foulness. The paradox is, however, natural, and should not astonish. To be superlatively effective in depicting horror and anguish does not imply a liking for these things, but rather the reverse. It is the thin-skinned, the tender-hearted, who receive the most scorching impressions, and are hence better able to excite the same feelings in others. Apparent callousness may be only an attitude consciously or instinctively assumed by the over-sensitive in self-defence. Smollett could tell a pathetic story in a most touching albeit not an effusive way—witness, for instance, the little episode in *Humphry Clinker* of the captain returning with his money from the East Indies, and finding his old father reduced to indigence and working as a pavior, and his brother in gaol. Before the old man can realize the situation, " a decent old woman, bolting out from the door of a poor habitation, cried: 'Where is my bairn? Where is my dear Willy?' The captain no sooner beheld her, than he quitted his father, and ran into her embrace." [1] It reminds one of the story how Smollett himself was recognized by his mother, by the twinkle in his eye, in spite of his attempt to pass himself off as a stranger. In fact, all the personal anecdotes support the view that Smollett was rather abnormally sensitive. [2]

Swift laid himself open to a similar charge; he, too, was guilty of the same indulgence in the horrifying and the disgusting. And his case exhibits the same paradox. Both men were extremely sensitive and tender-hearted. Both were exceptional in their anxiety about personal cleanliness in an age that was pretty lax in such matters; judged by their contemporaries, they were eccentrics in their addiction to cold water. The hater of filth will be the foulest in his stigmatization of foulness. The most sensitive will be the most outrageous in exposing horror and suffering. An irritable man like Smollett, or a man of fierce indignation like Swift, naturally, when he gets into a rage, flings out with just those things that he finds most nauseating and repulsive. In neither case was it prurience. The most probable explanation of both men's offences against literary decency seems to be this.

[1] Mr Melford to Sir Watkin Phillips, 12th September.

[2] Yet probably Dr Buck forgot certain passages when he wrote: "There is of course more goodness of heart in Parson Adams and in Fielding's works generally than in any character or work of Smollett's; but in point of pathetic incidents and strokes of characterization which affect us emotionally, the advantage is all the other way" (*Smollett as Poet*, 81; *cp.* the even more emphatic remarks on p. 84). Did he not forget the story-teller's meeting with his little daughter in the other world, in *A Journey from this World to the Next*, and many scenes in *Amelia*, especially that of Mrs Booth's forgiveness of her erring husband?

CHAPTER X

STERNE

*Nonsense
fiction
before
Sterne*
No sooner was fiction provided with a structural form and a set of canons firmly co-ordinated, than the form began to be knocked to pieces and the canons flouted. So handy a vehicle for sentiments and idiosyncrasies was bound to be seized upon and employed for the most heterogeneous purposes by solemn eccentrics—such as Thomas Amory and Henry Brooke—and for burlesque and extravaganza by irresponsible wags. The freakish deviations from the norm typified by *Tristram Shandy* and *A Sentimental Journey* were not, however, a thing entirely new, but on the contrary a revival of nondescript kinds of fiction that had been common enough before Richardson and Fielding took hold of the novel and put it in order. Nonsense fiction had been much in vogue during the sixteenth century. The one towering classic among the facetious writers was Rabelais; but there were also minor classics—Béroalde de Verville, author of *Le Moyen de Parvenir*, Bruscambille, with his *Pensées Facétieuses*, Guillaume Bouchet, with his *Serées*, and other Frenchmen, not excepting the more modern author of *Le Paysan Parvenu* and *La Vie de Marianne*, whose *marivaudage* was a kindred variety of humour. All Swift's fictions belonged to this class, and more recently the mock-biography of Martinus Scriblerus had appeared in print about the same time as the first works of Richardson and Fielding. Goldsmith, Brooke, author of *The Fool of Quality*, and others of less eminence, were to keep up the practice of unorthodox fiction, after Sterne had demonstrated the infinite malleability of the novel and its aptness for any impression that the hand of genius might think fit to give it. Whilst it was well that the newly accredited art should not be allowed to become a thing of rigid rules and regulations, the existence of the rules gave an extra piquancy to licence, whether comic or serious.

Sterne's immediate predecessor, though also half an Irishman, *Thomas* was no jester, but made that singular book, *The Life and Opinions* *Amory's* *of John Buncle Esquire* (1756-1766), a receptacle for his manias *nondescript* in heavy seriousness. It is one of the most laughable books ever *romances* written, but the humour appears to be absolutely unconscious. Not much is known about Amory beyond what is vouchsafed in his books, which are, however, like Sterne's, full of autobiography, though in an oblique sense. He was a devout Unitarian, and a man of the most varied erudition; and both learning and Unitarianism are poured wholesale into his books, with complete indifference to form, relevance, or the frailty of the average intelligent reader. For Amory wrote two books, and it is possible that even the first consists more of fiction than of fact. This, which came out in 1755, bears the formidable title, *Memoirs : containing the Lives of several Ladies of Great Britain. A History of Antiquities, Productions of Nature and Monuments of Art. Observations on the Christian Religion, as professed by the Established Church, and Dissenters of every Denomination. Remarks on the Writings of the greatest English Divines : with a variety of Disquisitions and Opinions relative to Criticism and Manners ; and many extraordinary Actions.* According to the " Advertisement," it was to be an account of some twenty ladies who were " a glory to Great Britain, and an honour to womankind; for their fine understandings, their valuable learning, their strong judgments, and their good lives." But of the twenty announced only two or three, with the saintly and beautiful Mrs Benlow at their head, actually appear; and, after many conversations, much theology, and a few picturesque incidents charmingly related, the rest of the book—about half of it—is taken up with Mrs Benlow's " Transactions and Observations in a Voyage to the Western Islands. In the year 1741."

Perhaps we may recognize most of the other ladies in those *"The Life* who figure in *John Buncle* as that hero's successive wives or *of John* brides to be, all of them uniformly cut off in the flower of their *Buncle"* beauty and erudition, leaving him disconsolate, at least for one or two weeks. The plan of this second book is just as haphazard ; the digressions always have the best of it, and the unlikeness to a novel or any work intended for amusement is enhanced by

Amory's addiction to voluminous footnotes. Buncle sallies out to try his fortune in the world, "not like the Chevalier La Mancha, in hopes of conquering a kingdom, or marrying some great princess; but to see if I could find another good country girl for a wife, and get a little more money; as these were the only two things united, that could secure me from melancholy, and confer real happiness." He quickly finds the woman, who is always the fairest of her sex, the most learned, accomplished, and, above all, the most religious. Buncle and she are married, or about to be married, after the briefest courtship, and then the blow descends. Take the case of Miss Noel:

This world is a series of visionary scenes, and contains so little solid, lasting felicity, as I have found it, that I cannot call life more than a deception; and, as Swift says it, "He is the happiest man, who is best deceived." When I thought myself within a fortnight of being married to Miss Noel, and thereby made as completely happy in every respect as it was possible for a mortal man to be, the small-pox stepped in, and in seven days' time, reduced the finest frame in the universe to the most hideous and offensive block. The most amiable of human creatures mortified all over, and became a spectacle the most hideous and appalling. This broke her father's heart in a month's time, and the paradise I had in view, sunk into everlasting night.[1]

But no sooner is one charmer dead and buried than the insatiate John shakes off sorrow and goes on his way in quest of another. He puts the case with inimitable gravity:

In the next place, as I had forfeited my father's favour and estate, for the sake of christian-deism, and had nothing but my own honest industry to secure me daily bread, it was necessary for me to lay hold of every opportunity to improve my fortune, and of consequence do my best to gain the heart of the first rich young woman who came in my way, after I had buried a wife. It was not fit for me to sit snivelling for months, because my wife died before me, which was, at least, as probable, as that she should be the survivor; but instead of solemn affliction, and the inconsolable part, for an event I foresaw, it was incumbent on me, after a little decent mourning, to consecrate myself to virtue and good fortune united in the form of a woman.[2]

[1] *John Buncle*, ed. E. A. Baker, 35.   [2] *Ibid.*, 297-298.

The love-making consists of learned conversations, on the *A non-* mysteries of religion, the more remote arcana of Biblical exegesis, *descript* entomology, mathematics—the last-named illustrated by elaborate *miscellany like* diagrams and equations. These scenes are hugely entertaining, *"Tristram* but the entertainment was never so designed. What coy maiden *Shandy"* was ever wooed after the manner that won the " illustrious Statia "? Indelicacy almost ceases to be indelicate when it becomes so elephantine.

" Ponder, illustrious Statia, on the important point. Consider what it is to die a maid, when you may, in a regular way, produce heirs to that inestimable blessing of life and favour, which the munificence of the Most High was pleased freely to bestow, and which the great Christian mediator, agent, and negotiator, re-published, confirmed, and sealed with his blood. Marry then in regard to the gospel, and let it be the fine employment of your life, to open gradually the treasures of revelation to the under-standing of the little Christians you produce. What do you say, illustrious Statia? Shall it be a succession, as you are an upright Christian? And may I hope to have the honour of sharing in the mutual satisfaction that must attend the discharge of so momentous a duty? " [1]

The book is a literary curiosity and something more. It fascinated Lamb, Hazlitt,[2] and Leigh Hunt, chiefly, no doubt, by the frankness and literary vigour with which an extraordinary man reveals the whole of his character. Buncle is an eccentric in the sense that he carries very common traits to a strange excess. In his love of good living, his sensuality combined with a pharisaic animus against vice, in his blind egotism and invincible arrogance, may be perceived an exaggeration of certain national characteristics with which the author shows his sympathy by exalting them to the pitch of absurdity. John Bull—at any rate one side of him—is unintentionally caricatured in John Buncle, as perhaps it was caricatured in the author himself. Along with the rest, the sectarian spirit that is so deeply ingrained in the national character is faithfully portrayed in Buncle the Unitarian, with his dogmatism and intolerance, and his delight in wordy

---

[1] *John Buncle*, 244-245.
[2] Hazlitt was daring enough to hail in John (*sic*) Amory " the soul of Francis Rabelais."

argument untempered by the slightest capacity for understanding his adversary's point of view. Of his utter obtuseness to the comic—a quality which he unwittingly provided in abundance— let a last quotation stand as voucher. He is reporting on the opinions of Jack Gallaspy, another original:

As to swearing, he thought it was only criminal when it was false, or men lied in their affirmations; and for whoring he hoped there would be mercy, since men will be men while there are women. Ravishing he did not pretend to justify, as the laws of his country were against it; but he could not think the woman was a sufferer by it, as she enjoyed without sinning the highest felicity. He intended her happiness; and her saying No, kept her an innocent. [1]

It is improbable that Sterne ever read either of Amory's books; but they must be mentioned here as a miscellany of strange and incongruous elements parallel to, though so unlike, Sterne's own salmagundi of odds and ends recklessly compounded. *John Buncle* is soberly absurd as *Tristram Shandy* is playfully so.

Laurence Sterne   Laurence Sterne (1713-1768) was the son of an ensign in an infantry regiment, and was born at Clonmel, soon after the regiment had arrived there from Dunkirk, some little time after the Peace of Utrecht. His father, Roger Sterne, though he never rose above the rank of subaltern, was the grandson of an Archbishop of York, and, himself poor, had well-to-do kinsmen. He was a younger son, and had done his prospects no good by marrying a widowed Frenchwoman, who was the step-daughter of a sutler, very well known in the army. The regiment was soon disbanded, then re-enrolled, and for ten years Mrs Sterne and her children followed it about—to Ireland from the family seat at Elvington, near York, then as far as the Isle of Wight, whence the troops embarked on the Vigo expedition, and then back to Ireland, where they moved from place to place, until Roger, after serving at Gibraltar during the siege and fighting a duel, was sent to Jamaica, where he died. Laurence was then eighteen. He afterwards described Roger Sterne as " a little smart man," very active, patient of fatigue and disappointments, in temper

[1] *John Buncle*, 291.

" somewhat rapid, and hasty—but of a kindly, sweet disposition, void of all design." He was as innocent as Uncle Toby, who is often said to have been drawn from him. At any rate, Sterne's familiarity with military life, so evident in *Tristram Shandy*, was a product of the years when the little family wandered about with the regiment, whilst he picked up the rudiments of an education intermittently.

When the boy was about ten he was sent to a grammar school near Halifax, where he was under the kindly eye of his uncle Richard, of Elvington and Woodhouse. This protector died a year before Laurence went to Cambridge,[1] being admitted to a sizarship at Jesus College, where his great-grandfather, the Archbishop, had been a master. One of Sterne's fellow-collegiates was John Hall, afterwards Hall-Stevenson, with whom he struck up a friendship that was to have some consequences in later years, when the incumbent of the quiet Yorkshire parish was to be a regular visitor to Hall-Stevenson, the Eugenius of *Tristram Shandy*, at the notorious Crazy Castle.

In January 1736 the young man took his B.A., was ordained, *Life at* and as soon as he was in priest's Orders received, through the *Sutton-in-* influence of his uncle, Jaques, the benefice of Sutton-in-the *the-Forest* Forest, about eight miles from York. Jaques Sterne was an energetic and ambitious clergyman, who held a number of livings and was an active politician on the Whig and Hanoverian side. For some years he helped his nephew materially, securing him two prebends at York though not the more substantial preferment Sterne coveted. He induced the young vicar to take a hand in politics and local journalism; and then, finding him not too amenable, and probably annoyed by his erratic and humorous disposition, suddenly broke with him.[2] Sterne spent more than a score of years in his sequestered village in the vale of York, the chills and damps of which did not suit his weakly constitution. He obtained an additional small living at Stillington, the duties

---

[1] His son, another Richard Sterne, now supervised the youth's education. From this cousin Richard, says Mr Sichel (*Sterne, a Study*, 20), Sterne seems to have derived his character of the elder Shandy.

[2] These early episodes in Sterne's career are the subject of a recent study, *The Politicks of Laurence Sterne*, by Lewis Perry Curtis (1929). The writer has managed to exhume some of Sterne's work from the *York Gazetteer*.

of which he performed himself without a curate, and still was able to preach fairly often at York Minster. He had married Elizabeth Lumley in 1741, after two years of sentimental rather than ardent courtship. Some of the love-letters sent her came in useful, characteristically, when years later he was in love with someone else. That same year, according to a passage in *Tristram Shandy*, he was travelling on the Continent as governor to a young man of fashion, but on this episode information is lacking.[1]

Inter-course with Hall-Stevenson

For the most part Sterne seems to have found life in his rural parish humdrum and depressing. Preferment was long in coming. He was sometimes friendly and sometimes at variance with the few neighbours of his own class. He tried farming, but only lost money after persistent efforts, and he had some rows with his humbler parishioners, who were not likely to comprehend a pastor who was a " humorist " in the old-fashioned sense. The neighbourhood of the minster city was some relief; he indulged his taste for music by going there for concerts, and he amused himself, not only with politics but also with the intrigues going on in the cathedral chapter, at a time when jobbery was probably more rampant than ever before or since. Then not far away was Crazy Castle, the home of his friend, Hall-Stevenson, who aspired to be a wit, and made his house the headquarters of a boisterous circle calling themselves the Demoniacks. It was a sort of junior to the Hell Fire Club, then performing their childish antics, their mock-diabolism, in the ruins of Medmenham Abbey, to the scandal of well-behaved society. Hall-Stevenson had a library rich in curious literature, which Sterne no doubt used freely, as he probably did also the minster library at York, laying the foundations of that far-fetched learning which was such a strong ingredient in his books. But all the time he was unconsciously amassing material. There were few things in his life, public or private, that did not somehow or other find their way into his books; there was little in his books without an origin in fact or in the authors from whom he was to plagiarize without restraint.

Not long after his marriage Sterne's mother and sister, believing or pretending to believe that he had espoused a fortune,

---

[1] *Tristram Shandy*, I. xi., and Cross, *Life and Times of Laurence Sterne*, 52-53.

came from Chester and tried to plant themselves upon him. He *Personal* was too poor to help them much, but appears to have done what *troubles* he could. Nevertheless, his uncle, Dr Jaques Sterne, tried to *and* make out that the son had treated his mother inhumanly, and so *cathedral broils* started a slander which was given further currency by Walpole, and still survives. This was but one of many incidents which were so interpreted by people who knew him as to mount up in time to a grievous record against " poor Yorick "; the apology which he afterwards interweaved in *Tristram Shandy* was not uncalled for. The affair which was the actual prelude to that work occurred later. A certain ecclesiastical lawyer, Dr Topham, who held as many offices in the diocese as any clerical pluralist, had been worsted in a scheme for installing his own son in a lucrative post, and among his exultant opponents was Sterne, who a year or two earlier had come in for another office coveted by Topham. The dispute made a great noise in the York chapter, and has its echoes in *Tristram Shandy*, in the scenes where the disputatious Didius appears, and especially in the incident of the hot chestnut at the visitation dinner, where, perhaps, Topham is hit at in Phutatorius.[1] But the direct sequel of the Topham disturbance was singularly important. Sterne concocted a fabulous history of " a good warm Watch-coat," in which the rapacious sexton, Trim, who by trickery appropriates the watch-coat that had been bequeathed in perpetuity to all who succeeded to the office, was easily recognized for Topham.[2] The laughter with which this skit was greeted determined Sterne to write something more ambitious in the same style, and *Tristram Shandy* was begun forthwith.

The work went ahead rapidly. Sterne had his miscellaneous *Origin of* experiences of the last twenty years in Yorkshire, his agricultural *"Tristram* enterprises and the consequent differences with his neighbours, *Shandy"* the misunderstandings and reproofs he had met with as a pastor, the intrigues in the chapter and the recent contest, the doings at Crazy Castle, and a grudge to discharge against an obnoxious local physician, Dr John Burton, whose unpopularity was mainly

[1] Cross, 239-240.
[2] The satire was entitled *A Political Romance, Addressed to* ——, *Esq., of York. To which is subjoined a Key*, York, 1759 (Cross, i. 159). It was afterwards entitled *The History of a Good Warm Watch-coat*.

due, it seems, to his being a papist and of Jacobite sympathies—
and of unpleasing appearance. All this local history and these
local scandals are brought in by a kind of allegorical transposition.
Burton comes on the stage as Dr Slop, Topham as Didius, Hall-
Stevenson as Eugenius, Sterne as Yorick. With the Shandy family,
Mr Shandy senior and his wife, Uncle Toby and his henchman,
Trim, and the whole household at Shandy Hall, a set of originals
not to be so closely identified, Sterne led out a troupe of comedians
whose antics might go on indefinitely. It was a tale—if a tale it
can be called—that would grow with the telling. When he was
well under way, and found the reading public eager for more of
the same fare, he seriously proposed to keep it up as long as he
lived. Since he died leaving the book unfinished, it may be said
that he actually did so.

Sterne in London   *Tristram Shandy* was begun in January 1759, and by June two
volumes were finished. After some alterations these appeared in
January 1760 with the imprint of a York bookseller, and the
name of the great Dodsley underneath. Sterne was dying to
know how the world of London would receive it; the appreciation of some acquaintances at York and the protests of others at
his treatment of Dr Burton were beneath his notice. The chance
occurring of a visit to London, he seized it. He found everybody
talking about his book. It was approved by Garrick, and Garrick
was the arbiter of taste. Sterne made favourable terms with
Dodsley for a second edition and the continuation of the work,
and also for two volumes of his sermons. He was lionized by
society and complimented by the great. He sent for Miss Four-
mantelle,[1] a young singer whom he had philandered with at York,
the latest object of many flirtations, to come up and witness his
triumph, and then had to neglect her through more urgent demands
upon his time. When he returned home, Sterne was a different
man : his poverty was at an end, he could afford to laugh at those
who objected to his unclerical levity or resented his jests, and
moving from Sutton to Coxwold—a living to which he had been
presented whilst in London—he settled down in an old house re-
christened Shandy Hall, laid in an ample store of books, and went
ahead with the next two volumes.

[1] The Kitty or Jenny of his novel.

This brief summary of the events in Sterne's life bearing *Sterne in* directly or indirectly on the genesis of the extraordinary book *France* which he had launched upon the world may from this point be still briefer. By the middle of 1761 four more volumes of *Tristram Shandy* had been published. Sterne's health was steadily growing worse. He was told that the only way to save his life was to betake himself to a warmer climate; so in 1762 he went to Paris, in spite of difficulties due to our being at war with France. His reception there was even more flattering than that he had met with in London. But it was imperative that he should go farther south. Accordingly, his wife and his daughter Lydia came over and joined him, and together they took the journey through the Midi to Toulouse, which Sterne chronicled in his free-and-easy style in his seventh volume. He was abroad two and a half years, and in 1765 went again to the Continent, going over some of the same ground once more and then traversing the Alps into Italy, visiting Turin, Milan, Florence, Rome—his receptions at which are recorded in his letters—and wintering at Naples. This second tour, with some experiences from the earlier one, forms the subject of his *Sentimental Journey*. *Tristram Shandy* came to an abrupt end with the ninth volume, issued in 1767. His strength was failing. He got no farther than the second volume of the other work, which was to have been much longer. Barely were the two volumes out when Sterne was taken with sudden illness, and died in his lodgings in Bond Street, his wife and daughter both absent.

Tristram Shandy and *A Sentimental Journey* are our only *His* direct concern here, but there is a huge quantity of biographical *Sermons* and other material by or about Sterne which is of greater or less importance for a complete study of his peculiar genius. He published several sets of sermons, and more appeared after his death. The first lot were those he had with him on his first visit to London, which he astutely foresaw would benefit by the prestige of the new novel. They were doubtless the best of those he had preached in the minster at York. Everybody has read the sermon on Conscience in the second book of *Tristram Shandy*: that one is a little too good to be selected as a fair sample. They may be described generally as moralizing essays, admirable for reading, but hardly so well adapted for effective use in the pulpit. The moral and religious teaching is unexceptionable, and the lessons are illustrated with human incidents and the strokes of character and by-play that Sterne referred to when he called them dramatic. Later sermons were more expressly composed for publication, and the stamp of Yorick had to be impressed. These are still more dramatic, much less like the conventional sermon, often deliberately quaint and Shandean, made very piquant and provocative by the freshness with which old matter is revivified. The character-sketches of Bible worthies are pointedly illustrated with allusions to the life of the present. He analyses motive with the acuteness of a past master of fiction, and his very free handling of questions of casuistry is similarly enlivened by modern applications. Naturally, the sentimental vein comes out strongly in the retelling of pathetic stories, and he often gave a loose to fancy in arraying with colour and romance some incident only too familiar in its bald outlines. Sterne's out-of-the-way reading gave him a store of illustrations often as surprising as they are apt.

His "Letters" and the "Journal to Eliza"   Masses of correspondence have also been preserved, including those letters which enable us to fill up the gaps in his *Sentimental Journey*, as originally projected, though not quite as he would have filled them. From others may be reconstructed the history of some of his amorous experiences. On that side of his biography the most important document is the *Journal to Eliza*, in which, for some months in 1767, he kept a record of the transports and daydreams of his last love affair.[1] Many letters also were addressed to this lady, Mrs Draper, and are extant in divers editions. *A Sentimental Journey* was in hand at the time he was keeping his *Journal to Eliza*; the latter consequently throws light on the composition of the former, showing the crude emotionalism out of which was refined and harmonized the exquisite music of his masterpiece. How painfully and with what infallible tact he laboured to catch the most fugitive shades of sentiment and to adjust his subtle rhythms and cadences is witnessed by the correc-

[1] Cross (ii. 265-298) gives a full bibliography, to which may now be added Laurence Sterne's *Second Journal to Eliza*; *hitherto known as Letters supposed to have been written by Yorick and Eliza, but now shown to be a later version of the Journal to Eliza*; transcribed by Margaret R. B. Shaw, 1929. The *Journal to Eliza* can be read in Walter Sichel's *Sterne, a Study* (1910).

tions in part of the manuscript preserved in the British Museum.[1]
He made correction on correction, substitution for substitution,
before he left well alone.

In the fourth book of *Tristram Shandy*, Sterne tells us for what *What*
object the work was written : *was the*
purpose of

> If 'tis wrote against anything—'tis wrote, an' please your *"Tristram*
> Worships, against the spleen; in order, by a more frequent and *Shandy"?*
> more convulsive elevation and depression of the diaphragm, and
> the succussations of the intercostal and abdominal muscles in
> laughter, to drive the *gall* and other *bitter juices* from the gall-
> bladder, liver, and sweetbread of his majesty's subjects, with all
> the inimicitious passions which belong to them, down into their
> duodenums.[2]

It was in the first place, then, an outlet for his humour, not a
satire of anything or anybody in particular, nor a mere burlesque
of an accepted literary form. True, Sterne went out of his way
at the outset to pillory Dr Burton, the caricature of whom is
a blemish in a work that shows no other trace of malice. He
had not yet freed himself entirely from the local animosities in
which he had been plunged, years before, by his uncle's rabid
Protestantism and Whiggism. So far as can be made out now,
Dr Burton was a disagreeable but comparatively harmless person,
who was brutally persecuted by Dr Jaques Sterne for his loyalty
to his church and his probable sympathies with the Jacobites,
and unfairly maltreated by the author of *Tristram Shandy*. No
one else is caricatured except in the way of legitimate comedy.[3]

Was the book meant as a travesty of the regular novel, the *Was it an*
main lines of which had been so carefully drawn and the theory *intentional*
so ably expounded by Fielding? To this question the answer *caricature*
is both yes and no. Obviously, placed side by side with any of *fiction?*

---

[1] Egerton MSS., 1610 (see Cross, ii 149-154).
[2] Book IV., c. 22.
[3] Sterne showed that a sharp claw was hidden under his sleek fur again in
A Sentimental Journey, where he has a playful stroke at Smollett (see above,
p. 226). His satirical prowess was feared. There is the well-known story
of Warburton's terror. The great bishop is reported, and the report is
probably true in part, to have given Sterne a purse of guineas—to induce him
not to carry out his supposed design of sending Warburton abroad in *Tristram
Shandy* as the young squire's tutor. The present may well have been for the
purpose of forestalling ridicule, though Sterne refused to acknowledge the
imputation.

the serious works of fiction reviewed in the foregoing chapters, *Tristram Shandy* is a mere caricature of a novel. But, obviously, it is also much more. There would, of course, be little entertainment in irregularity and disorder unless there was an established order to turn topsy-turvy. To take what had been so thoughtfully and laboriously built up, pull it to pieces, play ducks and drakes with the architect's plans, and then put it all together again according to his own whims and fancies, was a first-rate joke. No doubt Sterne played the fool with the structure of the novel for the sheer fun of playing the fool; but he also knew that he would provide himself with an incomparable screen on which to shadow forth his freaks and vagaries without the constraint of any rules.

Sterne's method in "Tristram Shandy"
It is constantly said that he had no plan or method. Plan he did not require, but he had a method. Deny it he may. He says, for instance:

> Of all the several ways of beginning a book which are now in practice throughout the known world, I am confident my own way of doing it is the best.—I'm sure it is the most religious, —for I begin with writing the first sentence,—and trusting to Almighty God for the second.[1]

And again, he remarks, of Corporal Trim's habit of standing with his lame knee behind Uncle Toby's chair, "Why did I mention it? Ask my pen: it governs me;—I govern not it." But these are humorous sallies to amuse the reader. Sterne's method is not really concealed. Fiction as now established and as Fielding had explained it has the same three objects of æsthetic imitation as Aristotle had specified for drama: characters, actions, sentiments. Now Sterne had no use for actions; he had no story to tell. Nothing really happens in *Tristram Shandy*, there are incidents but no events. The book is a huge improvisation for the display of the characters and the sentiments—sentiments, of course, including humour—and its connecting thread is simply that great principle, as Sterne considered it, of his master Locke, the association of ideas. This it is which leads him, when about to give " the great outlines of my Uncle Toby's most whimsical

[1] Book VIII., c. 2.

character," on " a vagary some millions of miles into the very heart of the planetary system." It is continually being illustrated. When Obadiah announces the death of the young master—" A green-satin nightgown of my mother's, which had been twice scoured, was the first idea which Obadiah's exclamation brought into Susannah's head.—Well might Locke write a chapter upon the imperfections of words." Even the word *mourning* failed of doing its office; " it excited not one single idea, tinged either with grey or black—all was green. The green-satin nightgown hung there still." [1] So, too, when the party are going to the Abbey of St Germain, and Mr Shandy remarks that the bodies they are about to see are all mummies: " Then one need not shave," is the first thought that occurs to his brother Toby. [2] The same principle, combined with Locke's theory of time, is the whole basis of the humorous dissertation on the machinery of the book, in which two contrary motions are shown to be introduced and reconciled, so that the work is digressive and progressive too, at the same time. [3] Yet the mode of articulation, how things will be associated, is so entirely his own secret that Sterne can defy the reader to foresee what is coming.

And in this, Sir, I am of so nice and singular a humour, that if I thought you was able to form the least judgment or probable conjecture to yourself of what was to come in the next page—I would tear it out of my book. [4]

Well might Mr Whibley describe this sort of fiction as the " picaresque of the intellect." It is a " rhapsodical work," " a civil, nonsensical, good-humoured, Shandean book, which will do all your hearts good—— And all your heads too,—provided you understand it."

Underlying the movement of the whole book is another philo-sophical conception derived from Locke. The two and a half hours between Dr Slop's and Obadiah's arrival and the moment

---

[1] Book V., c. 7.

[2] *Cp.* the remark in *A Sentimental Journey* upon La Fleur: "The young fellow, said the landlord, is beloved by all the town; and there is scarce a corner in Montriul where the want of him will not be felt. He has but one misfortune in the world, continued he, He is always in love. I am heartily glad of it, said I; 'twill save me the trouble every night of putting my breeches under my head " (*S. J.*, " Montriul ").

[3] Book I., c. 22.

[4] *Ibid.*, c. 25.

Locke's theory of duration an essential element

when the physician takes the green-baize bag and trips upstairs have seemed to Mr Shandy "almost an age." Though he said "he knew not how it happened," yet he knew very well how it happened, and "was pre-determined in his mind to give my Uncle Toby a clear account of the matter, by a metaphysical dissertation upon the subject of *duration, and its simple modes,* in order to show my Uncle Toby by what mechanism and mensurations in the brain it came to pass that the rapid succession of their ideas, and the eternal scampering of the discourse from one thing to another, since Dr Slop had come into the room, had lengthened out so short a period to so inconceivable an extent.—' I know not how it happens,' cried my father,—' but it seems an age.' —It is owing entirely, quoth my Uncle Toby, to the succession of our ideas." [1]

The dissertation on time and infinity

Then follows the dissertation on time and infinity, and "the idea we have of duration," which is taken almost bodily from Locke's *Essay concerning Human Understanding.* [2]

For if you will turn your eyes inwards upon your mind (continued my father), and observe attentively, you will perceive, brother, that whilst you and I are talking together, and thinking, and smoking our pipes, or whilst we receive successively ideas in our minds, we know that we do exist: and so we estimate the existence, or the continuation of the existence, of ourselves, or anything else, commensurate with the succession of any ideas in our minds, the duration of ourselves, or any such other thing co-existing with our thinking; and so, according to that pre-conceived. . . . You puzzle me to death, cried my uncle Toby.

Mr Shandy then explains the distinction between the idea of duration so perceived and "our computations of time" by "minutes, hours, weeks, and months." "I wish there was not a clock in the kingdom," he exclaims; when he is interrupted by the mention of a train—of ideas—as he was going to say, calling up a different association in the mind of Toby. " 'A train of Artillery?' said my uncle Toby. . . . 'A train of a fiddlestick!' quoth my father." [3]

[1] Book III., c. 18.   [2] Book II., c. 14, "Of Duration and its Simple Modes."
[3] One is continually reminded in *Tristram Shandy* of the modern school of novelists in France, who have made a constructive use of the theories of duration they have learned from Bergson.

This concept of a background of duration distinct from the *This* psychic time perceived in the passage of ideas through the mind *supplies the* is extremely useful to Sterne and an essential factor in his method. *background* Clock time and the other are incommensurable. The story is *to the* interrupted, everything going on is pretermitted, between the *comedy* opening of chapter twenty-one in the first book and chapter six in the next. Mr Shandy asks a question, which receives no answer till the story is resumed, all between being taken up by random digressions and a zigzag account of the Shandys. Sterne can play any pranks he likes with time, putting the clock back or putting it on, with the same ludicrous results as in his other departures from the normal method of relating a story. All this gives additional piquancy to his demonstration in the fourth book, that at his way of advancing, since by the time he has finished his account of his first day's life he finds he is a year older, " 'tis demonstrative that I have three hundred and sixty-four days more life to write just now than when I first set out," so that " I am just thrown so many volumes back," and since " at this rate I should live 364 times faster than I should write,—it must follow, an' please your Worships, that the more I write the more I shall have to write." [1] Against this background of time that goes regularly on and can be measured out like space in minutes, hours, and years, Sterne sets his comic pantomime, his dance of ideas, for which time exists not. The play runs forward at lightning speed, it stands still, it may even go backwards, if Yorick the stage-manager so directs—more arbitrary than Joshua in the valley of Ajalon.

Not born till the end of the fourth volume, which is half-way *The* to the place where the author's pen dropped from his hand, the *characters* hero at length announces: " It is from this point, properly, that *in* the story of my LIFE AND OPINIONS sets out." [2] But the hero is a *"Tristram* nonentity; he is merely the peg for his father's absurd philosophy *Shandy"* and the naïve remarks of his uncle. His begetting, birth, and upbringing are the matters round which the comedy revolves but hardly advances; there is no need for it to advance. The real characters are his father and mother, his uncle and his uncle's body-servant, and some of less consequence, Dr Slop and the

[1] Book IV., c. 13.   [2] Book IV., c. 32.

various domestics, and occasional figures like Eugenius, Didius, Kysarcius, and Phutatorius, suggested by personages in the Crazy Castle circle or that of York. When the hero takes a hand himself, as he does in the travels through France, in the seventh book, he remains the same nonentity.[1]

The leading characters may be arranged in pairs. First, there are Mr and Mrs Shandy, carefully devised to be a foil to each other; then Mr Shandy and his brother stand in a parallel relation, Toby is Sancho to the quixotic idealist; at the same time, Corporal Trim is Uncle Toby's Sancho. For, though the book in general owes much more to Rabelais than to Cervantes, yet the central notion and recurring topic of the Hobby Horse is essentially Cervantic, and more profoundly akin to the philosophy of *Don Quixote* is the immeasurable incongruity and mutual incomprehensibility of human individuals typified by these contrasted pairs. Still it is Yorick alone among his characters that the author actually likens to " the peerless knight of La Mancha," on the score of his " spiritual and refined sentiments " and his innocent aberrations.[2]

Mr Shandy

Mr Shandy, that " great motive-monger," who delighted in subtleties of any kind,[3] and, incessantly refining on intellectual distinctions, has a theory for everything in life but a theory absurdly out of all relation to fact and reality, is the exponent of Shandeism, and it must not be overlooked that Sterne himself is at least half a Shandean. He loved these subtle and far-reaching speculations as fondly as Mr Shandy loved them, and was just as likely to tie himself up in a knot if he unwound the metaphysical skein too far.[4]

Mr Shandy, my father, Sir, would see nothing in the light in which others placed it;—he placed things in his own light;— he would weigh nothing in common scales:—no,—he was too refined a researcher to lie open to so gross an imposition.[5]

[1] Professor Cross discusses the question of Sterne's originals (Cross, i. 183-185).
[2] Book I., c. 10.   [3] Book IV. 29.
[4] Sterne had imbibed at Oxford a violent antipathy to the logic of the schools, which he caricatured in the well-known excursus on the *Argumentum Fistulatorium*, the *Argumentum Baculinum*, etc., where he drops the witty saying about the end of disputation being " more to silence than convince " (Book I., c. 21).   [5] Book II., c. 19.

There was that infinitude of oddities in him, and of chances along with it, by which handle he would take a thing—it baffled, Sir, all calculations. The truth was, his road lay so very far on one side from that wherein most men travelled, that every object before him presented a face and section of itself to his eye altogether different from the plan and elevation of it seen by the rest of mankind. In other words, 'twas a different object, and, in course, was differently considered.[1]

Yet, though his way was " to force every event in nature into an hypothesis, by which means man never crucified *Truth* at the rate he did," as Yorick observed, " there was a seasoning of wisdom unaccountably mixed up with his strangest whims; and he had sometimes such illuminations in the darkest of his eclipses as almost atoned for them." There is a trait that relates him to Smollett's Mr Bramble in the cheerfulness which he draws even from a mishap, since it provides such opportunity for showing his wit and eloquence.

A blessing which tied up my father's tongue, and a misfortune which set it loose with a good grace, were pretty equal: sometimes, indeed, the misfortune was the better of the two; for instance, where the pleasure of the harangue was as *ten*, and the pain of the misfortune but as *five*,—my father gained half in half; and consequently was as well again off as if it had never befallen him.[2]

The conjugal comedy of the philosopher who was " master of one of the finest chains of reasoning in nature," and had a wife, " with such a head-piece that he cannot hang up a single inference within-side of it, to save his soul from destruction," is comic enough; but the humour of the juxtaposition of the two brothers is infinitely finer. No characters were ever " cast or contrasted with so dramatic a felicity." Superfluous to observe that Toby is never an object of satire; neither indeed is his brother: both are figures of the purest comedy. But Captain Shandy is drawn with a tenderness that confers a rare beauty on his gentleness and simplicity, his humility, his exquisite obliviousness of self. He is finer even than Fielding's Parson Adams, and much finer than

Mrs Shandy

Uncle Toby

any of his spiritual offspring, Dr Primrose, Colonel Newcome, and the rest.

He is a kindly-hearted gentleman, said Obadiah, as ever lived. . . . Ay, and as brave a one too, said the Corporal, as ever stept before a platoon.—There never was a better officer in the King's army—or a better man in God's world; for he would march up to the mouth of a cannon, though he saw the lighted match at the very touch-hole;—and yet for all that, he has a heart as soft as a child for other people.[1]

Toby and his brother are beings that live in different mental worlds. They love each other, they long to bridge the chasm, but each remains, and must remain, totally inaccessible, an enigma to his nearest friend. A delicate pathos mingles with this comedy of affectionate misunderstanding, of idiosyncrasy at cross-purposes, and, happily, it is seldom tinged with Sterne's usual excess of sentimentality. One of the finest traits in his art is how out of things that verge on the grotesque he educes an undefinable beauty.

Corporal Trim   " The Corporal—Tread lightly on his ashes, ye men of genius, for he was your kinsman: Weed his grave clean, ye men of goodness, for he was your brother." The corporal is subtly differentiated from that other great simple nature, his master the captain. Yet, again, there is the same sort of difference, the same incomprehension, though in this case, instead of the anxious straining to join hands across the gulf, the difference becomes a natural ground for the lowly admiration and respect of another innocent and loyal soul for his great-hearted master.

Sterne's sentiment-alism   Sterne prided himself more on his faculty for experiencing and expressing sentiment than on any other gift. Early in *Tristram Shandy* he defines his sentimentalism in a passage that may be accepted as essentially autobiographical; it is his comment on the famous incident of Uncle Toby and the fly:

I was but ten years old when this happened: but whether it was that the action itself was more in unison with my nerves at that age of pity, which instantly set my whole frame into one vibration of most pleasurable sensation;—or how far the manner

[1] Book **V.**, c. 10.

and expression of it might go towards it;—or, in what degree, or by what secret magic—a tone of voice, and harmony of movement, attuned by mercy, might find a passage to my heart, I know not;—this I know, that the lesson of universal good-will, then taught and imprinted by my uncle Toby, has never since been worn out of my mind.[1]

It was the luxury of feeling that captivated Sterne, feeling, in particular, of a sorrowful tendency, above all, compassion. Richardson through his minute analysis of the sensibilities arrived at a more momentous theme, the intrinsic value of personality. Sterne was content to spend his life toying with the emotions, of sympathy, pity, thwarted affection, melancholy. Melancholy, but not dejection, for Sterne was never really depressed; few men with such a wretched constitution as his have enjoyed such a fund of vitality and buoyant spirits; he went on sentimentalizing—it is his own word—and chasing tearful experiences until his hand had no longer the strength to write them down. In the amazing *Journal* he tells Eliza how he felt " a pleasure in this kind of resigned misery arising from that situation of heart unsupported by aught but its own tenderness." He should have been in his grave years before; the doctors gave him up when he first went to France. But he dosed himself with melancholy as some invalids dose themselves with poisonous drugs, and it kept him alive and cheerful. Or was it the humour lurking beside the sensibility in his strange constitution that saved him— humour so intimately bound up with the sensibility? Assuredly it is not dejection that sits on his brow in the extant portraits, but rather a genial and inextinguishable humour. The likeness of the Carmontelle water-colour to Voltaire is striking. Hence to call his sentimentalism morbid seems absurd; it might be morbid for the generality of people, it was evidently hygienic to Sterne.

That, however, is a question for the pathologist; it is the *A* literary aspect of his sentimentalism which is our problem. *cultivated* Sincerity, in the thing written if not in the writer, is a primary *emotional-* requirement in literature, of whatever kind. Anything false, *ism* affected, overcharged, or merely equivocal, excites suspicion, misses the mark, fails to impress in the way intended. Sterne's

[1] Book II. 12.

too often strikes the ordinary cold-blooded reader as false sentiment; he appears to be constantly working himself up into the
required mood, forcing the tears to come; and, since he thoroughly
enjoyed a weep, no doubt that is just what he is doing. And, as
he was first and foremost a purveyor of sentimental experiences,
all this was a part of the literary process. Sterne lived his pages
before he wrote them, and for the express purpose of writing
them. Instead of looking round for fresh material he went out
and manufactured it. Hence the posturing over the dead ass,
which provoked Thackeray's ire: "Psha, mountebank! I'll not
give thee one penny more for that trick, donkey and all!" Such
sentimentalism as this is bound to be self-conscious, and radically
different from the pathos of classical art, which is the natural
result of events, not the object of a quest or cult. Sterne, busy
fondling his emotions, cries: "Look at me; what a tender-
hearted fellow I am!" He makes a spectacle of his compassionate
feelings, whereas true pity, genuine sympathy, concentrate on
the object. And this theatrical tendency spoils many scenes and
incidents which otherwise would have been flawless; an obvious
instance is the rhetorical touch at the end of Le Fevre's story:
"The pulse fluttered;—stopped;—went on,—throbbed,—stopped
again;—moved, stopped.—Shall I go on?—No."

Sentiment-
alism the
basis of his
philosophy
of life

Sentimentalism was much more to Sterne than a form of self-
indulgence or a literary plaything; it was an integral part of his
philosophy, which in this respect was diametrically opposed to
Fielding's. Fielding held that healthy feelings were necessary for
right living, and that good impulses could and should be cultivated;
he also showed that prudence, good sense, heed to the lessons of
experience, were equally necessary. Sterne inculcates obedience
to the feelings alone. He prefers to listen to the heart rather than
the intelligence, even though perchance the heart may say too
much.[1]

"When the heart flies out before the understanding, it saves
the judgment a world of pains."[2] Man disquiets himself by
consulting the reason only:

---

[1] "In transports of this kind, the heart, in spite of the understanding, will
always say too much" (*Sentimental Journey*, "Amiens").
[2] *Ibid.*, "The Remise Door."

Surely, this is not walking in a vain shadow,—nor does man disquiet himself in vain by it—he oftener does so in trusting the issue of his commotions to reason only.—I can safely say, for myself, I was never able to conquer any one single bad sensation in my heart so decisively as by beating up as fast as I could for some kindly and gentle sensation to fight it upon its own ground.[1]

Here lies the source of generosity and happiness. " Dear sensibility ! source inexhausted of all that's precious in our joys, or costly in our sorrows ! . . . But that I feel some generous joys and generous cares beyond myself;—all comes from thee, great —great *Sensorium* of the world ! which vibrates, if a hair of our heads but falls upon the ground, in the remotest desert of thy creation." [2] Thus Sterne transcendentalizes feeling as Coleridge afterwards transcendentalized the reason. Was it reason or sentiment, we may well inquire, that checked impulse in the affair of the *fille de chambre* ? What was it that reproached him after the famous outburst of sentimental fervour when Madame de L. drove away with her brother ?

Then I will meet thee, said I, fair spirit ! at Brussels ;—'tis only returning from Italy, through Germany to Holland, by the route of Flanders, home ;—'twill scarce be ten posts out of my way ; but were it ten thousand ! with what a moral delight will it crown my journey, in sharing in the sickening incidents of a tale of misery told to me by such a sufferer ! to see her weep, and, though I cannot dry up the fountain of her tears, what an exquisite sensation is there still left in wiping them away from off the cheeks of the first and fairest of women, as I'm sitting with my handkerchief in my hand in silence the whole night beside her !
There was nothing wrong in the sentiment ; and yet I instantly reproached my heart with it in the bitterest and " most reprobate of expressions." [3]

In spite of the incessant parade of sensitiveness, which is tiring " *A Senti-* and, when overdone, repellent, *A Sentimental Journey* has that *mental* which was to seek in the travel-books of this era—and they were *Journey* " legion—sympathy for all sorts and conditions, not only of men,

---

[1] *Sentimental Journey*, " The Passport—Versailles."
[2] *Ibid.*, " The Bourbonnois."
[3] *Ibid.*, " Amiens."

but of every living thing.[1] Sterne enumerates the various sorts:
" Idle Travellers, Inquisitive Travellers, Lying Travellers, Proud
Travellers, Vain Travellers, Splenetic Travellers." [2] There are
some others, but these are the chief, and the last include Smollett,
whose recent performance was peculiarly antipathetic to Sterne.
This last and ripest of his books is an exquisite symphony
of sight, sound, and feeling. He did not go on long enough
to take the reader with him across the Mont Cenis; the story
breaks off when he has travelled from Calais to Paris and from
Paris to the Bourbonnais, where, near Moulins, he meets again
" the poor Maria my friend Mr Shandy met with " in the ninth
book of *Tristram*. But the fact that he had already dealt with
many of the same matters, which were now twice alembicated,
gives to *A Sentimental Journey* a perfection of form and surface
which is marred by very few falsities and pretences. Among these,
however, must be enumerated, not perhaps the episode of the lady
at Calais just cited, which is entirely in character with all we
know of Sterne, but certainly the rhapsody over the dead ass at
Nampont, worked up, it is plain, to outgo the admirable colloquy
on the live one in the doorway at Lyons,[3] and also the more
lachrymose and stagy version of the Maria incident.[4] These are
the aberrations of sentimentalism, losing all touch with reality in
transports of self-admiration. But where Sterne is content to set
down his impressions just as they came, coloured with the feelings
rising spontaneously in a mind exquisitely sensitive and delicately
attuned, the people, the incidents, the whole moving scene of the
traveller's progress is brought before us, with all its atmosphere,
in a series of incomparable pictures. And the vignettes of those
with whom he has passing adventures: the postilion La Fleur,
the Franciscan monk, the *fille de chambre*, the grisette, and her

---

[1] The association of ideas reminds us that he could be tender-hearted even
about a thing that was not alive, like the *désobligeante* at Calais—an incident
that exasperated Thackeray ("this luxury of generosity, this gallant rescue
of Misery—out of an old cab "), and roused Traill in Sterne's defence to argue
solemnly that it was "an obvious piece of mock pathetic" (H. D. Traill,
Sterne, 157). Traill forgot to mention that Sterne's expedition in concluding
the extortionate bargain with M. Dessein was due to his anxiety to hasten
after the lady.

[2] *Sentimental Journey*, " Preface in the Désobligeant."

[3] *Tristram Shandy*, Book VII., c. 32.

[4] *Ibid.*, Book IX., 24, and *Sentimental Journey*, "Maria, Moulines."

husband who interrupts him in the occupation of feeling his wife's pulse and thanks him for doing him too much honour, even the gigantic German and the persecuted dwarf in the little incident at the Opéra Comique, and the crowd of beggars, landlords, abbés, officials, and notables of Paris, all these in spite of the smallness of scale, are among Sterne's happiest evocations of character. It is a masterpiece of a new style of art, impressionism.

Impressionism is the right if not the only method of presenting himself and the world open to the sentimentalist. Sensation and emotion constitute his mental life; they are also the box of colours with which he paints. Though of all Sterne's work *A Sentimental Journey* is the finest example of the style, the rest, not excluding the letters or the sermons, are of the same make. Even his reasoning is in the main only a stringing together of impressions. Himself incapable of philosophic thought, he loved to think that he understood Locke, and would have justified his method by appealing to the great empiricist's theory of sensation. But Sterne's impressionism was not a matter of theory or of deliberate choice; to him it was the one inevitable method. When he was vicar of Sutton, one of his recreations was painting, and the scanty specimens of his efforts that remain are enough to show that he might have excelled in this art, as he might perhaps have excelled in music. Visual sensations were to him the keenest. He disparaged that of touch, although he could experience such ecstasy from counting the pulsations in a fair lady's wrist. " Let it suffice to affirm that, of all the senses, the eye (for I absolutely deny the touch, though most of your *Barbati*, I know, are for it) has the quickest commerce with the soul—gives a smarter stroke, and leaves something more inexpressible upon the fancy than words can either convey—or sometimes get rid of." [1] Hence his contagious delight in pictorial effects, more vivid than any narrative: Mrs Shandy in the dark passage with her ear at the chink, " as my uncle Toby pronounced the word *wife* "; " the listening slave, with the goddess of Silence at his back, could not have given a finer thought for an intaglio "; Trim about to read the sermon, " so swayed his body, so contrasted his limbs, and with such an oratorical sweep throughout the whole figure, a statuary

Impressionism the natural method of the sentimentalist

---

[1] *Tristram Shandy*, Book V., c. 7.

might have modelled from it "; Mr Shandy elaborately drawn in such an attitude that, " Reynolds himself, great and graceful as he paints, might have painted him as he sat "; or the arrival of Dr Slop, depicted as if by one of the primitives in a succession of views—Dr Slop on his diminutive pony encountering Obadiah on his monstrous coach-horse, plunging like a devil towards him in the muddy lane; Dr Slop, mired from head to foot, entering the back parlour where Mr Shandy and my uncle Toby were discoursing. Scores of similar pictures leap to the eye as one turns the pages of either *Tristram Shandy* or *A Sentimental Journey*.

Technique of impressionism   This kind of art is entirely subjective. Instead of describing " things " so that they may be instantly recognized by the intelligence, the writer simply sets down the impressions received by an onlooker, the reactions of his consciousness to outward things. Instead of recounting an incident in such a way that intelligent anticipation is alternately invited and gratified, he presents the series of concrete images as they strike one after another upon the senses.

'Tis a pity, said my father, that truth can only be one side, brother Toby, considering what ingenuity these learned men have all shown in their solution of noses. . . . Can noses be dissolved? replied my uncle Toby.

—My father thrust back his chair—rose up—put on his hat— took four long strides to the door—jerked it open, thrust his head half-way out—shut the door again—took no notice of the bad hinge—returned to the table—plucked my mother's thread-paper out of Slawkenbergius's book, went hastily to his bureau—walked slowly back, twisting my mother's thread-paper about his thumb —unbuttoned his waistcoat—threw my mother's thread-paper into the fire—bit her satin pincushion in two—filled his mouth with bran—confounded it;—but, mark, the oath of confusion was levelled at my uncle Toby's brain;—which was even confused enough already;—the curse came charged only with the bran;—the bran, may it please your Honours, was no more than powder to the ball.[1]

Told in this fashion, even such a frivolous anecdote as that of Francis the First and his diplomatic invitation to the Swiss to stand sponsor to his next child, becomes a little masterpiece of

[1] *Tristram Shandy*, Book III., c. 41.

point and neatness. After some delay the answer comes; the Prime Minister informs His Majesty that the invitation has been accepted. " And what name has the republic fixed upon for the Dauphin? . . . Shadrach-Meshach-Abednego, replied the minister." What can be done? There are no funds in the treasury to pay for a compromise. " I'll pawn the best jewels in my crown, quoth Francis the First. Your honour stands pawned already in this matter, answered Monsieur le Premier. Then, Monsieur le Premier, said the king, by —— we'll go to war with 'em." [1] The method accounts for the abrupt beginnings of so many chapters, especially those in which there is some dramatic action. Here are a few such exordiums: " Then reach my breeches off the chair, said my father to Susannah "; " Your Honour, said Trim, shutting the parlour door before he began to speak, has heard, I imagine, of this unlucky accident "; " But can the thing be undone, Yorick? said my father,—for in my opinion, continued he, it cannot "; and the famous " ZOUNDS! . . . Z—ds! cried Phutatorius," in the chapter that presently tells the woeful tale of the hot chestnut. The drama is visualized, and we gather the meaning of what is going on exactly as we do in real life. The peerless beauty of such a story as that of Le Fevre lies not only in the tender and delicate feeling but also in the method of its unfolding, as it comes bit by bit from the artless Trim, interrupted by Captain Shandy's comments and interrogations. *A Sentimental Journey* opens in the middle of a dialogue and goes on in a succession of scenes; there is nothing of the nature of a formal transition between them, yet we glide from one episode to the next with never a jolt. But, nearly flawless as *A Sentimental Journey* is, it has nothing quite so consummate as the dance with Nannette and the peasants on the road betwixt Nismes and Lunel, or the tale of Le Fevre, two gems of impressionist art, which owe more than half their beauty to the perfect naturalness with which the scene enacts itself, stroke after stroke falling gently on the sensorium, as if life itself were passing before our very eyes.

Thus, instead of a reasoned and coherent picture of the world, as if contemplated by the eye of omniscience, Sterne gives the

[1] *Tristram Shandy*, Book IV., c. 21.

The
opposite to
intellectual
realism

impressions of sight, sound, contact, atmosphere, as they strike upon the mind. We experience them in the manner and order in which they arrived, and we become aware of their mutual bearing as they combine into a definite image. Reflection comes after, if it comes at all. This is the opposite of the method of Fielding, who was intent, not merely on a truthful representation of reality, but also on making reality intelligible. The representation, indeed, was subsidiary to the interpretation. What has here been called intellectual realism submits a definite view of life to the understanding. Whatever the object, a thing, a person, an act or complication of acts, it must be recognized, understood, fitted into its place in an existing scheme, our generalized knowledge of the world. The intellectual realist must be periodically abstracting, generalizing, discovering relations of cause and effect. Probability and lifelikeness, his touchstones of veracity and insight, can be reduced ultimately to this, a plausible appearance of causality. Whereas the impressionist shuns abstractions and generalities, has no interest in causes, no motive to question probabilities; he is wholly absorbed in his multitudinous sensations, and sensations authenticate themselves.

The danger is that the intellectual realist, engrossed in the work of generalization and abstract analysis, may let life, in its concreteness and infinite variability, fade away. The intelligible world so constructed, in which there is a reason for everything and a universal concatenation of causes and effects, may be, and did become in the hands of certain followers of Fielding, who had not his sure eye for actuality, a distortion or an empty simulacrum of the real world. Impressionism counteracts such tendencies. Not that it offers a better understanding of things in themselves. But by seizing impressions at their very birth, in all their freshness and vividness, we become conscious of a thousand aspects unnoticed in our ordinary perfunctory view of things, in which generalization has rubbed out differences and tended to suppress individuality. The impressionist is not impatient to comprehend the world; he prefers to enjoy it. Happily intent upon the shifting impressions that stream through his mind he invites the reader's imagination to merge itself with his and see with the same vividness.

Sterne's prose, which has been condemned by this critic and acquitted by that, was a most appropriate medium for his impressionism, and shows the same passivity, the same responsiveness to the influence of the moment, as the rest of his technique. It was moulded by the fluctuations of mood and idea. Sterne's inspirations came from far as well as near, and the style responded and changed its note accordingly. There are plenty of fantastic passages as wild in vocabulary and syntax as Rabelais at his most licensed. Sterne could echo any author you please, as well as quote from him without thanks. But he had a style of his own, the limpid, dulcet, conversational style that is at its best in *A Sentimental Journey*, where he took more care than usual to correct—at least, to alter for the better. Its slovenliness, and in *Tristram Shandy* especially there is often no other word for it, has scandalized purists. Much Sterne would have cared! " A pretty story! Is a man to follow rules—or rules to follow him?" Some of the corrections he actually made show that he would coolly ungrammaticize a sentence, if he could suit it better to his meaning; he would even disable a predicate to improve a cadence. Like the Greeks, he perceived that incorrectness might be a virtue. He led out the Muse in deshabille, but no one could fail to recognize the Muse.

"Writing, when properly managed, is but a different name for conversation." That is his theory of style, in which he sought the same graces of informality and intimacy which characterized his whole attitude towards the reader. Even his epigrams and aphorisms have a colloquial turn. " 'Tis known by the name of perseverance in a good cause, and of obstinacy in a bad one." " Sciences may be learned by rote, but Wisdom not." "We lose the right of complaining sometimes by forbearing it;—but we often treble the force." " If the old man be yet disputing and inquiring concerning wisdom—what time will he have to make use of it?" They are pruned and polished, yet retain an air of unstudied grace, these charming little commonplaces. " Heat is in proportion to the want of true knowledge." Or take that delightful phrase characterizing the postilion La Fleur, "the festivity of his temper "—what an exquisite misuse of language! His " shorn lamb " dictum he adapted from a clumsy French stanza, and tried it in two or three shapes before it was smoothed down to this last melodious stave. For it was the ear of the musician that gave the final increment of beauty to his wit. Music is the proper art of the impressionist: painter or writer, there must be something of the essence of music in the work of either. *A Sentimental Journey* has the effect of a piece of music running limpidly along through varied modulations, the words and phrases often laden with musical suggestion as unanalysable as a melody. But the more specific Shandean quality is to be found in the humorous colloquies, monologues, letters, and the like, in *Tristram Shandy*. The most quotable, after the epigrams already cited, are perhaps the mock-aphorisms in the letter on love addressed by Mr Shandy to the enamoured Uncle Toby.

A just medium prevents all conclusions.

Whatever thou hast to say, be it more or less, forget not to utter it in a low soft tone of voice;—silence, and whatever approaches it, weaves dreams of midnight secrecy into the brain; for this cause, if thou canst help it, never throw down the tongs and poker.

Avoid all kinds of pleasantry and facetiousness in thy discourse with her, and do whatever lies in thy power, at the same time, to keep her from all books and writings which tend thereto: there are some devotional tracts, which if thou canst entice her to read over,—it will be well; but suffer her not to look into Rabelais, or Scarron, or Don Quixote.

They are all books which excite laughter; and thou knowest, dear Toby, that there is no passion so serious as lust.[1]

Sterne's plagiarisms   *Tristram Shandy* is a huge miscellany,[2] and a considerable part of it is a patchwork of extracts, literally or otherwise adapted from other men's books. Sterne can hardly be said to have plundered surreptitiously, for many of the passages are lifted from authors very familiar at that day; those, for instance, already mentioned from Locke. Ozell's revision of Urquhart's *Rabelais*, which lay always at his elbow, was only twenty years old, two editions having come out in 1737 and the following year. Allusions to this could not escape notice. But he imitated the rambling

---

[1] *Tristram Shandy*, Book VIII.
[2] "This rhapsodical work," as he calls it.

method of Rabelais and the Rabelaisian burlesque without actually quoting much; his levity was something very different from the fundamental seriousness of Rabelais' satire of scholasticism. In 1798 Dr John Ferriar, a Manchester physician who was an admirer of Sterne, brought out a book, *Illustrations of Sterne*,[1] indicating his place among the comic writers and to what a large extent he had borrowed from his predecessors. In *Le Moyen de Parvenir* of Béroalde de Verville, in Bouchet, Scarron, and "Gabriel John," doubtfully identified by Professor Cross with Tom D'Urfey, the wit and dramatist, Sterne had models for the portraiture of low life, in the anti-romantic way, and for the nonsensical travesty of pedantry and useless erudition in which the French delighted. Bruscambille supplied more tomfoolery, and his prologue on noses may have suggested that great topic and Slawkenbergius's tale. But Ferriar traces the philosophy of noses back to the ancients, and finds a possible source in a treatise by Gaspar Tagliacozzi, physiologist in the University of Bologna. Aretino, Marivaux, and Crébillon are other probable sources or models; as already noted, the humour of the Shandean style is of a very similar nature to *Marivaudage*, especially in the studied ambiguity that was one of its characteristics. The mock-heroic theme of the *Tristra-pædia* points to an origin in the histories of Gargantua and Pantagruel; but there was a nearer one, both in date and in similarity. *The Memoirs of Martinus Scriblerus*, put together by Dr John Arbuthnot, with contributions from Pope, Gay, Swift, and other members of the Scriblerus Club, had been published with the prose works of Pope in 1741, as a satire on learned fools. It gives a Rabelaisian but matter-of-fact account of the "suction and nutrition" of Martin, and his education, his father's extravagant pedantry being contrasted with the sober and practical good sense of his uncle, Albert, just as Mr Shandy's manias are contrasted with his brother's simplicity. The burlesque dissertations on logic, philosophy, anatomy, and other erudite subjects also may well have given hints to Sterne, who improved upon them enormously. The art of digression had been nobly practised by Swift, particularly in *A Tale of a Tub*, and Sterne needed no other suggestion, though he could have

---

[1] Second edition, in 2 vols., 1812.

found plenty in almost any of the writers named. Finally, there is the group of learned philosophers and essayists from whom Sterne cut large excerpts and reproduced them, often word for word. First, as by far the largest creditor, comes Burton, from whose *Anatomy of Melancholy* he levied wholesale; Locke has been mentioned next come Bacon, Montaigne, and Bishop Hall. And, last of all, for the technicalities in the episodes of Captain Shandy's fortress-building and sieges, Sterne supplied himself with a number of military treatises that have been identified.[1]

The admirable way in which he used them Opinions will, of course, always differ on the ethics of these loans or depredations. The best defence of Sterne is that he used the results for the finest purposes, and out of books that very few read extracted materials for one never likely to be forgotten. To which must be added that he did not proceed in a clandestine way. When he stands before us, as it were, red-handed, with the spoils of one foray behind him and another unacknowledged raid in view on the subsequent page, he unburdens himself of the following harangue on the very point at issue:

> Tell me, ye learned, shall we be for ever adding so much to the *bulk*,—so little to the *stock*?
> Shall we for ever make new books, as apothecaries make new mixtures, by pouring only out of one vessel into another?
> Are we for ever to be twisting and untwisting the same rope! for ever in the same track,—for ever at the same pace?
> Shall we be destined, to the days of eternity, on holy-days as well as working days, to be showing the *relics of learning*, as monks do the relics of their saints—without working one—one single miracle with them?[2]

What shall be said of such candour, which some would call impudence? But it is of a piece with his sly and provocative, but, if taken in the right spirit, admirably humorous references to other peccadilloes.

Far more serious in the eyes of many respected critics were his offences against decorum. In his own day Sterne had enemies or

[1] For a very full account of Sterne's plagiarisms or legitimate appropriations see Cross, i., "The Parson in his Library," pp. 126-148. Professor Cross has discovered another important source in "the mad book" of John Dunton, *A Voyage round the World . . . containing the Rare Adventures of Don Kainophilus* (1691).
[2] *Tristram Shandy*, Book V., c. 1.

ill-disposed critics enough. The people who decried Fielding *The* were not likely to be more lenient towards a clergyman telling *charge of* bawdy tales, even in the most discreet and harmless manner. *immorality* Many who denounced him were, no doubt, actuated by honest motives. Richardson, for instance, could hardly be expected to approve of *Tristram Shandy*, and, in fact, he saw in it nothing but " unaccountable wildness; whimsical incoherencies; un- common indecencies." [1] Others, who were not so prudish, had not the sense of humour to read him intelligently, or exacted vengeance for personal, clerical, or other grudges by affecting moral indignation. Sterne's reputation was not in good odour even in the eighteenth century. In the next his reception was still more mixed. Coleridge was speaking for himself and moral theology when he ponderously anatomized Sterne's licentiousness, which he considered as proven. Carlyle's genius was too closely akin to Sterne's for any such narrow judgment. But the general attitude of the early, middle, and later Victorian periods is summarily represented by three critics—Thackeray, Bagehot, and H. D. Traill. Thackeray, in the same collection of lectures, *The* *Thack-* *English Humourists*, in which he had done his worst for Fielding, *eray's* undertook in the one on " Sterne and Goldsmith " to deal faith- *view of* fully with the delinquent author of *Tristram Shandy* and *A* *Sterne* *Sentimental Journey*. He could not shut his eyes to the merits of Sterne at his best, but scoffed at what he considered mere buffoonery, and at his sentimental attitudinizing. He served up again the old strictures on Sterne's sentimental affairs, the alleged neglect of his mother and his wife, and the immorality of his books. The novelist who learned his own excellent style from Sterne repaid him by a few compliments, many gibes, and the concluding sentence : " There is not a page in Sterne's writing but has some- thing that were better away, a latent corruption—a hint, as of an impure presence."

Bagehot's study is of no critical importance, but is a striking *Bagehot* revelation of the sanctimonious attitude of the majority in that *on Sterne* period towards any literature that was not strictly " on the side of the angels," the period when Archdeacon Grantly might indulge a taste for Rabelais, but only in the privacy of his study,

[1] Cross, i. 216.

slipping the wicked volume into a secret drawer when his wife came in.[1] Bagehot, whose article, " Sterne and Thackeray," appeared as a review (1864), probably could not read Rabelais. He says: " Much of *Tristram Shandy* is a sort of antediluvian fun, in which uncouth Saurian jokes play idly in an unintelligible world." Sterne was a pagan and a sensualist, and his sensibility was a temperamental affliction that demands our pity. Bagehot obscurely discerned the rare virtue of Sterne's impressionism, but opined that this was vitiated by his irregularity and incoherence and his " *un*natural " style. Then he comes to the main charge. Sterne is indecent " for indecency's sake," he " gloats over " that which is " disgusting and improper," he revels in " ugliness," which " is always a sin in art." He admits that some doubtful scenes in *A Sentimental Journey* have " nothing displeasing to the natural man in them . . . to those whose æsthetic nature has not been laid waste by their moral nature, they are attractive." Bagehot did not notice how easily that last phrase might be used against himself. But he unwarily betrayed the hypocrisy of the view he was defending in a summary of the change which had come over the world in regard to such matters since the eighteenth century.

Much which would formerly have been blameless would now be censured and disliked. The audience has changed; and decency is of course dependent on who is within hearing. A divorce case may be talked over across a club-table with a plainness of speech and development of expression which would be indecent in a mixed party, and scandalous before young ladies. Now, a large part of old novels may very fairly be called club-books; they speak out plainly and simply the notorious facts of the world, as men speak of them to men. Much excellent and proper masculine conversation is wholly unfit for repetition to young girls; and just in the same way, books written—as was almost all old litera- ture—for men only, or nearly only, seem coarse enough when contrasted with novels written by young ladies upon the subjects and in the tone of the drawing-room.[2]

Apparently the male sex is immune from infection; or is it that men have the right to be chartered libertines—at least, in the

---

[1] *The Warden*, by Anthony Trollope, c. viii. ; this novel appeared in 1855.
[2] *Literary Studies*, ii. 297.

smoking-room? That seems to have been the accepted idea in the Victorian age, the humbug and smugness of which are so frankly though unconsciously revealed in this exquisite lucubration. Bagehot was wrong, however, in supposing that the enlightened nineteenth century had a monopoly of this anxiety about other people's morality and this unassailable confidence in one's own. It was at doctrines like this and at all similar pretences that Sterne was poking fun in the passages to which Bagehot and his like objected.

H. D. Traill, with less clumsiness and obtuseness than Bagehot, *H. D.* renewed the indictment in a monograph published eighteen years *Traill* later.[1] He laments that Sterne—and he takes it for granted *on the* that no one will contest the statement—"is of all writers the *question* most permeated and penetrated with impurity of thought and suggestion." A serious satiric purpose may sometimes justify even "offences against cleanliness"; but Sterne had no such object, and, further, if weighed in the balance with Rabelais or Swift, "he must be condemned on a *quantitative* comparison of indecency," whatever may be the "quality of their respective transgressions."[2] Traill would have found it hard, at any rate, to substantiate his quantitative comparison. It would be a pity to attempt this; but if anyone would assemble all the passages in Sterne's writings to which, on their own principles, Bagehot and Traill could reasonably object, the meagreness of the result would be rather surprising.

The charge of foulness and grossness may, indeed, be refuted *Is Sterne* out of the mouth of this latest censor himself. Traill could not *guilty?* help being impressed by the "purity" and "delicacy" of Sterne's humour, so devoid of any touch of the "physical grotesque," at the same time deploring his impurity and indelicacy in another sense. But this will not do. Foulness and grossness are so incompatible with refinement of humour they can never exist in the same individual. If such a writer be immoral, it can only be that

[1] *Sterne* (English Men of Letters), 1882.
[2] Pp. 147-148; Traill castigates Sterne for inaccuracy, and himself describes David Hume as "the author of the *Wealth of Nations* (*Ibid.*, 85); he makes fun of Sterne's bad French, but invariably employs the solecism, a *double entendre*. Much of his criticism is highly ingenious but transparently unsound. Nevertheless the book has merits, whereas Bagehot's article has none.

by lewd suggestion or complacent approval he condones or incites to immorality. Was Sterne guilty of this? It is the question with which we are left, after clearing away the fictitious articles of the arraignment. Now it could reasonably be argued that *Pamela* or *Clarissa* might have an evil effect upon susceptible readers, through Richardson's luscious treatment of certain incidents and of the feelings and motives involved. But there is nothing whatever of this nature in either *Tristram Shandy* or *A Sentimental Journey*. Is the mischief to be traced, then, in the sentiments? Unhealthy sentimentalizing may easily lead imperceptibly into the danger zone. Yet, if anywhere, it is not in the sentimental parts that Sterne transgresses, but almost entirely in his humorous scenes and the accompanying word-play. The forbidden topics that are objected to, the alleged lewd suggestion, and all the rest of it, pertain to the humour; they are not products of his sentimentalism. Had it been the other way about, his detractors might have had a case.

Sterne's laughter at puritanical reticence　They did not pay due regard to this circumstance, or they might have realized the truth, that Sterne is not an offender against morality at all, but only guilty of finding a subject for mirth in the demureness and pretences of those who identify morality with propriety. His favourite jests were directed at that puritanical foible, of inviolable reticence on certain subjects and everything connected with them. He loved to make the flesh creep by uttering the forbidden word, pointing an impish finger at the very thing that ought to be ignored. The exaggerated and often hypocritical reticence of the formalist was too much for his risibility, and he made fair game of it. When the censorious complain of his leering and sniggering, they fail to see that he is rallying those who look askance at any daring allusion, and that his humour may rebound upon those who snigger complacently, like Bagehot's friends round the club table at their conversations "for men only." They have no suspicion that they themselves are perhaps the very people hit by his verbal innuendoes, his simulated bashfulness, his admirable mimicry of offended propriety. The beauty of human absurdities had an inexhaustible fascination for Sterne, and there was no reason why one of the commonest and most inveterate absurdities should escape ridicule. And he loved to skate on thin ice. Once, when he was vicar of Sutton-in-the-Forest, he tumbled through the ice in the middle of a pond, and we are told that none of his parishioners loved him enough to help him out.[1] An obstetrical romance was a rather risky performance, but it is the short-sighted reader who comes to grief over it. That is the point of the little anecdote of Bevoriskius describing the love-making of two sparrows on his window-sill, and Sterne's comment:

Ill-fated Yorick! that the gravest of thy brethren should be able to write that to the world which stains thy face with crimson to copy, even in thy study.[2]

And of the ironical:

I have something within me which cannot bear the shock of the least indecent insinuation; in the sportability of chit-chat I have often endeavoured to conquer it, and with infinite pain have hazarded a thousand things to a dozen of the sex together,—the least of which I would not venture to a single one to gain heaven.[3]

It has recently been said: "What is pornography to one man is the laughter of genius to another."[4] The converse is equally true: what is the laughter of genius to one man is pornography to another.

A good deal of the influence usually attributed to Richardson *Sterne's* on the novelists of the subsequent generation is due rather to *work and* Sterne. Many of them took his sentimentalism over-seriously, *influence* and were blind to his humour, which goes along with it. He was more intelligently appreciated by De Quincey and Carlyle, and the novelists, Dickens, even the ungrateful Thackeray, Peacock, and Peacock's son-in-law, Meredith, all of whom show traces of Shandeism or of a native quality cognate with it. Some foreigners, Jean Paul Richter, for instance, Xavier de Maistre, and several much later French novelists, were imitators or else consanguineous.

Sterne was at once a wholesome corrective to Richardson and his complement. The older man treated sensibility with tragic seriousness, Sterne made it yield not only pathos but humour.

[1] Cross, i. 62.
[2] *Sentimental Journey*, "The Passport, Versailles."
[3] *Ibid.*
[4] D. H. Lawrence, "Pornography and Obscenity" (*Criterion Miscellany*), p. 5.

He was more akin to Smollett, in spite of mutual dislike, than to Fielding, whose realism, the kind of realism that was to prevail in English fiction for at least a century, he seems to be trying to subvert and demolish. He really added something that it lacked. He opposed sentiment to reason, sensation to reflection, and with his impressionism revived that joy in the passing show which the graver spectator of the human drama runs the risk of letting slip. His name will appear again many times in the later history of the novel.

SELECT READING AND REFERENCE LIST

GENERAL

BAKER, E. A. *A Guide to the Best Fiction in English.* 2nd edition. 1913. (New edition in preparation.)

BALDWIN, C. E. *Marivaux' Place in the Development of Character Portrayal.* (Publications of the Modern Language Association of America, xxvii, pp. 168-187. 1912.)

BIRKHEAD, EDITH. *Sentiment and Sensibility in the Eighteenth-Century Novel.* (Essays and Studies by Members of the English Association, xi.) 1925.

BRANDES, GEORGE. *Main Currents in Nineteenth-Century Literature.* 6 vols. 1902.

CAZAMIAN, LOUIS. *L'Evolution psychologique et la Littérature en Angleterre (1660-1914).* 1920.

CHANDLER, F. W. *The Literature of Roguery,* vol. ii. 1907.

CROSS, WILBUR L. *The Development of the English Novel.* 1899.

ERNLE, LORD. *The Light Reading of our Ancestors : Chapters in the Growth of the English Novel.* 1927.

FORSTER, E. M. *Aspects of the Novel.* 1927.

HAZLITT, WILLIAM. *Lectures on the English Comic Writers.* 1819.
> Especially the chapter "On the English Novelists."

LANSON, GUSTAVE. *L'Art de la Prose.* 1911.

MASSON, DAVID. *British Novelists and their Styles, being a Critical Sketch of the History of British Prose Fiction.* 1859.
> On the novel as a form of literature—British novelists of the eighteenth century.

RALEIGH, SIR WALTER. *The English Novel . . . to the Appearance of "Waverley."* Second edition. 1904.

SAINTSBURY, GEORGE. *The English Novel.* (Channels of English Literature.) 1913.

THACKERAY, W. M. *The English Humourists of the Eighteenth Century.* 1853.
Especially Hogarth, Smollett and Fielding, Sterne and Goldsmith.

WARD, A. W., and WALLER, A. R. *The Cambridge History of English Literature*, vol. x. : "The Age of Johnson." 1913.

CHAPTERS I.-III.—RICHARDSON

BOAS, F. S. *Richardson's Novels and their Influence.* (Essays and Studies by Members of the English Association, ii.) 1911.

DOBSON, AUSTIN. *Samuel Richardson.* (English Men of Letters.) 1902.

RICHARDSON, SAMUEL. *Works.* Edited, with a prefatory chapter of biographical criticism, by Leslie Stephen. 12 vols. 1883.

RICHARDSON, SAMUEL. *Letters from Sir Charles Grandison.* Selected, with a biographical introduction and connecting notes, by George Saintsbury. Illustrated by Chris Hammond. Two vols. in one. 1904.

THOMSON, CLARA L. *Samuel Richardson : A Biographical and Critical Study.* 1900.

CHAPTERS IV.-VIII.—FIELDING

BLANCHARD, FREDERIC T. *Fielding the Novelist : A Study in Historical Criticism.* 1926.

CROSS, WILBUR L. *The History of Henry Fielding.* 3 vols. 1918.

DIGEON, AURÉLIEN. *Les Romans de Fielding.* 1923.
    Le Texte des Romans de Fielding (étude critique). 1923.

DOBSON, AUSTIN. *Fielding.* (English Men of Letters.) 1889.

FIELDING, HENRY. *Works.* Edited by Leslie Stephen, 10 vols. 1882.

> *Works.* Edited, with introduction, by Edmund Gosse. 12 vols. 1898-1899.
>
> *Works.* Edited, with introduction, by George Saintsbury. 12 vols. 1893.
>
> *Works.* Edited by G. H. Maynadier. 12 vols. 1903.

FIELDING, HENRY. *The Adventures of Joseph Andrews and his Friend, Mr Abraham Adams.* Edited, with introduction and notes, by J. Paul de Castro. Scholartis Press. 1929.

These are valuable for their editorial matter.

FIELDING HENRY. *An Apology for the Life of Mrs Shamela Andrews, in which the many Notorious Falsehoods and Misrepresentations of a Book called Pamela are Exposed.* By Conny Keyber. 1741.

FIELDING, SARAH. *The Adventures of David Simple.* With Introduction by E. A. Baker. 1904.

> *The Lives of Cleopatra and Octavia.* Edited by R. Brimley Johnson. 1928.

GODDEN, G. M. *Henry Fielding : A Memoir.* 1910.

Including newly discovered letters and records, with illustrations from contemporary prints.

WELLS, J. E. *Fielding's Political Purpose in Jonathan Wild.* (Publications of the Modern Language Association of America, xxviii, pp. 1-55. 1913.)

CHAPTER IX.—SMOLLETT

BUCK, HOWARD SWAZEY. *Smollett as Poet.* 1927.

Interesting on the verses contained in the novels.

> *A Study in Smollett, chiefly " Peregrine Pickle."* 1925.

CHAMBERS, ROBERT. *Smollett : his Life and a Selection from his Writings.* 1867.

HANNAY, DAVID. *Life of Tobias George Smollett.* (Great Writers.) 1887.

Smollett, Tobias. *Miscellaneous Works ; with Memoirs of his Life and Writings.* By Robert Anderson. 6 vols. 1796.

> *Works ; with Memoirs of his Life.* By John Moore (1797). 8 vols. 1872.
>
> *Works.* Edited by George Saintsbury. 12 vols. 1895.
>
> *Works.* Edited by W. E. Henley. 12 vols. 1899-1901.
>
> Valuable for the introductory matter.
>
> *Letters.* Edited by E. S. Noyes. 1926.
>
> *Travels through France and Italy.* 2 vols. 1766. With an introduction by Thomas Seccombe. (The World's Classics.) 1901.

CHAPTER X.—STERNE

Amory, Thomas. *The Life and Opinions of John Buncle Esquire.* With an introduction by E. A. Baker. (Library of Early Novelists.) 1904.

Bagehot, Walter. *Literary Studies.* Edited by R. H. Hutton. 3 vols. 1905.

Vol. ii. contains an article from *The National Review* (April 1864) which expresses the righteous indignation of the mid-Victorians at Sterne's "immorality" in an amusing manner.

Barton, F. B. *Étude sur l'Influence de Laurence Sterne en France au XVIIIᵉ Siècle.* 1911.

Cross, Wilbur L. *The Life and Times of Laurence Sterne.* 2 vols. 1825.

By far the fullest biography ; contains an excellent bibliography of works by or attributed to Sterne.

Ferriar, John. *Illustrations of Sterne.* 1798. Second edition. in 2 vols., 1812.

Memoirs of the Life, Works, and Discoveries of Martinus Scriblerus. 1741.

By Arbuthnot, Gay, Pope, and other members of the Scriblerus Club.

Sichel, Walter. *Sterne : A Study.* 1910.

Gives the *Journal to Eliza.*

STAPFER, C. *Laurence Sterne, sa Personne et ses Ouvrages : Étude précédée d'un Fragment inédit.* 1870. Second edition, 1882.

STERNE, LAURENCE. *Works ; with a Life of the Author written by Himself.* Edited by J. P. Browne. 4 vols. 1813.
> *A Sentimental Journey.* Edited, with introduction, by Herbert Read. 1929.
>> Specially interesting on Sterne's prose and his punctuation (see the bibliographical note.)

> *A Sentimental Journey.* With an introduction by Virginia Woolf. (The World's Classics.) 1929.
> *A Sentimental Journey and the Journal to Eliza.* With introduction by George Saintsbury (Everyman.) 1926.
> *The Life and Opinions of Tristram Shandy, Gentleman.* [Introduction by Charles Whibley.] 1894.
>> A text containing numerous misprints, but a good introduction.

TRAILL, H. D. *Sterne.* (English Men of Letters.) 1882.

INDEX

INDEX

A

C

D

S

This book may be kept

FOURTEEN DAYS

A fine will be charged for each day the book
time.